THE
PATH
OF
TRUE
GODLINESS

Classics of Reformed Spirituality

This series offers fresh translations of key writings from the seventeenth and eighteenth centuries, making them accessible to the twenty-first century church. These writings from the "Further Reformation" in the Netherlands offer a balance of doctrine and piety, a mingling of theology and life that has seldom been equaled in the history of Christianity. Each book in this series will provide invaluable insight into a vibrant part of the Christian heritage.

Initial titles to be released are:

Jean Taffin, *The Marks of God's Children,* 1586
Jacobus Koelman, *The Duties of Parents,* 1679
Gisbertus Voetius and Johannes Hoornbeeck, *Spiritual Desertion,* 1659
Willem Teellinck, *The Path of True Godliness,* 1636

Additional titles are under consideration.

THE
PATH
OF
TRUE
GODLINESS

Willem Teellinck

TRANSLATED BY ANNEMIE GODBEHERE
EDITED BY JOEL R. BEEKE

Baker Academic

A Division of Baker Book House Co
Grand Rapids, Michigan 49516

© 2003 by the Dutch Reformed Translation Society

Published by Baker Academic
a division of Baker Book House Company
P.O. Box 6287, Grand Rapids, MI 49516-6287
www.bakeracademic.com

Printed in the United States of America

Library of Congress Cataloging-in-Publication Data
Teellinck, Willem, 1579–1629
    [Noord-Sterre, aawijzende de juiste richting van de ware godzalighed. English]
    The North Star, showing the right direction of true godliness / Willem Teellinck ;
translated by Annemie Godbehere ; edited by Joel R. Beeke.
        p.   cm.—(Classics of Reformed spirituality)
    ISBN 0-8010-2633-4 (pbk.)
    1. Christian life—Reformed authors. I. Beeke, Joel R., 1952– II. Title. III. Series.
BV4501.3.T4413 2003
249.4′842—dc21   2003043657

Illustrations are used with permission of Den Hertog, the Netherlands.

Scripture quotations are from the King James Version of the Bible.

Contents

Series Preface

———————— ✳ ————————

The *Nadere Reformatie* (a term translated into English as either the "Dutch Second Reformation" or the "Further Reformation") paralleled the historical and spiritual development of English Puritanism in the seventeenth and eighteenth centuries. From its teachers came the watchword of post-Reformation piety: *Ecclesia reformata semper reformanda* ("The church always being reformed").

Proponents of the *Nadere Reformatie* used that phrase to indicate their commitment to the doctrinal and ecclesiological reforms of the Reformation of the sixteenth century as well as to the ongoing reformation of the church. Their intent was not to alter Reformed doctrine. Rather, they proposed the development of a life of piety based on that doctrine within Reformed churches that, in turn, would impact all spheres of life.

Dutch scholars responsible for a periodical on the *Nadere Reformatie* recently formulated the following definition of the movement:

> The Dutch Second (or "Further") Reformation is that movement within the Dutch Reformed Church during the seventeenth and eighteenth centuries, which, as a reaction to the declension or absence of a living faith, made both the personal experience of faith and godliness matters of central importance. From that perspective the movement formulated substantial and procedural reformation initiatives, submitting them to the proper ecclesiastical, political,

and social agencies, and pursued those initiatives through a further reformation of the church, society, and state in both word and deed.[1]

To further their program of active personal, spiritual, ecclesiastical, and social reformation, the writers of the *Nadere Reformatie* produced some of the finest, most profound literature in the Protestant tradition. Furthermore, because the Dutch Reformed piety of the seventeenth century grew out of Reformed orthodoxy and included among its founders and exponents several erudite orthodox theologians—such as Gisbertus Voetius, Petrus van Mastricht, and Johannes Hoornbeeck—the works of the *Nadere Reformatie* do not give evidence of the kind of antagonism between theology and piety that belonged to the Pietist phase of German Lutheranism. Rather, the proponents of the *Nadere Reformatie* offered a balance of doctrine and piety as well as theology and life that has seldom been equaled in church history.

The *Nadere Reformatie* has generally been overlooked in English-speaking circles due to the lack of primary sources in English. The works of Jean Taffin and Willem Teellinck, two early *Nadere Reformatie* authors, were translated into English in the late sixteenth and early seventeenth centuries, but those now-antiquated translations have not reappeared in more recent times. Moreover, the larger body of works of famous dogmaticians such as Voetius and Hoornbeeck or of pastors such as Theodorus à Brakel, Jacobus Koelman, Jodocus van Lodenstein, Wilhelmus Schortinghuis, and Godefridus Udemans remained untranslated until now. Two exceptions are Alexander Comrie's *ABC of Faith*, first published in English in 1978, and Wilhelmus à Brakel's *Christian's Reasonable Service*, translated into English and published in four volumes in 1992–95.

The present series addresses the need for further translation of these "old writers," as they are affectionately called by those who know them in Dutch. It also contributes significant biblical and historical insights to the contemporary emphasis on discipleship and spirituality.

In this series, the editors and translators present a representative sampling of the writings of this vibrant movement, along with introductions that open both the texts and the lives of the various authors to the modern reader. The series is intended for the lay reader as

1. *Documentatieblad Nadere Reformatie* 19 (1995): 108.

well as for pastors and scholars, all of whom should benefit from this introduction to the literature of the *Nadere Reformatie* movement, much as the Dutch have benefited from the translation of numerous English Puritan works into their language.

On behalf of the Dutch Reformed Translation Society,
Joel Beeke
James A. De Jong
Richard Muller
Eugene Osterhaven

Willem Teellinck (1579–1629)

Introduction

―――――――――― ✼ ――――――――――

Christians know that the practice of godliness is no easy task. They want to glorify God but often do not know how to go about it. They know they need "to put on the whole armour of God" (Eph. 6:11) but often have little understanding of what it is or how to use it. For example, how does the believer use the Word of God to arm himself, to uncover the schemes of the enemy, and to press on to victory? How do we use prayer in this battle? Should we tell God in prayer how strong our enemies are, how weak we are, and how desperately we need his Son to help us? How do believers flee from temptation? What can they do to purge their minds of blasphemous thoughts and selfish pride? How should they battle a sense of despair when affliction strikes? How can they learn from mature Christians how to fight the good fight of faith? What is the proper role of self-examination in this fight? How does the believer open his heart to God's promises?

These are questions that Willem Teellinck answers. This book is packed with scriptural and practical guidance for Christians who earnestly desire to live holy lives focused on God and his glory.

Teellinck is often called "the father of the Dutch *Nadere Reformatie*" (usually translated as the "Further" or "Second Reformation"), much as William Perkins is called the father of English Puritanism. The *Nadere Reformatie*, on occasion also translated as Dutch Precisianism, Pietism, or Puritanism, was primarily a seventeenth- and early eighteenth-century movement that roughly paralleled English Puritanism. It dates from such early representatives as Jean Taffin (1528/9–1602) and Willem Teellinck (1579–1629) to its last

The Banbury church in the eighteenth century

major contributors, Alexander Comrie (1706–74) and Theodorus van der Groe (1705–84). Like English Puritanism, it stressed the necessity of a vital Christian piety, true to the teachings of Scripture and the Reformed confessions and consistently worked out in all aspects of one's daily life.

Education and Family Life

Willem Teellinck was born January 4, 1579, in Zerikzee, the main town on the island of Duiveland, Zeeland, to a godly, prominent family. He was the youngest of eight children. His father, Joost Teellinck (1543–94), who served as mayor of Zerikzee two years prior to Willem's birth, died when Willem was fifteen years old. His mother, Johanna de Jonge (1552–1609), survived her husband by fifteen years but was often sickly when Willem was young. Willem was well educated in his youth; he studied law at St. Andrews in Scotland (1600) and at the University of Poitiers in France, where he earned a doctorate in 1603.

The following year he spent nine months with the Puritan community in England. His lodging with a godly family in Banbury and his exposure to Puritan godliness—lived out through extensive family worship, private prayer, sermon discussions, Sabbath observance, fasting, spiritual fellowship, self-examination, heartfelt piety, and good works—profoundly impressed him. At that time, Psalm-singing could be heard everywhere a person walked in Banbury, particularly on Sabbath days. These Puritans did not feel at home in the established church; they believed that the Reformation had been shortchanged in England, and they greatly admired Calvin's Genevan model for church, society, and family life. Godly Puritans in England such as John Dod (d. 1645) and Arthur Hildersham (1563–1632) were their mentors, and the people lived what these divines taught. Teellinck would later write about the fruits of their holy living: "Their Christian walk was such that it convinced even their most bitter foes of the sincerity and wholeheartedness of their faith and practice. The foes saw faith working powerfully through love, demonstrated in their straightforward business dealings, charitable deeds to the poor, visiting and comforting the sick and oppressed, educating the ignorant, convincing the erring, punishing the wicked, reproving the idle, and encouraging the devout. And all this was done with diligence and sensitivity, as well as joy, peace,

Some old houses on High Street, Banbury

John Dod (d. 1645)

Arthur Hildersham (1563–1632)

and happiness, such that it was obvious that the Lord was truly with them."

Teellinck believed the Lord converted him in England. A zeal for God's truth and Puritan piety that was never quenched was born in his heart. He surrendered his life to the Lord and considered changing his field of study to theology. After consulting some astute theologians in England and holding a day of prayer and fasting with his friends, Teellinck decided to study theology at Leiden. He trained there for two years under Lucas Trelcatius (1542–1602), Franciscus Gomarus (1563–1641), and James Arminius (1560–1609). He felt most attached to Trelcatius and tried to stay neutral in the tensions that had developed between Gomarus and Arminius.

While in England, Teellinck met Martha Greendon, a young Puritan woman from Derby, who became his wife. She shared Teellinck's life goal of living out the Puritan *praxis pietatis* ("practice of piety") in family life as well as in parish work. Their first son, Johannes, died in infancy. They were then blessed with three sons— Maximiliaan, Theodorus, and Johannes—all of whom became Reformed ministers with emphases similar to their father's. They also had two daughters: Johanna, who married an English minister, and Maria, who married a political official at Middelburg. The oldest son, Maximiliaan, became pastor of the English-speaking church at Vlissingen in 1627, then served at Middelburg until his death in 1653. Willem Teellinck did not live to see his younger sons ordained into the ministry. None of the sons became as renowned as their father, although Johannes drew some attention as pastor at Utrecht through his book *Den Vruchtbaarmakende Wijnstock* (Christ, the Fructifying Vine) and a sermon on God's promises. In both he tried to move the Second Reformation in a more objective direction.

Teellinck edified his family by his godly example. He was hospitable and philanthropic, yet he stressed simplicity in furnishings, clothing, and food. He generally steered conversation at mealtimes in a spiritual direction. Foolish conversation was not tolerated. Family worship was scrupulously practiced the Puritan way. Once a week, Teellinck invited a few of the godliest members of his congregation to join his family for devotions. Overnight guests were always welcome and were expected to participate in family worship. Once or twice a year, the Teellincks observed a family day of prayer and fasting. Teellinck regarded this practice as helpful for moving himself and his family to dedicate themselves entirely to God.

Pastoral Ministry

Willem Teellinck was ordained into the pastoral ministry in 1606 and served the Burgh-Haamstede parish on the island of Duiveland for seven fairly fruitful years. There were several conversions, but Teellinck, much like his predecessor, Godfridus Udemans (c. 1580–1649), struggled with village life, which was rough and undisciplined. The classis minutes of that time frequently address the problems of alcohol abuse, Sabbath desecration, fighting, carnival attendance, and a general disorderly spirit.

During this pastorate, Teellinck wrote his first books. In his first publication, *Philopatris ofte Christelijke Bericht* (The Love of Fatherland, or A Christian Report), published in 1608, he stressed the Dutch government's need to implement strict laws to combat the sins and faults of the populace. In 1610, Teellinck visited England to renew ties with his Puritan colleagues Thomas Taylor, Dod, and Hildersham. During that stay, he preached to the Dutch congregation in London. In 1612, he was delegated by Zeeland to go to The Hague to lobby the National Estates General for a national synod dedicated to resolving the growing problems associated with Arminianism.

From 1613 until his death in 1629, Teellinck served as pastor in Middelburg, a flourishing city that had six Reformed churches—four Dutch, one English, and one French. People were drawn to his ministry by his sincere conversation and preaching, faithful visiting and catechizing, godly walk and selfless demeanor, and sim-

The interior of the Reformed church at Haamstede. Teellinck preached from this pulpit, which was installed in 1610 during his ministry there.

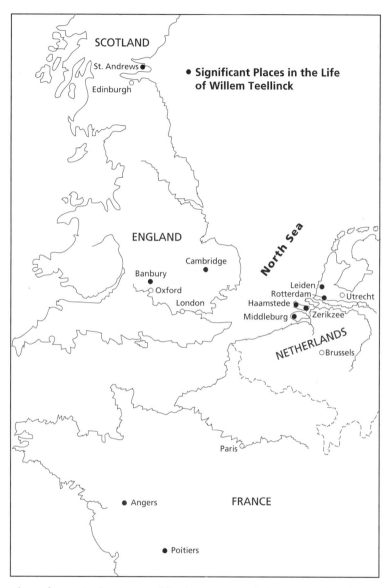

ple and practical writings. He demonstrated the conviction that a pastor ought to be the godliest person in the congregation—and his godliness involved self-denial. When a pestilence swept through Middelburg in 1624, for example, Teellinck not only called people to public and private repentance but also visited numerous infected homes, even as he urged others not to put themselves at risk by doing so.

Teellinck's hard work in Middelburg bore fruit. Five years after his arrival, he wrote to his congregation in his *Noodwendig Vertoogh* (Urgent Discourse): "We have every reason to thank the Lord. You come to church in large numbers each Sunday; our four church buildings cannot contain all the people. Many of your families may be called 'little churches.' There is good order according to good rules. Many of you use the means of grace diligently and you gladly listen to our admonitions to exercise godliness." Yet Teellinck remained burdened for the indifference in and beyond his flock. The "constant hurt and pain" that he carried in his heart because of the spiritual laxity and carnality that prevailed in church and society moved him to use his prodigious energies and gifts in speaking and writing to bring about a comprehensive reformation in every sphere of life.

The new church at Middelburg

Near the end of his life, Teellinck developed a mystical emphasis that had surfaced only occasionally in his earlier writings. That mysticism became evident in the posthumously published *Soliloquium* (Soliloquy) and *Het Nieuwe Jeruzalem* (The New Jerusalem). The latter book is reminiscent of the writings of Bernard of Clairvaux. Feelings and emotions are accented more than faith; the believing soul becomes one with Christ in tender communion.

Teellinck battled ill health for most of his ministry. He passed away on April 8, 1629, at the age of fifty. He was mourned by thousands and was buried in the churchyard of St. Pieters Church in Middelburg.

Sermons

In his preaching, Teellinck infiltrated the Dutch scene with English Puritan pathos. His sermons focused on the practice of godliness, and he preached often on the necessity of repentance. He had the gifts to rebuke sin and pronounce God's impending judgments while simultaneously drawing people to the love of God and wooing them to Christ. He despised trivialities from the pulpit, which included flowery expressions and petty illustrations. He was blunt and forthright in expressing himself, even to the point of coarseness. Not everyone appreciated his reference to God as the "first tailor" or to Paul as a *voor-vrijer* of Christ—that is, one who would deliver a suitor's overture to a young woman.

Teellinck was a practical preacher who addressed current events. For example, when Admiral Piet Hein captured the Spanish Silver-fleet and all of the Netherlands rejoiced, Teellinck preached from 1 Timothy 6:17–19, stressing that the riches of this world are counterfeit and that only the riches of Christ are authentic. Teellinck also addressed the current trends and fashions of the day. At times he was criticized for being legalistic in his sermons against luxury in dress, amorous literature, excessive drinking, dancing, traveling on the Sabbath, overindulgence in feasting, and the neglect of fasting. However, that was only one strand of a complex web of practical godliness that Teellinck sought to weave in the hearts and lives of his parishioners. Though he castigated the eth-

William Perkins
(1558–1602)

ical insensibilities of some professing believers and deplored spiritual deadness in the church, his overarching emphasis was to build
up the believer's "most holy faith" and to move the church toward
a "new life in Christ."

Homiletically, Teellinck was influenced by William Perkins
(1558–1602), who advocated the Puritan "plain method" of preaching. After exegeting a text, Teellinck drew out various doctrines,
explained how these doctrines should benefit the hearer by means
of comfort and admonition, and then applied wisdom gleaned from
the text to saved and unsaved hearers. Though not an eloquent ora-
tor, Teellinck was an effective preacher. After hearing Teellinck
preach on a few occasions, Gisbertus Voetius wrote, "Since that time
my heart's desire has been that I and all other preachers of this land
could duplicate this kind of powerful preaching."

The Netherlands was not as ready for Teellinck as England had
been for Perkins, however. Teellinck's insistence on connecting
the fruits of love with the acts of justifying faith did not appeal to
some of his peers. They found his call for renewal in church,
school, family, government, and society too intense. So on the one

hand, Teellinck's preaching against dead Reformed orthodoxy brought him under suspicion by the orthodox Reformed, while on the other hand, Arminians censored him for his devotion to that same Reformed orthodoxy and resented his popularity with laypeople.

Writing Ministry

Teellinck's goals for the reformation of the church are most evident in his writings. His numerous works sought to build up people in the faith by moving the Reformed Church beyond reformation in doctrine and polity to reformation in life and practice. Even more than Perkins, Teellinck stressed godly living, fruits of love, marks of grace, and primacy of the will.

Teellinck produced 127 manuscripts in all, sixty of which were printed. Those sixty included twenty full-length books. Franciscus Ridderus published a representative anthology of Teellinck's works in 1656 titled *Uyt de Geschriften en Tractaten van Mr. Willem Teellinck* (From the Writings and Tracts of Mr. Willem Teellinck). Three years later Teellinck's sons began printing his works, but they never got beyond three folio volumes titled *Alle de wercken van Mr. Willem Teellinck* (The Works of Mr. Willem Teellinck). Most of Teellinck's writings can be divided into five categories:

• *Exegetical*. Teellinck's exegesis of Romans 7 was published posthumously as *De Worstelinghe eenes Bekeerden Sondaers* (The Wrestling of a Converted Sinner). He published commentaries on Malachi, Judges 13–16, and Isaiah 9:5. His commentary on the Pentateuch, *Verklaeringe Over de Vijf Boecken Moses* (Exposition of the Five Books of Moses), which was ready for print shortly before his death, was lost. All of his exegetical works were written on a popular level. His concern was always for the genuine practice of Christianity.

• *Catechetical*. Teellinck's catechetical writings include his *Huysboeck* (Family Manual), a commentary on the Compendium of the Heidelberg Catechism intended for family devotions, and *Sleutel der Devotie openende de Deure des Hemels voor ons* (The Key of Devotion Opening the Door of Heaven for Us), a two-volume work of dialogues that addresses many questions about spiritual and practical Christian living.

• *Edificatory.* The majority of Teellinck's books were written to edify and instruct believers and usually focused on a single theme. *Een getrouwe Bericht hoe men sich in geval van Sieckte Dragen Moet* (A Faithful Account of How One Should Conduct Oneself in Time of Sickness) provides practical guidance for coping with affliction. *Den Christelijcken Leidsman, Aanwijzend de Practycke der Warer Bekeeringhe* (The Christian Guide, Showing the Practice of True Conversion) was written to challenge Calvinists spiritually and to warn them about Arminian ideas. *Noodwendigh Vertoogh Aengaende de Tegenwoordigen Bedroefden Staet van Gods Volck* (Urgent Discussion Regarding the Present Sad State of God's People)—one of his most important books, written shortly before his death—strongly emphasizes the need for reform of Christian life.

• *Admonitory.* In *Wraeck-Sweert* (Sword of Revenge), Teellinck warns of divine judgments that will descend upon the people who fail to repent and turn to God. In *Zions Basuijne* (The Trumpet of Zion), he tells representatives of the provinces that the Netherlands cannot be saved without a spiritual and moral reformation. Teellinck often wrote short books to warn against specific sins. In *Timotheus* (Timothy), he warns about the use of images, and in *Den Spiegel der Zedicheyt* (The Mirror of Morality), he opposes immodesty and extravagance in dress.

• *Polemical.* In *Balaam,* Teellinck warns against Roman Catholicism, and in *Den Volstandigen Christen* (The Mature Christian), against Arminianism. In *Eubolus,* Teellinck opposes Arminians for their man-centered doctrine, though he also points out faults of the Calvinists. Teellinck believed that most Calvinists focused on sound doctrine at the expense of practical godliness. He thought that Calvinists should read practical writers *(practijk-scribenten)* such as William Perkins and Jean Taffin. He also stressed that staunch orthodoxy is worthless if confession is not made from the heart. Because of this emphasis, some Reformed leaders charged Teellinck with being too emotionally subjective and put him in league with the Arminians. Teellinck responded to these charges by saying that he emphasized both soundness of doctrine and godliness of life.

Major Themes: Sanctification, Devotion, Sabbath-Keeping, the Lord's Supper

Teellinck's writings focused on four major themes: sanctification, devotion, the Lord's Supper, and Sabbath-keeping. The present book, *The True Path of Godliness,* is his major work on sanctification.

Teellinck's most extensive work, *Sleutel der Devotie* (The Key of Devotion), offers nearly eight hundred pages on the subject of devotion, which is, for Teellinck, one aspect of sanctification. Teellinck's preface explains devotion as commitment to God in Christ, which is man's highest calling.

Teellinck also wrote extensively about the Lord's Supper, particularly in his *Het Geestelijk Sieraad van Christus' Bruiloftskinderen, of de Praktijk van het H. Avondmaal* (The Spiritual Ornament of Christ's Children of the Bridechamber, or The Use of the Holy Supper), which was reprinted eleven times from 1620 to 1665. The book consists of four lengthy sermons, the first of which details a believer's duty toward the Lord's Supper; the second, preparation for the Supper; the third, partaking of the Supper; and the fourth, conduct after the Supper.

Teellinck was offended by how easily the Lord's Day was profaned in the Netherlands. In 1622, he wrote *De Rusttijdt, ofte Tractaet van d'onderhoudinge des Christelijcke Rustdachs, diemen gemeynlijck den Sondach Noemt* (The Time of Rest, or A Tract about Maintaining the Christian Day of Rest, Which Is Generally Called the Sunday). Divided into seven books, *De Rustijdt* urges strict observance of the Sabbath and includes details from Teellinck's own experience on how to prepare for the Sabbath.

Sanctification and *The Path of True Godliness*

Teellinck's first love was to promote the Puritan ideal of the sanctification of life in all its aspects, nurtured by heartfelt devotion. That is why *The Path of True Godliness* was chosen as the first of his writings to be translated into English.

The Path of True Godliness, originally titled *Noord-Sterre, aawijzende de juiste richting van de ware godzalighed* (North Star, Showing the Right Direction of True Godliness), was printed four times

Noord-sterre/

Aen-wijsende

De rechte streke

Van de vvare God-
salicheyt.

DOOR

Willem Teellinck , Bedienaer des H.
Evangelij, binnen M I D D E L B V R G H.

TOT MIDDELBVRGH,

Ghedruckt by Hans vander Hellen :
voor Geeraert vande Vivre woonende by de
nieuwe Beurse in de Druckerie/ 1621.

Title page of the
first edition of
North Star

in Dutch: in 1621, at Middelburg by Hans van der Hellen; in 1636,
at Groningen by Nathanael Rooman; in 1642, at Groningen by Jan
Claesen; and in 1971, at Dordrecht by J. P. van den Tol. This last
edition, edited by J. van der Haar (from the 1636 edition), was used
as the basis for this translation. The translation does not include
Teellinck's lengthy foreword to his brother Ewoud (in which he
complains that many professing Christians are too worldly and forget God), his preface to the "Receiver General of Their Noble
Mighty Lordships, the Estates of Zeeland," or his address to the
Christian reader, none of which contributes to the substance of this
volume.

The Path of True Godliness, Teellinck's major work on sanctification, is a Puritan-style manual on how to practice godliness. Teellinck divided this work into nine sections, which he called "books," then subdivided the books into eighty-one "chapters." We have kept the book divisions, only shortening the titles, and used the chapter titles as subdivision headings.

Book 1. Since many people boast of their faith but have no saving knowledge of the truth, Teellinck feels a need to address three matters in this book: (1) what true godliness is, (2) how believers should conduct themselves in practicing godliness, and (3) why the exercise of true godliness is of utmost importance.

Book 2. The second book discusses the realm of darkness that opposes the practice of godliness. The three main powers of this realm are our own depraved flesh, the world, and the devil.

Book 3. Teellinck shows how the kingdom of grace, in contrast to the realm of darkness, promotes godliness. The kingdom of grace possesses three powers: the renewed spirit, which wars against the flesh; the church of God, which fights against the world; and the Spirit of God, who opposes the devil. Each of these powers possesses three gifts that oppose and overcome its enemy in the realm of darkness.

Book 4. The fourth book shows us how to respond to these two realms. We must at all times keep life's three major purposes before us: the glory of God, the salvation of our own souls, and the promotion of the salvation of others. Teellinck then explains how the realm of darkness tries to divert people from life's real purposes by influencing them to live without ever knowing those purposes, to pursue wrong purposes, or to pursue the right purposes only halfheartedly.

Book 5. This book describes the means of achieving the true purposes of life: God's holy ordinances, God's works, and God's promises. It also describes people upon whom it is especially incumbent to use those means: civil authorities, church office bearers (especially pastors), and ordinary Christians.

Book 6. This book shows how Christians must attain the right purposes of life through the assistance of the right means described in the last book, all the while living consistently, watching diligently, and struggling against every hindrance.

Book 7. Here Teellinck provides us with a variety of God-centered motivations for practicing godliness. These include the Father's wisdom, omnipotence, and loving-kindness; the Son's incarnation, exemplary life, and kind invitations to come to him; and the Spirit's promise to give new hearts, to overlook weaknesses, and to graciously reward the practice of godliness.

Book 8. This book contains motivations for practicing godliness and is divided into three major sections: our natural condition, the manifold blessings of God, and the promises we make to God.

Book 9. The last book presents motivations for practicing godliness from the excellence of the godly life, including the glorious God we serve, the glorious work that is accomplished, and the glorious fruits that result; the misery of the godless life, including the awful master that is served, the detestable work that is accomplished, and the shameful fruits that result; and the emptiness of material things with regard to this life, to death, and to life after death.

Throughout this book, Teellinck insists on the need for personal religious experience and the detailed regulation of Christian conduct in life, especially in regard to prayer, fasting, Christian education, and Sabbath observance but also extending to mealtimes, clothing, dancing, carnivals, and card playing. Notwithstanding his intensely spiritual and practical emphasis on inward godliness, the modern reader may be somewhat taken aback by his repeated negative references to a number of these outward things. To understand Teellinck in these cases, one must understand two things.

First, Teellinck's stress on external sanctification must be understood against the backdrop of the numerous sins and faults of his generation that deeply troubled him. According to Teellinck and like-minded contemporaries, both society and the church were plagued by lasciviousness, which was promoted by dancing, immoral jokes, amorous literature, and card playing, often accompanied by gambling.

Teellinck also complained about the abuse of worship by church members. Preaching was not highly respected. Many attended church only out of custom. A fair number extended their dinner hour so that they could not attend the evening service. When they did come, some slept or yawned openly, and a few talked to one another during worship. Sacraments fared no better. Some people unnecessarily postponed the baptism of their children. Others would enter the service late, have their child baptized, and leave before the service concluded. Scores of parents were not fulfilling their baptismal vows to instruct their children in the doctrines of Scripture. Some church members presented themselves at the Table of the Lord without knowing the fundamental doctrines of the Christian faith, or they entered church after the sermon was over just in time to partake of the Supper. Few sacrificed in giving to the church; their offerings were usually meager and given thoughtlessly.

Sabbath days were ill-spent by many. Many people attended church only once on Sunday, even if they had no other obligations for the day. The remainder of the day was not spent in personal Bible study, self-examination, holy meditation, or spiritual conversation. Many would work at unnecessary occupations or take pleasure trips. Some would frequent taverns, even after attending the Lord's Supper.

Family life often followed little or no order. Discipline was minimal at best, and family and private worship were often neglected. Parents did not talk to their children about the sermons or about their catechism class. Some let their children dance, play cards, sing sinful love songs, and exchange jokes. There was little waging of war against the devil, the world, and the self.

Christian education was neglected. In many towns, the teachers themselves were ignorant of the basics of vital Christianity. Many young people from the church married unbelievers, staging grandiose wedding receptions at which guests drank too much. Wearing of immodest clothing was on the increase—even in the church. Many had an inordinate desire for keeping up with the latest fashions. The poor and the orphans were oppressed. Selfishness and idleness abounded.

These, then, were some of Teellinck's complaints that are repeated throughout his writings. Did he exaggerate his case? Many today might think so, but to understand history rightly we must always place ourselves in the era in which the author lived. We must not forget that many of Teellinck's contemporaries voiced similar complaints. As we read Teellinck's lists of admonitions against various evils, we must bear in mind the pastoral context in the midst of which he labored.

Second, like most Reformed forefathers who focused on a practical, vital religion of experience, Teellinck believed that true spirituality is inseparable from an outward walk of life that flees all kinds of worldliness. Whatever we may think of Teellinck's warnings against external forms of worldly behavior, we may be certain of one thing: He was motivated by a zealous desire for God's glory, not by legalism. Teellinck and nearly all those who stressed Reformed spirituality in the seventeenth century believed that serious admonitions against a worldly spirit were a natural outgrowth of scriptural teachings such as "By their fruits ye shall know them" (Matt. 7:20); "Be not conformed to this world: but be ye transformed by the renewing of your mind" (Rom. 12:2); "Whether therefore ye eat, or drink, or whatsoever ye do, do all to the glory of God" (1 Cor. 10:31); and "Love not the world, neither the things that are in the world. If any man love the world, the love of the Father is not in him" (1 John 2:15).

In Teellinck's day, the only way to travel long distances was by sea. Sea travel involved many dangers and problems of navigation; it was easy to lose one's way. Travelers looked to the north star as a fixed point to help them keep to a true course. Teellinck intended this book to be a north star to those laboring to practice godliness as they traversed the seas of life. Read this book, then keep it handy to refer to for spiritual problems you encounter. Let it assist you in your daily walk with God as you strive to stay focused on your ultimate North Star, Jesus Christ, who is our sanctification (1 Cor. 1:30).

Influence

Teellinck's major influence was injecting Puritan color into the Dutch Second Reformation. Though he never taught theology at a university, was no scholar at heart, and was not eloquent, his life, sermons, and writings helped shape the piety of the entire movement.

Teellinck was one of the most influential "old writers" *(oude schrijvers)* of the seventeenth century. More than 150 editions of his books were printed in Dutch. Moreover, his practical piety was carried on and reshaped by other major Dutch Second Reformation writers such as Voetius. Four of his books were translated into English in the 1620s but were never reprinted: *The Balance of the Sanctuary,*

Paul's Complaint against His Natural Corruption, The Christian Conflict and Conquest, and *The Resting Place of the Mind.* Several of Teellinck's books were also translated into German. One of Germany's most influential Pietists, Friedrich Adolph Lampe (1683–1729), often used Teellinck's writings to promote the practice of godly living. Thus, Teellinck left his mark on both continental and American pietism.

Teellinck's influence waned in the Netherlands in the eighteenth century when the Dutch Second Reformation became more of an introspective movement that stressed passivity rather than activity in practical Christian living. Only his *Het Nieuwe Jeruzalem* was reprinted in 1731.

Four of Teellinck's smaller works were reprinted in the nineteenth century. His writings drew the attention of Heinrich Heppe in 1879, Albrecht Ritschl in 1880, and Willem Engelberts, who wrote a doctoral dissertation on Teellinck in 1898. H. Bouwman's *Willem Teellinck en de practijk der godzalighed* (Willem Teellinck and the Practice of Godliness), written in 1928, defends Teellinck against the somewhat negative views of Heppe and Ritschl. More of Teellinck's major titles were reprinted in the twentieth century, beginning in 1969. Some scholars associated with the *Stichting Studie der Nadere Reformatie*—Willem op't Hof in particular—are now studying and writing extensively about Teellinck's life and writings. Teellinck is being increasingly read in the Netherlands today.

The Practice of True Godliness deserves a hearing in English at the present hour. Teellinck's positive emphasis in promoting biblical, Reformed spirituality serves as a corrective to much false spirituality being marketed today. It also serves as an important corrective to orthodox teaching that presents truth to the mind but does not apply it to the heart and daily life. Teellinck helps us link a clear mind, a warm heart, and helping hands to serve God with the whole person, which is our reasonable service. He fleshes out James's emphasis, saying to us on every page, "Show me your faith by your works" (cf. James 2:18).

Joel R. Beeke

BOOK
1

The Character of True Godliness

The apostle Paul assures us that the true Christian faith is knowledge that leads to godliness. Today, unfortunately, many are found who glory in the Christian faith but do not have even the barest knowledge of the truth. Additionally, many are found who have some knowledge of the truth but not enough to produce godliness. "They profess that they know God; but in works they deny him." Among those who have a form of godliness are many who deny its power, complains the apostle Paul in 2 Timothy 3:5.

Therefore, to instruct the simple, we intend to show how all those who glory in the Christian faith and possess some knowledge of the truth may use such knowledge to practice true godliness, which brings with it, in every way, great gain with contentment, since this godliness contains promises from almighty God for this life and the life to come. For our purpose, then, we will deal with the following three topics:

- what true godliness is and of what it consists
- how we should conduct ourselves in order to live in the practice of godliness
- why we should prefer to practice true godliness above all other works

What True Godliness Is

True godliness is a gift of God by which man is made willing and able to serve God. He no longer lives according to the lusts of the flesh, as the ungodly do, but according to the will of God, revealed to us in his Word. For this reason, the godly life, in which we give ourselves over to the service of God so that we live no longer for ourselves but for God, is called our reasonable service. That means we regulate our service to God according to the direction of the reasonable "milk" of God's Word, not according to our own notion or understanding (1 Peter 2:2).

They who sincerely render this reasonable service show in every respect how much they value, highly esteem, and treasure the Lord their God. Because these godly people (and they alone!) make the things of God their chief occupation in every way, they regulate and direct their whole conduct accordingly. They show thereby to the whole world that they subordinate all their own interests to the Word of the Lord and to his holy will, to their honor and to his service. This true godliness, which magnifies the Lord our God in every respect (which is how it shows itself), consists mainly of three things, three holy exercises, which we will now consider.

True Godliness Shows Itself in Three Ways

A Sincere Resolve to Live a Godly Life, according to God's Word, from Henceforth

The first holy exercise in which true godliness shows itself in a lively way is that one makes a sincere resolve, and comes to a firm decision, to walk from henceforth in all the ways of the Lord, always making God's good, acceptable, and perfect will a rule of life, and making God's glory the chief end of all one does. This was David's resolve according to Psalm 119:44: "So shall I keep thy law continually for ever and ever." And again in verse 106, "I have sworn, and I will perform it, that I will keep thy righteous judgments." In this, the good conscience of the godly shows itself. The apostle Paul was also of the same mind when he says, "For we trust we have a good conscience, in all things willing to live honestly" (Heb. 13:18). The first exercise of godliness consists of three parts.

1. We are firmly minded to cease from all evil, which we clearly know to be displeasing to God. Everyone knows that this is the duty to which the godly man is bound (Psalm 15). The Lord our God commands us to forsake, avoid, and shun

> all ungodliness, superstition, and profaning of his holy name, his holy ordinances, and his holy day of rest
> all disobedience or contempt for authority of father or mother, master or mistress
> all hate, envy, quarreling, anger, jealousy, and bitterness toward and unreconciled differences with our neighbor
> all lewdness and frivolousness
> all pomp, splendor, and excess in clothes and festive occasions
> all unchastity
> all idle talk, songs, and books
> all gluttony, drunkenness, and drinking
> all laziness, falsehood, and deceit in earning our living or in our calling
> all avarice and filthy lucre
> all lies, false witness, slander, and backbiting
> in short, all wicked and wrong practices and desires

When we read in the Word of the Lord that God detests such things, we must sincerely resolve, if we wish to show that we are godly people, to avoid and shun these things—yes, all of them.

So we must immediately cut ourselves loose from the sins that we, in fact, can leave off and forsake—for example, from those evil deeds and practices that are done with our bodily members, such as drunkenness, fornication, idle talk or songs, backbiting, deceit, and a thousand other evil things. These we *can* forsake immediately, if we are willing. We must both give these up and, as the saying goes, "keep our hands off" if we would abide before God the Lord with nothing for which to make excuses.

Surely, no one should accept the excuse of a thief who goes stealing and breaking into homes at night and then claims that he should be excused because he just can't stop. Frankly, the same applies to those who get drunk, fornicate, slander, or indulge in idle talk, since these things are done with the members of the body. A fornicator or drunkard can and must stop his fornication or drunkenness just as the thief must stop his stealing. All these things stand on the same level before God, however much the judgment of men may regard one sin more shameful than another.

Concerning other sins such as anger, envy, evil lusts, and all other sins of the inner man that are not committed with our bodily members but burn deep in our heart and cling to us as spots to a leopard—these we should surely forsake with a most heartfelt determination. For these sins we should daily humble ourselves, and we must constantly fight against them, crying out with the apostle in all sincerity, "O wretched man that I am! Who shall deliver me from the body of this death?" (Rom. 7:24).

If we would show that we are truly godly people, then we must absolutely not indulge ourselves in such things as the godless are accustomed to use. As soon as we learn how displeasing such things are to God, and if we are really serious and want to show that we are indeed godly people, we must be found fighting against them all. We should therefore deny ourselves for God's sake, even if we loved some of these sins as much as our own right eye, yes, even if some sin seems as necessary and as profitable to us as our own right hand. Nevertheless, in such cases we must cut sin off for God's sake.

2. We are sincere in performing all the good works that we already know are pleasing to God. Who doubts that this, too, is what the godly are bound to do? In his Word, the Lord commands us

to believe in him and in his Son Jesus Christ; to fear him, love him, and cleave to him to pray to him, to read his Word diligently, to meditate on it, to keep it in our heart, to speak about it, and to glorify him and praise him in song

to be meek and patient in all he sends upon us

to remember and keep his holy day of rest

to love the assemblies of the faithful and attend them frequently

to have a heart for the concerns of his church and people

to humble ourselves and to mourn not only for our own sins but also for those of the nation and to rejoice greatly when we see progress

to submit to and obey those who have been placed in authority and to have a care for those who are under our authority, to lead them to the fear of God

to show love to our neighbors, to give alms to help the needy, and to visit the sick and the prisoners

to return no evil for evil but to do good to those who cause us grief and to bless those who curse us

to be humble, modest, chaste, discreet, and temperate in our manner of life

to be diligent, prudent, and upright in the pursuit of our calling

to season our words with salt, to defend the innocent, and to shame the evil tongue and oppose it

in short, ever to practice "whatsoever things are true, whatsoever things are honest, whatsoever things are just, whatsoever things are pure, whatsoever things are lovely, whatsoever things are of good report; if there be any virtue, and if there be any praise, think on these things" (Phil. 4:8)

To that end, we should also endeavor to fill our hearts with many holy desires, to hunger and thirst after righteousness, and, indeed, to desire the Spirit's gifts. Above all things of the world, we should seek to experience the power of Christ's death in order to put to death our members, which are upon the earth, and all evil desires and to feel the power of his resurrection in order to rise again in newness of life and so express the life of Christ in our own life.

When we read in the Word of God that these and the like things please God, we should determine to practice them in earnest—yes, all these things—and to live accordingly. What we can in fact do we should cultivate and practice right away, everything in its season, and not first sleep on it for a night. What we cannot so easily take in hand, there we must exert ourselves and strive to receive the gift of God by which we are enabled to perform these praiseworthy things as well.

3. We must also heartily wish and sincerely desire to understand as much as we can of the revealed will of God concerning us. If any unknown sin still lodges in our heart, if there is anything wrong in our conduct or that lies hidden in us without our knowledge, we must desire with utmost sincerity to have it revealed and made known to us in one way or another so that we may correct it. Such was the mind of godly David, who always prayed to his God this way: "Search me, O God, and know my heart: try me, and know my thoughts: And see if there be any wicked way in me, and lead me in the way everlasting" (Ps. 139:23–24). Such was also the mind of godly Job, who inquired of his God, "How many are mine iniquities and sins? Make me to know my transgression and my sin" (Job 13:23).

This deserves careful attention. One meets with people who are "willingly ignorant" and don't want to know God's righteous will for their lives. In ignorance, they willingly continue in a particular sin from which they derive some profit or comfort. It grieves them if a man of God comes to testify against them from the Word of the Lord, as John to Herod, that "it is not lawful for thee to have thy brother's wife" (Mark 6:18). That means they should not persist in this or that sin (which they love, even as Herod loved his Herodias) but should break off from and forsake it if they would please God with their conduct.

Yes, some become very angry when told that they are not godly people. When they are chastened in this manner, they become downright irate. They begin to resist with all their cleverness and intelligence. With a thousand contrived and dim-witted evasions, they try to get out from under this yoke and put matters in a good light, saying that their conduct, if it is not especially virtuous, is at least unobjectionable. When they are confronted even more strongly, and they begin to realize to some extent that their behavior is not quite right, still they are far from hating their sins and from thanking those who take the trouble to warn them.

They are more likely to hate the man of God in their heart and to slander him. And what does this prove but that these people do not esteem godliness to be great gain! If they did, they would regard as profit and gain whatever is revealed and made known more clearly to them regarding the things that inhibit godliness. All this shows that such people are no champions of godliness! Who cannot see that the conduct of these people fully agrees with the thoughts of the ungodly, who say to God, "Depart from us; for we desire not the knowledge of thy ways" (Job 21:14)?

These ungodly thoughts should be far removed from the defenders of godliness. Together with David, we should all say to God, "Teach me, O LORD, the way of thy statutes; and I shall keep it unto the end" (Ps. 119:33).

One Does His Utmost to Carry Out His Hearty Resolve to Live a Godly Life

The second holy exercise by which the practice of true godliness shows itself is this, that having made the resolve, one does his utmost to put that holy resolve into effect. This was the practice of godly Paul, who speaks on behalf of all the godly as follows: "Wherefore we labour, that, whether present or absent, we may be accepted of him" (2 Cor. 5:9). Furthermore, he testifies of himself, "Herein do I exercise myself," making it his whole endeavor "to have always a conscience void of offence toward God, and toward men" (Acts 24:16).

Surely, it is only mocking God when someone insists that he has a sincere and wholehearted intention to live a godly life and a determination to do so yet at the same time does not take any trouble and is not zealous to live a godly life here and now! If someone announced that from this moment on he will take up surgery or the sale of goods and yet day after day you see him do nothing about it, would anyone put stock in his words? Similarly, whoever wants to be regarded as a godly person must not only resolve to live a godly life but must do his utmost to demonstrate that he esteems godliness as his greatest gain. Now this exercise consists of three parts:

1. We must abstain from and avoid everything that can impede us in the practice of godliness. This was godly David's practice: "I have refrained my feet from every evil way, that I might keep thy

word" (Ps. 119:101). By nature, man is so constituted that he will, to the best of his ability, endeavor to avoid anything that hinders his reaching a desired goal. We see this clearly in misers, lovers, glory seekers, and all worldly people, once they earnestly set their minds on something. The weightier and more important the matter is, the more zeal and foresight they use to preclude or avoid whatever may hinder them. Since to the godly, godliness means the greatest gain and the most important work, they try most diligently to anticipate and to ward off every hindrance and obstacle in their path.

The man who boasts that he earnestly intends to practice godliness, while at the same time gives no evidence that he abstains from or avoids the hindrances and obstacles to godliness, clearly shows that his intentions are not genuine and indeed that his resolves are merely feigned. Therefore, everyone who wants to demonstrate that he is a godly person should abstain as much as possible from and avoid all hindrances and obstacles to godliness. The chief obstacles and hindrances to true godliness will be discussed in detail as this work continues, for we are obliged to investigate this further in its due place.

2. We must also make use of and strive after everything that can be useful in the practice of godliness. Godly David exerted himself greatly in every respect and availed himself of all known means and tried to add to these, thus enabling him to take hold of and advance in true godliness (see Psalm 119). Human nature is like that. We see that newborn babies by nature clamor for milk that can feed and strengthen them. Every day we see the same thing with worldly men: When they have set their minds on something, they leave no stone unturned and use every means to achieve their goal. If they do not succeed with one technique, they try another. If it happens that many means are needed, they take hold of them all in order that they may reach their goal. If worldly men do this now to obtain some puny thing in the world that perishes with use, should not God's children make much more use of every means to advance in true godliness, which brings great gain and eternal satisfaction?

In just this way, does not he who makes no effort and neglects the zealous use of the means that can strengthen him in true godliness show openly that he does not genuinely hold godliness as his greatest gain? Therefore, everyone who would pass for a truly godly person should make diligent use of every means that can promote godliness. The chief means to that end are shown in detail in books 4 and 5, to which the reader is referred.

3. We must therefore begin to practice all this, not in our own strength, which means absolutely nothing, but in the power of our Lord and Savior Jesus Christ, who is the strength of our life and by whom we can do all things. See how the godly Paul counsels us: "Be strong in the Lord, and in the power of his might" (Eph. 6:10). This was his own practice, as it was of all the godly in his time. He therefore says, "For we are the circumcision, which worship God in the spirit, and rejoice in Christ Jesus, and have no confidence in the flesh" (Phil. 3:3). Take note that before we believed we were powerless and totally unable to do good, and after we believe we are not "sufficient [able] of ourselves to think any thing as of ourselves; but our sufficiency [ability] is of God" (2 Cor. 3:5). Therefore, the good that is in us through regeneration serves only to make us more and more inclined to expect and to cultivate the good help and power of God. He strengthens us and works all our works for us, even he who "is able to make all grace abound toward you; that ye, always having all sufficiency in all things, may abound to every good work" (2 Cor. 9:8).

Take careful note of this, for surely many a man begins the practice of godliness and then gives up in discouragement and withdraws from his work. Since he began it in his own strength, he makes a mess of things. It's exactly the same thing as when a little child, in his own strength, wants to build a big castle. It is a fact that our own strength means nothing in the building up of the Christian life. Unless the power of the Almighty comes upon us, we cannot build anything that will last. That is why we call it godliness; it reminds us that without *God* and his holy help we would never be able to accomplish this work.

How the devil tries to keep this fact hidden from the eyes of men! That is why there are found everywhere so many who now and then put on holy airs as if they henceforth want to be godly, but you see after only a short time that they have returned to the world, having so very quickly lost interest. This happens because they began in their own strength; therefore, they found their work too much for them and quickly tired of it because they found no more joy in it. Therefore, all students of true godliness who wish to begin this work well and truly wish to bring it to completion must renounce their own strength. They must surrender themselves entirely to the Lord Jesus Christ, who is "the author and finisher of our faith" (Heb. 12:2), that they may be strengthened through him to hold fast their good resolutions, to put them into practice, and, indeed, to bring them to full effect. We will explain in books 3 and 6 how the Lord Jesus brings this about in those who deny themselves and cast themselves upon him. All who wish to practice true godliness thoroughly, to their comfort, are advised to take particular notice of what is written there.

One Prepares to Be What God Intends Him to Be

The third way that true godliness reveals itself is that in practicing true godliness with heart and mind, we prepare to be all that God wants us to be. We are willing to do this both in temporal and spiritual things. This means letting God's Spirit lead and work in us as he pleases and according to what he considers best. David showed this kind of willingness when he was pursued by Absalom and said to Zadok the priest, "Carry back the ark of God into the city: if I shall find favour in the eyes of the LORD, he will bring me again, and shew me both it, and his habitation: But if he thus say, I have no delight in thee; behold here am I, let him do to me as seemeth good unto him" (2 Sam. 15:25–26). Joab, David's general, learned from his godly master that when he had done his utmost in the battle against his enemies, he left the outcome of the matter completely in God's hands. He therefore said to his soldiers, "Be of good courage, and let us play the men for our people, and for the cities of our God: and the LORD do that which seemeth him good" (2 Sam. 10:12).

In the same way, a godly person must be content to be whatever God wants him to be, whether rich, poor, sick, healthy, honored, insulted, rejected, or privileged. He must be willing to be tall or short of stature, strong or weak in faith, free from or full of temptation—all according to what the Lord God considers best. This does not mean that he should not distinguish between sickness and health, or between weakness and strength in faith, for if he could choose, he would clearly decide to be strong rather than weak in faith and to be healthy rather than sick (1 Cor. 7:21). However, this means that we must be willing to do the will of the Lord our God, whatever the circumstances. For example, if God's will is that a godly person be sick rather than healthy and weak rather than strong in faith, then the godliness of that person is also proved by whether he accepts God's will in this, for true godliness is revealed not only in fulfilling what God commands or forbids but also in willingly putting up with those things God sends our way. We are to be content with whatever God arranges for us, for this shows true godliness.

The godly should particularly submit themselves to the holy exercises and activities of the good Spirit of God so that they may be brought to where the Spirit of the Lord leads them, just as his Word decrees (Rom. 8:4). For example, when the Spirit of the Lord strongly admonishes us to slow down in our worldly affairs and gently rebukes our inward hearts for being far too busy with the things of this world, indicating that he grieves over this, we should gladly listen to him. We should humble ourselves and learn to deny our earthly cares and concerns. When the Spirit of the Lord admonishes us to regulate our family better—to read the Word of God with members of our family, to catechize our children, to reinstate family prayers that we may have neglected for a time, and to start praying regularly and perseveringly with our family—then we should gladly comply, for this means that we have freed ourselves from our own activities and are willing to deny ourselves in order to surrender completely to God, to be ruled by him, and to be led by his Holy Spirit in the way that seems right to him. True godliness is clearly shown in this kind of submission as well as in the ways mentioned above.

So we see that true godliness consists of not only doing what we can to serve God but also of exerting ourselves, rousing ourselves, encouraging ourselves, and stirring ourselves to strive to put into practice what we have now learned. We must submit ourselves to the good will of God in whatever way it may be made known to us and let ourselves be ruled by him. Indeed, we should conduct ourselves before the Lord our God as clay in the hand of the potter in order to be completely turned, kneaded, and molded by the Lord, our good God, who knows what is best for us (Isa. 45:9; Jer. 18:6).

We bring this up so often because we have seen how many godly people take no notice of this. Their hearts are thus greatly confused, with the result that they often become depressed. However, they would have been strengthened and would have continued the race had they paid careful attention to the Word of God. Notice that this activity consists of three parts.

1. Humbly judging ourselves. Even when we have done all we could do, we should not be satisfied, for we are still unprofitable servants (Luke 17:10). We are still totally unworthy, wanting to have things our own way. Indeed, we deserve and often badly need to have our desires frustrated so that we do not get our own way and do not have the desires of our heart fulfilled but instead are visited by the rod and afflicted by many difficulties. This was the case with the godly apostle Paul. Even when he did everything he could, he wrote, "For I know nothing by myself; yet am I not hereby justified: but he that judgeth me is the Lord" (1 Cor. 4:4). All godly people should think like this.

2. Trusting that everything is done for our good. We should often remind ourselves that the Lord our God knows what is best for us. That should assure us that, come what may, everything will be all right in the end, for the Lord God takes it upon himself, whatever may happen to us, to make all things work together for our good (Rom. 8:28). Thus, godly Paul testified in the middle of all his difficulties, "For the which cause I also suffer these things: nevertheless I am not ashamed: for I know whom I have believed, and am persuaded that he is able to keep that which I have committed unto him against that day" (2 Tim. 1:12). All godly people should have the same attitude when they are surrounded with difficulties. They should try to affirm and experience how God's strength is made perfect in weakness (2 Cor. 12:9).

3. Availing ourselves of every means. When we experience great suffering and distress, we must submit to God's holy will in the way that we have already explained. We must then diligently avail ourselves of all the means that God has revealed in his Word and has placed at our disposal in this temporal life to help deliver us from our difficulties. The apostle Paul applied every lawful means as much as possible, and these were permitted so that he might be helped and delivered from his difficulties (see 2 Cor. 12:8–10). David and other godly people did likewise. Indeed, Scripture says of the Lord Jesus himself, "Who in the days of his flesh, when he had offered up prayers and supplications with strong crying and tears unto him that was able to save him from death, and was heard in that he feared" (Heb. 5:7), and he prayed, "If it be possible, let this cup pass from me: nevertheless not as I will, but as thou wilt" (Matt. 26:39).

We need to take careful note of this. It is a praiseworthy Christian quality to commit our ways to the Lord in all our sorrows and to be content to "let patience have her perfect work" (James 1:4). We are to be cheerful about whatever plans God has for us. However, we should not think that it is ungodly to do whatever we can to be delivered from difficulties that sorely press us, as long as we do not resort to the wrong means. This does not contradict godliness at all; rather, it is a sign of true godliness to call upon God in the day of trouble and ask to be delivered (Ps. 50:15), provided we do it in humble submission of ourselves to the will of God in all circumstances. Like the Lord Jesus Christ we may say, "O my Father, if it be possible, let this cup pass from me: nevertheless not as I will, but as thou wilt" (Matt. 26:39).

Some people do not pay attention to this. As a result, they become greatly hardened and insensitive in their grief. That is because they have disregarded and neglected this clear command of God. It is also due to the cunning work of Satan, who deceived them into believing that it is actually most exemplary to lie passively under God's rod and let him do his work. All godly people should be on their guard against this deceit and gladly avail themselves of every good means to be delivered. Then they should leave the outcome to God. The spiritual means for deliverance (the physical cannot be counted) are mainly these:

1. Be humble in affliction. We must humble ourselves when we are oppressed under the hand of God and, as it were, kiss the rod with which we are afflicted. This humility is to be shown in various ways:

In wholehearted and public confession that we deserve to suffer all the pain that the Lord has laid upon us because of our sinfulness. We will suffer a thousand times over if he thinks this best for us. Like true people of God we will say, "We have transgressed and have rebelled: thou hast not pardoned" (Lam. 3:42).

Expectantly believing that we will be delivered from all our sorrows because of Christ's merits and by the mighty hand of God, who has chastised us (Micah 7:8–9). We and all creatures are humbled so we may exalt God alone, for we truly believe that only God can help us without anyone's aid (Ps. 123:3; Hosea 14:4).

With cheerful thanksgiving for all the good that we, such unworthy people, have enjoyed from God in the past and still enjoy today. This is how Jacob acted as he stood in awe before his God (Gen. 32:10; see also 2 Sam. 22:4).

2. Pray for deliverance in our sorrow. If we want to experience God's helping hand, we should lament from a humble heart. We should avail ourselves of prayer to promote a gracious deliverance. To make that prayer most effective, we should pray:

According to God's will (1 John 5:15). That means that in prayer we surrender our will to God's will, bending our will to God's will more than God's will to ours. We should be careful that in praying for deliverance we do not lay down the law to God in the measure of grace, for even if he does not deliver us from suffering, indeed, even if he puts us to death, we still have our hope in him. We should also trust him in the timing of deliverance, for he knows best the most appropriate time to help us (Heb. 4:16). We should trust him, too, in the manner and means of deliverance, for great things can be done by simple means, or without means, or even by means that appear to have the opposite effect. Nothing is impossible for God.

In faith. That means we should be firmly convinced that God's will is always the best for us, that God will in time deliver us from our distress, and that he will truly comfort and strengthen us in our distress.

With persistence. Scripture says, "And he spake a parable unto them to this end, that men ought always to pray, and not to faint" (Luke 18:1). That means we should not quit praying, even if it seems that we are not receiving immediate deliverance, strength, or comfort in the things we have prayed for in faith and in accordance with God's will. We should remember that the man who perseveres in all sincerity will prevail (Gen. 32:24–28). So we should pray fervently and frequently and, if necessary, add fasting to our prayer.

3. Seek the face of God in our sorrow (2 Cor. 7:4). This means we should seek assurance of God's favor in our heart and mind, even more than immediate deliverance from our difficulty. Indeed, we should be like the prodigal son, who sought the favor of his father more than food and clothes—even though initially lack of food and clothing drove him to return to his father (Luke 15:21).

Seeking God's face greatly increases when we repent of our evil ways and turn to God. That means abandoning our plotting and scheming and forsaking our wicked sins so we may be completely led and ruled by God from now on. We must practice this if we truly seek deliverance, for the Lord primarily sends oppression so that we will repent. Listen to what he says in Revelation 3:19: "As many as I love, I rebuke and chasten: be zealous therefore, and repent." When affliction brings us to repentance, the Lord will immediately end the oppression, acting as a skillful physician of our souls who sends us oppression to lead us to repentance. This repentance is especially shown in these ways:

With clear understanding of what sins have led to this. We should not be satisfied to say in a general way that we deserve these afflictions because of our sins, as worldly people do. Rather, like David and the church of God, we should meditate on our suffering and our ways, earnestly considering for which specific sins—even calling them by name—God is chastising us and wanting us to repent, for we can turn our feet to the testimonies of the Lord only when we have determined what those sins are and repent of them before the Lord (Ps. 119:59).

Asking forgiveness for specific sins. After we have identified specific sins for which we justly think the Lord is chastising us, we should be more sorrowful for these sins than for the suffering itself. We should diligently strive to forsake the sins that are causing us this grief more than we should strive to be delivered from this oppression. Remember, once the wound of sin has healed and dried up, the scab of distress will soon fall away by itself. We should therefore take care that we transform carnal and worldly sorrow, which we all feel by nature over things that disappoint us, into godly sorrow, for godly sorrow works repentance to salvation and is not to be repented of, but the sorrow of the world (namely, a sorrow over worldly things, without having any scruples over sin) works death in us (2 Cor. 7:10). We must thus judge ourselves in order not to be condemned with the world (1 Cor. 4:3–5).

Promising to be more zealous in serving God. When God has delivered us from affliction, we should promise him with a holy vow that from now on we will be more diligent in his service than before. David often made a promise to God when he was afraid or in trouble (see Pss. 50:14–15; 66:13–14). Commitment to a vow will contribute much to our sanctification. This particularly applies to things that we are not able to accomplish very well because we are hindered by suffering. When we are delivered, especially from illness, we should do the following: thank God in the great congregation of many people (Ps. 35:18), teach sinners and transgressors about our experience (Ps. 51:13), and start hating sin more and more throughout our life because sin has indeed caused us all this grief (Ps. 34:13–15).

If we practice these things faithfully when we are having difficulty, then God will not fail to accomplish the purpose he has for our chastisement. We will enjoy great benefits and be giving a positive witness, which is no small comfort to our soul! For although we experience the same afflictions as worldly people, we are not afflicted in the same way, nor do we endure suffering the same way they do. The oppression of worldly people is clear evidence of their eventual damnation and a foretaste of the pangs of hell they will suffer, whereas oppression for us is evidence of our salvation, which is from God alone (Phil. 1:28).

Additional Proofs of Godliness

A Prompt Forsaking of Sin

In the three holy exercises we have described, we have seen how true godliness powerfully reveals itself. Yet we know that the godliness of the most holy saints in this life is still imperfect. It is very defective, for we all stumble in many ways (James 3:2). Even the best of us are sometimes overcome by a certain sin. However, there are three additional holy exercises in which true godliness further proves and reveals itself.

The first exercise is that when we have been overtaken by a sin, whether great or small, we do not remain or persist in our transgression as ungodly people do, for they feel comfortable living in their sins (1 John 5:19). By contrast, as soon as we discover that we have been overcome by some sin, we must jump back from it as quickly as if we had fallen into a fire or had been taken like a fish out of water (Jude 23). We must consider how awful it is that we have become so ensnared in sin, and we must be reproached by it just as David was when he fell into sin. When he came to his senses and realized what he had done, he saw the awfulness of it. We read in the Psalms that he was in a sorrowful state from the time he had sinned. His sap changed into summer dryness long before the prophet Nathan approached him. All that time, David had tried to forsake his sins, but he was not able to do so because his fall was so great (Psalm 32).

The godly therefore will gladly make use of these three means to help them more promptly forsake their sins.

1. They see the wickedness of sin. They eagerly and earnestly consider what foul and loathsome corruption sin is. They also see how the devil uses sin to defile their hearts and make them more offensive to God. They also understand that the longer they live in sin, the more polluted they will become. When we fall into sin, we are just like someone who falls into a filthy gutter filled with garbage or manure. The longer he rolls around in such filth, the dirtier he will get and the worse he will smell.

2. They remember their vow to forsake sin. They gladly consider the holy confession that they received in baptism and in the Lord's Supper and remember that they are committed and obligated to immediately forsake sin as soon as they realize that they have fallen into it. It is bad enough that heathens stay and wallow in their sins, but to find true Christians doing so is inconceivable. It should not be so in Israel. We must do our utmost to forsake our sin immediately (Romans 6).

3. They look to God for grace. They realize that by quickly forsaking their sins, they may still find God's grace and be reconciled and restored to his favor. They keep in view that the Lord God, whose Spirit is grieved because of sin, is still ready to have compassion on them because of his great grace. He will have mercy on them, forgetting and forgiving their sins as soon as they wholeheartedly turn to him.

This hope, this trust, this loving-kindness of God affects them so greatly that they immediately and with all their strength tear themselves away from sin and return to the Lord, for they now realize that it is far better to live with him than to live in sin.

The Search for Reconciliation with God

The second exercise that reveals true godliness is that, when we have sinned, we not only forsake sin and refuse to remain in it but also try above all to be reconciled with God. Ungodly people ignore this matter. Indeed, when they have greatly sinned, they ask defiantly what they have done wrong. That is not so with the godly. When they have been overcome by a great sin, their greatest concern is to find out how they can be reconciled to God. We see this clearly in David, who reveals his ways in Psalm 51. Godly people diligently try to be reconciled to God as soon as they notice that they have fallen into a specific sin. They particularly apply these means:

1. They are sorry for their sins. They not only immediately forsake sin when they have transgressed but also sincerely weep over their sins, just as David did in his sorrowful search for God (Psalm 51). They know they cannot be reconciled to God as long as they do not weep and lament and sincerely grieve over their sins. They also realize that there are more than enough reasons for doing this. They think, "If I had merely been selfish and greatly offended some respectable person, who is also a faithful friend—if I had ignored and insulted and provoked him—would this not greatly concern me? Well, then, should I esteem my great, good, and merciful God so little that I would not feel sad and weep if I had sinned against him?" (see Jer. 30:14; James 4:9). Is this great God just someone we can treat with contempt and pay no attention to? This thought cuts the godly to the heart and makes them weep and lament before God.

2. They promise to forsake sin. The godly pray for mercy and forgiveness and solemnly promise the Lord God that they will not repeat that sin (Hosea 14:3), just as good-natured children usually promise their parents to be good after they have done something wrong. The parents expect this of the children before they restore them to favor. In the same way, the godly know very well that it would only be mocking God to seek reconciliation with him because of their sins and yet have no intention to forsake them. Should an adulterous wife achieve anything when she seeks reconciliation with her husband, who knows very well that she has no intention of refraining from adultery? Remember, God knows our thoughts afar off. He knows long before we do what we plan to do (Deut. 31:21).

If we have sinned and want to be reconciled to God, then we must sincerely plan to forsake that sin and pray for mercy and grace.

3. They seek forgiveness in Christ. Like the repentant David, their faith is stirred up when their sins are forgiven by the blood of Christ (Rom. 3:25). They understand well that the great guilt and awful stain brought upon them as fallen sinners by evil and sin cannot be removed by mere tears, even if they cried both their eyes out (Jer. 2:22). They clearly understand that nothing other than the lifeblood of Christ can accomplish this. Therefore, they will not allow their souls to rest until they have their hearts sprinkled by faith with the blood of God's Son, which alone can cleanse them from dead works (Heb. 9:14). They seek reconciliation with God through Jesus Christ, the beloved in whom God is well pleased and who is their propitiation.

Ungodly people know nothing of this experience. Therefore, they generally ignore the matter of reconciliation. If they have suffered a little heartache and perhaps have shed a tear or two for their sins, they think everything is fine; God should now be completely satisfied. But such ungodly thoughts are far removed from the godly. When the godly sin, their souls cannot be comforted until they are reconciled with God, and reconciliation with God is possible only through true faith in the blood of God's Son.

Obtaining Spiritual Gain from Falling into Sin

The third exercise that reveals true godliness is that, when we are overcome by some transgression, we not only forsake it and reconcile ourselves to God but also try to make an effective antidote out of its venomous poison. We try to use our stumbling as a motivation to stimulate within us the following special virtues because of our fall:

1. More prudence in our conduct. We try to guard ourselves better against that sin and against all sin in the future. That means that now that we have discovered, to our own shame and through restoration, how easily we can fall into sin if we are not on our guard, we avoid opportunities to sin from the start and more diligently use the means to godliness. That is what David did (Ps. 119:37–38).

2. More humility before God and men. Because of our great weakness and sin, we acknowledge that we deserve all punishment, scorn, and contempt. We learn to put our nose in the dust with the rest of the church of God when the Lord visits us with some trial. We patiently bear his chastisement, knowing that we greatly deserve it because we have sinned against God. Moreover, we know that it is necessary for us to be pruned in that way since our carnal nature is responsible for so much destruction. That is how David felt about his sin (Psalm 51). We should therefore be patient with our fellow men when they sin against God or perhaps against us, taking care that we do not rebuke them too sharply. Rather, we should bear with their sin with a spirit of meekness by comparing them to ourselves, for we may also have similarly transgressed in the past. We still stumble in many things and might also unexpectedly be overcome by such a transgression in the future (Gal. 6:1).

We should also get used to thinking, when something happens that is not quite to our liking, that it is no surprise that things do not go according to our own will since we do not always behave according to God's will. Why should we, poor sinful people, be roused to anger because of some mischief or slander committed against us? Surely, we often deserve it. We have earned it and need to be treated poorly to humble ourselves and hate the sins that bring all this upon us.

3. More zeal in building God's church. Our sin ought to inspire more zeal in us to build up God's church and edify our neighbors. We ought to consider that our sins have offended the people of God. We have also selfishly slandered the good name of God. Then, too, if we have committed a secret sin, we have grieved the good Spirit of God. Thus, we should now counter this by magnifying God's name and edifying our fellow men. We should also sincerely walk in godliness so we may please God's Spirit anew. By a more diligent exercise of godliness, we can help restore whatever has been disturbed by our stumbling. This also was David's intention after his fall (Psalm 51).

Godliness is nurtured by these virtues as well as by means of other spiritual exercises. Just as great care and attention helps newborn babies, if they are basically in good health, to grow and develop, so these practices increasingly develop godly life in us and cause it to grow.

Three More Excellent Virtues

From the previous discussion, we conclude that when God's will is observed, true godliness possesses three most glorious and excellent virtues. Those are to be steadfast, immovable, and abounding in seeking to do God's will. We will discuss these three attributes in reverse order.

1. It teaches us to abound in doing God's will. True godliness does not strive after God's will for any other reason than that it is God's will. True godliness teaches us that we should not hold on to even one sin, making it our pet sin, but we should refrain from all sin because the Lord loathes and forbids all sin (Ps. 119:101). This kind of godliness also teaches us that we should not neglect even one virtue or Christian duty, making it, so to speak, an outcast. We should honor and observe all virtues because they all please the Holy Spirit and he commands them all.

The godly person will not, like Herod, gladly do many things that John taught and at the same time hold on to one pet sin. Instead, like David, he will keep his feet from every evil way. Unlike the hypocritical Israelite, he will not say to a man of God that he will do everything he has been taught in the name of the Lord and then, after having understood the will of God, refuse to obey it. Like Abraham, he will try to be obedient in all of his duties. That is what the apostle calls abounding in the work of the Lord.

Some choose to do otherwise, embracing some virtue or duty but neglecting or completely ignoring another. For example, some are baptized and have their children baptized but will not go to the Lord's Supper. Or some privately pray but do not teach their households to pray nor pray with them in the fear of the Lord. That kind of person does not submit himself to God's law but makes himself a judge over God's law, as is explained in James 4:11, for he dares to take away from and reject all that the law praises and approves.

On the other hand, those who refrain from some sins or wrong whims while still holding fast to some pet sin that they cherish do not submit to God's Word either. For example, some refrain from prostitution or rolling dice but not from drinking and idle talk at mealtimes or from bitterness or strife. They are not submissive, for God's Word forbids all those sins. Indeed, that kind of person has begun to judge God's law as being too narrow, therefore making himself a judge over the law. His deeds cannot please God; he is declared guilty of breaking all the commandments because of his attitude.

The godly person, however, is of a different mind. He sincerely tries to refrain from all the sin he can. He continually fights against those sins that cling to him against his will. He laments, deplores, fights, and prunes these sins as much as he can. He practices all the virtues and holy duties that he is able to perform and strives to develop those virtues that may be obtained only by long practice and much effort, making use of the means God offers.

Ungodly people fall miserably short in this. They, like Herod, think that they do well if they repent of many things, but they still hold on to some pet sin like a lover, having no intention of letting it go (Job 20:12–13). They should heed this warning and consider the consequences of their actions. As long as they continue to hold on to this sin, no reconciliation is possible between them and God, for they hold on to the sin that God most hates in them. It is similar to an occurrence of adultery. When there is talk about the reconciliation of a respectable man with his adulterous wife, the husband is most hostile to the lover with whom his wife has most played the harlot and with whom she is still infatuated. If reconciliation between her and her husband is ever going to take place, she should above all else discard and forsake this lover.

2. It teaches us to steadfastly do God's will. We do his will not only when it coincides with bringing us comfort, profit, or reputation and when everything goes well but also when we can expect only great ingratitude, loss, or humiliation from the world—indeed, opposition and hostility from all sides. For in this, true godliness will teach us to place God's will above pleasure, profit, or reputation; we will do whatever pleases God in spite of gratitude or ingratitude, honor or dishonor, profit or loss. The apostle calls this being "stedfast, unmoveable, always abounding in the work of the Lord" (1 Cor. 15:58).

True godliness taught the three godly men, Shadrach, Meshach, and Abednego, to answer King Nebuchadnezzar by saying, "If it be so, our God whom we serve is able to deliver us from the burning fiery furnace, and he will deliver us out of thine hand, O king. But if not, be it known unto thee, O king, that we will not serve thy gods, nor worship the golden image which thou hast set up" (Dan. 3:17–18).

The apostle Paul was of the same mind (see 2 Corinthians 6). So were all those godly people who did not value their lives above martyrdom but kept the faith of Jesus and the commandments of God (Revelation 12:17). It is certainly true that only good soil persistently "bring[s] forth fruit with patience" (Luke 8:15). The righteous and the truly godly are this good soil. Listen to what the prophet says about this: "Who said unto his father and to his mother, I have not seen him; neither did he acknowledge his brethren, nor knew his own children: for they have observed thy word, and kept thy covenant" (Deut. 33:9).

It is also clear that those who are faithful in God's service and are truly godly people do not merely practice godliness when it pays to do so in a worldly sense but regard godliness itself as great gain. They are steadfast in godliness even when it causes them much worldly loss. They therefore prove that they love godliness for its own sake.

What kind of poor religion does someone practice when he gives up serving God every time opposition comes along? What do we think of a servant who serves his master only when everything suits him but deserts the master as soon as some difficulty arises? Solomon's proverb certainly applies here: "If thou faint in the day of adversity, thy strength is small" (Prov. 24:10). They are like disloyal soldiers who turn their backs on their commander and sneak away in retreat when they see the enemy approaching.

Those who walk steadily in God's way only as long as great numbers of people go along with them should also take heed. As soon as the crowd wants something different, for example, a big party, a great dinner, a wedding feast, or something similar, then they lack the courage to resist. They allow themselves to drift along with the current flood of disorder. In those circumstances in which the Lord God most needs their service and in which he demands and expects to be honored and served, they desert him. Such people certainly do not produce fruit with patience (Luke 8:15).

3. It teaches us to be steadfast in doing God's will. This means not doing his will just sometimes, when we're spiritually motivated or when we're in the mood, for example. We do God's will then with great earnestness, diligence, and perseverance. But at other times, when we're not in the mood, we often let things slip and slide for a while. True godliness teaches us that it is wise and right to

always be steadfast in the Lord and not to waver. Indeed, true godliness sees to it that we do well in God's service and that we make
up our minds to remain with the Lord forever. Like a Hebrew servant, we would gladly have our ears pierced at the doorpost of the
house of the Lord in order to remain in God's service.

The godly life is not like the morning dew, which soon disap-
pears (Hosea 6:4). Rather, it is like a fountain from which living
water flows (John 7:38). It is indeed a life that never dies; it begins
in this life and continues in the life to come, where it continues eternally. As Christ the Lord says, "Verily, verily, I say unto you, If a
man keep my saying, he shall never see death" (John 8:51). In that
spirit, David calls out to the Lord, "So shall I keep thy law continually for ever and ever" (Ps. 119:44).

Those who do not persevere in practicing true godliness but
abandon it and become entangled in worldliness again are like a
dog that returns to its vomit and as a washed sow that goes back to
wallowing in the mire. They have the form but not the power of
true godliness. Clearly, they are at best no better than dogs that,
only because of the nagging ache in their stomach, temporarily forsake the filth of sins. They are like pigs that have not changed inside
but have been washed only outwardly of their filth (2 Peter 2:22).
But whoever has truly received the power of godliness perseveres
to the end. That person rejoices in the Lord so much that he is able
to say what Peter said when asked if he wanted to forsake his God:
"Lord, to whom shall we go? Thou hast the words of eternal life"
(John 6:68).

BOOK
2

The Kingdom of Darkness Opposes the Practice of Godliness

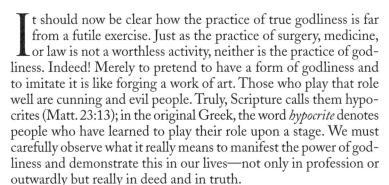

It should now be clear how the practice of true godliness is far from a futile exercise. Just as the practice of surgery, medicine, or law is not a worthless activity, neither is the practice of godliness. Indeed! Merely to pretend to have a form of godliness and to imitate it is like forging a work of art. Those who play that role well are cunning and evil people. Truly, Scripture calls them hypocrites (Matt. 23:13); in the original Greek, the word *hypocrite* denotes people who have learned to play their role upon a stage. We must carefully observe what it really means to manifest the power of godliness and demonstrate this in our lives—not only in profession or outwardly but really in deed and in truth.

Many do not pay attention to this and regard the matter as if the practice of godliness consisted of only confessing the Christian faith, diligently attending church and the Lord's Supper, being careful not to commit offensive sins, and living amiably with one's neighbors. In this way, many people have deceived themselves all too quickly in thinking that they are truly godly, while they really only have the appearance of godliness.

If we do not want to be deceived in this important matter, we should accept that the practice of godliness is a very strenuous undertaking that spreads like a good leaven until it has permeated every part of life, including the entire thought and the entire conduct of a person.

It is therefore necessary to apply good counsel as well as great diligence and faithfulness. In particular, we should give heed to the following three things for practicing true godliness, and each of these should be examined according to its own nature:

- the kingdom of darkness, which opposes true godliness
- the kingdom of grace, which promotes true godliness
- the divine guidance that must be followed if we wish to withstand the kingdom of darkness and to establish the kingdom of grace more and more within us so that we may obtain true godliness

The Kingdom of Darkness in General

With regard to the kingdom of darkness, the Christian who wants to practice godliness in all sincerity should first and foremost be mindful of the existence of an undivided spiritual power of darkness. It opposes and besieges anyone who practices true godliness and seeks to obstruct and thwart everyone in their holy work (Matt. 12:26; Col. 1:13). Note that this kingdom of darkness is full of craftiness, treason, and deceit because it performs all its practices in the dark. It is full of venom, bitterness, and cruelty, full of relentless spirits that roam about day and night and tirelessly foster all kinds of ungodliness as they seek to corrupt souls.

This kingdom is presented to us as the kingdom of Egypt. Just think of how much opposition and resistance the powers of Egypt exerted in keeping Israel, God's chosen people, in servitude to them, even when the Egyptians were forced to let Israel go so that they might hold a feast to their God (Exod. 5:1). Observe with what madness and great frenzy they afterward pursued Israel to bring them back into their former bondage (Exodus 14). This is also what happens to Christians when they begin to practice true godliness. No sooner has the Christian made up his mind to serve the Lord God with all his heart than the kingdom of darkness is stirred up to resist him like a brutal jailer who immediately acts to stop his prisoners from escaping as soon as he discovers their plans. To whatever degree a person truly succeeds in freeing himself from the bondage of sin, to that same degree this kingdom of darkness will oppose the struggle most fiercely and mobilize all its forces against the person. It will do battle with all its power to bring that person back into bondage, if that were possible. It is just like the jailer who keeps quiet when his prisoners are firmly chained. But as soon as some of them throw off their shackles, free themselves, and escape from prison, the jailer mobilizes the entire town and surrounding area against them. In the same way, the kingdom of darkness is most fiercely aroused as soon as it discovers that a person is escaping the bondage of sin and is engaged in the service of the Lord our God.

Note that the most important allies of the kingdom of darkness are the three spiritual enemies of the believer: the devil, the world, and our carnal flesh, whose wisdom Scripture calls earthly, sensual, and devilish (James 3:15). These are sly, fierce, and tireless enemies who seek to bring frail people to sin at every possible opportunity and to bring them back into the bondage of sin, on which all the might and dominion of this kingdom's power and rule are based.

These three enemies and allies in the kingdom of darkness resolutely roam about day and night, seeking to lead us into sin. They never miss a chance or let any opportunity pass to seduce us and tempt us to sin. They use everything we possess as well as every event and circumstance to seduce us to sin. They pay attention to our hearts, minds, affections, memories, and consciences; to our eyes and ears, our mouths and tongues; to our hands and feet; indeed, to all our actions in order to deceive and seduce us. Our spiritual enemies are always seeking to corrupt us in whatever we undertake or begin to do and in all our endeavors and plans.

Moreover, they are present when we pray or engage in any holy exercise such as showing kindness to our fellow neighbor, giving to the poor, or visiting the sick. They hover about us when we go to work and when we relax a little and enjoy ourselves or when we want to prepare a meal for friends or buy some clothes or anything else we do in life. They hover when we want to give orders to others, in accordance with our position, or when we are under the orders of another; when we speak or keep silent; when we go to bed or get up. Are we taking care of business or our individual concerns? Are we in conversation, going to bed, or getting up? Are we in the company of others or alone? Whether we are successful or meeting with opposition, whether we are praised or rebuked, honored or despised, whether things are being done satisfactorily or not to our liking, in short, whatever happens to us, these spiritual enemies are always around us or in us. These warriors of the kingdom of darkness are constantly lying in wait to take every opportunity to outwit us and ensnare us into sin (Job 18:18).

You may be certain that such a kingdom of darkness exists and that it opposes the practice of true godliness. That is exactly how things really are. Do you sincerely desire to practice true godliness? Then you must pay careful attention to this, and you need to be constantly on guard. It is certainly true that many practice godliness poorly because they are not prepared for the strong power that exerts itself against the practice of true godliness. They imagine that it can be accomplished without any difficulty, but that is certainly not the case! It is therefore easy to understand how it is impossible for anyone who has so many tremendously crafty, fierce, and tireless enemies and yet is not on guard against them, fully aware of them, or does not watch carefully, to keep his soul from destruction.

Is it not true that the beautiful town of Laish (Judg. 18:27) was taken by surprise because it did not suspect that it could be besieged and surrounded by its enormously deceitful and strong enemies? Or that it was not aware of them and so made not the slightest preparation for its defense? That is exactly what happens to careless people who do not know that spiritual enemies who lie in wait for their souls surround them on all sides. They live as if this were not so. Surely, this will lead many a soul to destruction. Surely, this is why many go down to hell who had looked forward to going up to heaven. When it is too late, they are surprised to find themselves thrown into outer darkness. They had never concerned themselves in this life with that possibility, even though God's messengers had clearly informed them that they could expect the kingdom of darkness to attempt great disastrous overthrows. How could it be otherwise?

My dear friend, carefully consider this: Does not this hellish devil, as Scripture confirms, always go about in darkness like a roaring lion, seeking how he may devour our souls (1 Peter 5:8)? Is not the whole world, which lies in wickedness (1 John 5:19), always seeking to defile us (James 1:27) along with her own followers and to lead us away from the right path? Is not our carnal flesh, according to its own nature, always going in the wrong way, lusting against the Spirit like the Israelites of old (Ps. 95:10)? Should a frail man not be careful of this? Should he expect to escape when he offers no resistance? Surely, that is impossible! To be brief, who does not understand that a whole kingdom of crafty, tireless, fierce, and destructive spirits is much too strong for a single carnal, slothful, inattentive, easygoing, careless human who is oblivious to all things spiritual? Tragically, we find too many in this state everywhere!

We conclude, therefore, that it is impossible for a man to be saved from destruction or perdition, let alone to practice true godliness in all sincerity, unless he guards himself with zeal, care, and diligence against this kingdom of darkness. We should pay attention to this. The more the devil hides this from our eyes (for he always tries to keep us from being suspicious of him and to keep us from being on our guard when he carries out his works of darkness), the more diligent we need to be to arm ourselves against him. He always seeks to work in the dark so that we do not suspect this kingdom's existence, which makes it far easier for him to deliver his deadly blows. In what follows, we will discuss in more detail the characteristics of the aforementioned three allies of the kingdom of darkness.

The Three Powers of the Kingdom of Darkness

Our Carnal Flesh and Its Three Horns

As far as our flesh is concerned, we understand that inherent corruption and depravity of the entire human nature incline us to every evil and make us incapable of any good (Ps. 51:5). This also includes the corruption and the power of sin a depraved person increasingly brings upon himself during a career of sin (Jer. 13:23; Ezek. 18:30–31; Heb. 12:1).

This carnal flesh is a very evil, sinful, and disorderly monster in which various kinds of corruption are hidden that dovetail well with our individual traits and circumstances so as to bind and unite us with them as if they were our own. Thus, it tarnishes and pollutes everything that is within us and around us. If we want to remain unharmed, it is necessary to be continually on guard against this. This gruesome, destructive monster notably possesses what may be called three harmful horns with which it fatally wounds many souls and completely overthrows true godliness when no prompt action is taken against it. These horns are (1) a carnal or natural mind, (2) evil desires, and (3) a corrupt conscience.

1. The first horn: the carnal mind of the flesh. This horn is dead set against the wisdom and counsel of God, as revealed in his Word, and therefore is emphatically described as being at enmity against God (Rom. 8:7). It is so impertinent that it considers the practice of godliness, demanded by God in his Word, as pure madness and foolishness (2 Kings 9:11; 1 Cor. 1:18). Indeed, it regards the desire to live a holy life, as I have described the practice of godliness in my first book, as no better than prudishness, legalism, and hypocrisy. The carnal mind will never accept bending, yielding, and subjecting all things to the service of God in order to give first priority to the practice of true godliness. Anything rather than that! On the contrary, the carnal mind wants true godliness—indeed, everything—to bend, yield, and be made subject to its own plans and pursuits.

That is how it is! The carnal mind devises a certain way of Christian life through which it imagines that God as well as man can be satisfied. Carnal man is willing to do certain things that God requires, such as giving money to the poor, going to church, and even partaking of the Lord's Supper. However, other things that God also requires, such as instructing one's household in the fear of the Lord, regularly visiting the sick, and comforting the poor, are not considered necessary or important. Carnal man rejects those things, not taking the slightest interest in them. Yet the things he himself has chosen he regards as the only right and reasonable Christian way of life. He affirms this as a virtuous and wise way of life. Everything outside of this he calls insincerity, prudishness, narrow-mindedness, superstition, or hypocrisy. Everything that does not fit into his own self-approved program he considers lukewarm, careless, slothful, or ungodly. Truly, these people are foolish because they deceive their own hearts with false arguments, as the apostle

James explains when, for those very reasons, he declares that "this man's religion is vain" (James 1:26). Carnal people subject God's Word to their own minds and manipulate it as they see fit, according to their understanding, instead of subordinating and ordering their thoughts and minds so that they are brought into captivity to God's Word (2 Cor. 10:5).

Carnal reason clings to this as stubbornly and desperately as a thief to the gallows. A person with this cannot be separated from it except by the power of the Holy Spirit.

And so many worldly wise people who refuse to listen to the words of the apostle are corrupted. The apostle says, "Let no man deceive himself. If any man among you seemeth to be wise in this world, let him become a fool, that he may be wise" (1 Cor. 3:18). Worldly wise people also make no effort to read God's Word attentively, although it is God's wisdom. They learn in vain because they apply their own vain understanding to it (Prov. 3:5). Oh, how many a soul has been destroyed by this horn of his depraved flesh! I really do not know whether more people are lost by the deceitful instruction of the carnal mind (which we will study in more detail) or by the corruption of the depraved lusts and desires of the flesh, which we will consider next.

2. The second horn: the evil desire of the flesh. We understand this to be the perverseness of man's will and desires that not only resist the counsel of God but also are often contrary to the guidance of man's own mind. Therefore, man, inflamed by the evil desires of the flesh, boldly does things that he himself acknowledges to be wrong, evil, unprofitable, and vain (Titus 3:9; Jude 10).

With this horn, many have been brought under the acute pressure and bondage of detrimental cravings: some of drunkenness, others of fornication, still others of greed or ambition. This happens regardless of whether there is little or much opposition to what they do and whether what they want is just or unjust. Even when there is little or much debate over it being right or wrong, they stubbornly persist and apply everything to pursuing that specific lust. This lust overcomes all reason.

These people say in their hearts and show by their deeds that as far as God's laws are concerned, "We do not want to be subjected in this way" (cf. Jer. 2:20). They say, "Let us break their bands asunder, and cast away their cords from us" (Ps. 2:3).

These cravings of the flesh are extremely flattering and continuously press a man to get what they want. They are what Delilah was to Samson, despite his strength.

They are also very stubborn and unreasonable when we refuse them something. They do not want to be persuaded and are not appeased until their lust has been satisfied. They speak as Rachel did: "Give me children, or else I die" (Gen. 30:1). It would indeed be good if the matter ended there. Unfortunately, the cravings of the flesh become stronger to the extent that we try to appease them. The person who tries to appease a craving falls more and more under its spell by being drawn daily into satiating it; the more he does so, the more he becomes inflamed with his evil desires (Rom. 1:27). The result is that many souls are mortally wounded by this horn of evil desire.

3. The third horn: the depraved conscience. When a man acts badly through wrong thinking or the evil desire of the flesh, the carnal and corrupted conscience comes along to deceive him by saying that what he did wasn't really so bad and arguing that God will not reject him for it. After all, God is gracious. All men have faults, but God is merciful. God gives and forgives all. They further say that they may have certain faults yet they also have certain virtues to compensate for them. They believe that they are not the worst offenders and that God can easily overlook them and save them with the rest because, after all, they are not Turks or heathens but baptized Christians who regularly attend church.

This is how the depraved conscience flatters a poor man when he sins beyond measure. It rocks him into the sleep of indifference as if it were reasonably well with his salvation, when in truth it is far from being well. It does that even when a poor man is driven by his lusts and becomes frivolous, superficial, thoughtless, and extravagant; even when he does not pray with or instruct his own family in household catechizing and family devotions; yes, even when he is not serious about his prayer life in private or does not diligently read God's Word and neglects holy meditation. Indeed, a carnal conscience flatters even when he does not instruct others in a Christian way and fails to admonish or comfort where it is needed. Truly, even when he fails to do any of the above and also neglects to watch and pray in accordance with Christ's admonition (Mark 13) and recklessly abandons himself to a worldly existence, choking in its lusts, the deceitful, carnal conscience will still acquit him. It will bless him when he transgresses in this way, saying, "Now look, it's no problem. Everything will be all right in the end; all will be well."

We have seen this happen to many. If somehow the conscience is awakened a little and begins to accuse someone about this conduct, then the depraved monster, the corrupt flesh, tries to distract the person. It does so with many carnal pleasures and diversions, some that attract them to taverns, others that use family games or something like that to numb the conscience. And it succeeds! The corrupt conscience is then silenced while the problem for which it raised its voice has not diminished at all. Rather, it has grown larger.

Such people are like careless people who have amassed great debts in various taverns through their drinking habits and frivolity. When they are summoned to pay their debts, they visit other taverns where their credit is still good so that they can drown their problem. Everyone knows this does not alter their situation. They will be warned more strongly next time and summoned more firmly to pay. Conscience exhorts in the same way. Since worldly people do not take any notice, this horn, the debased conscience, completely corrupts many souls by rocking them to sleep. Their consciences say, "Peace and safety," but "then sudden destruction cometh upon them, as travail upon a woman with child; and they shall not escape" (1 Thess. 5:3). This is the nature of corrupt flesh. Clearly, we should take careful notice and guard against this if we desire to practice godliness well. Then eternal damnation and banishment from the presence of the Lord's countenance can be avoided.

The Evil World

By this evil world, we understand the common course of action of worldly people, as we have seen. This includes the type of lifestyle, conduct, and conversation that are common among worldly people. The apostle calls this "the course of this world" (Eph. 2:2). This wicked world is a particularly powerful and dangerous enemy of the soul. It rises powerfully against the practitioner of true godliness. It has three specific horns by which it mortally wounds many souls and completely overthrows godliness in many hearts when no appropriate action is taken against it. These three horns are (1) erroneous customs and traditions, (2) wrong yet celebrated and distinguished role models, and (3) mistaken and wrong premises for reward and compensation.

1. The first horn of the world: wrong old traditions and customs. These customs are entirely opposed to the right practice of true godliness that admonishes us not to be conformed to this world (Rom. 12:2). On the contrary, the old traditions and customs want us to do just the opposite: to be conformed to the world. The world thinks that it suffers a great injustice from our not conforming and strongly demands that the old traditions and customs be maintained and followed everywhere without allowing them to be examined and proved right or wrong. It declares bluntly that old customs must be maintained and practiced continually simply because they are the ancient traditions and customs, of whatever sort they may be. The world therefore creates pandemonium against those who try to eliminate any of the world's ancient traditions because they find these to be wrong and contrary to the practice of godliness. The world lashes out immediately and slanders those who reject such traditions, labeling them "legalists." "Why, if they were to get their own way, these people would make havoc of everything," the world says. "They must be watched, thwarted, and frustrated wherever possible and wherever lawful."

By this first horn, the world maintains many erroneous practices that fly straight in the face of godliness, such as idolatrous, pagan, and devilish festivities that should have been abolished long ago. What occasions they offer for drunkenness and frivolous dancing! What dancing and singing we see at wedding feasts and other merry gatherings, all indulged in with never a qualm of conscience or serious thought!

Even now, despite the light of the gospel, they still maintain as a custom the peculiar tradition of the bride and groom striding into church with a crowd of people, right in the middle of a sermon or at least coming in and being seated after the solemn church service has already started.[1] Or think of the tradition of the bride not attend-

1. In seventeeth-century Netherlands, weddings were usually conducted on Sundays in connection with a regular worship service.

ing church during her engagement. Or of asking irresponsible unchurched people from who knows where to be witnesses (godparents) at the baptism of a child, just as long as they are relatives. In addition, they postpone the baptism for three or four weeks until the witnesses arrive or whenever it suits them rather than choose devout and well-known Christians who live nearby.[2] There are many such sinful, capricious people who, though plainly opposed to God's will, judge and regard those who challenge them as extremists or narrow-minded souls. So the world succeeds in enticing the careless children of men with the glitter of the outward appearances of holiness found in old customs. It even seems to these careless, worldly people who still wish to be regarded as good Christians that the old traditions and customs of the present world, which lays in complete wickedness (1 John 5:19), actually possess more authority and have more respectability and honor than the holy, enduring, and eternal Word of God! Therefore, worldly people have no objection to negating and ignoring the express and clear explanation of Holy Scripture. They pay little attention to it, yet they highly esteem whatever is covered with the cloak of the world's ancient traditions and customs. They dare not make any changes, even when it is clearly shown to them, if they would but see, that in Israel, which means among the Christians and God's people, there were many traditions and customs that were certainly never the laws of Jacob's God (Ps. 81:4). On the contrary, they actually contradict the legislation of the God of Jacob. Yet worldly people ought to know very well that not one of those prescriptions or rules counts against the decrees and royal prerogatives of our God! No, not one of those ancient traditions or customs possesses any legitimacy, for, old as they are, they are opposed to the ancient Word of God.

2. The second horn of the world: wrong yet celebrated and very distinguished role models. The world uses many people to wound souls and hinder godliness. Certainly, it has many important and prominent persons in various places who daily have the nerve to do

2. The tradition of having witnesses or sponsors (sometimes called godparents) accompany parents at the time of baptism was allowed in the Reformed churches of the Netherlands until the eighteenth century, provided they were godly. Article 57 of the Synod of Dort (1618–19) says, "In congregations where sponsors or witnesses are taken at baptism beside the father (which custom, not being objectional in itself, is not easily changed), it is proper that such be taken who agree with the pure doctrine and are pious in their conversation."

many things that are not right and proper, and many more who
neglect the many things that they ought to do. The world does not
pay attention to whether these people do what they do out of a hidden depraved conscience or simply out of human weakness. The
example is good enough for others to follow their lead (Ps. 106:35;
John 7:48).

The world says, "Look, these people have no scruples about being
friendly and merry at a wedding;[3] they even have fun celebrating at
the fairs and carnivals. They think nothing of marrying their children off to Roman Catholics or to folks of some other religious per-
suasion." These are respectable people! They have no misgivings
about not going to church regularly, or not having family Bible study,
or about neglecting the Holy Supper. They regard strict observance
of the Lord's Day as being overly scrupulous because it prevents
them from going for a ride or preparing a big dinner. They make it
impossible for even their most important guests to attend church
in the afternoon because of the big and late Sunday dinner.[4] Yet the
world says these are intelligent and respectable people; they are
devout, revered, admired, and popular citizens! They value the salvation of their souls just as seriously as anyone else; surely, they
would not do anything to imperil their souls! What has gotten into
you that you want to be such spoilsports? Do you not understand
that what you are promoting is not true godliness but only obsti-
nacy, prudishness, and hypocrisy?

Note that the world knows well how she may wound many souls
and effectively hinder real godliness with this horn of wrong role models. Because of this, a poor, careless man becomes foolhardy in his miserable and reckless life. He thinks that he is beyond reproach if he can
quote the example of some celebrity who is highly regarded and popular and has done—or neglected—the same things that he himself
has done. If someone were to complain, or if his conscience were to
accuse him, then the man is able to justify his conduct by reminding
himself, "Well, I am not the only one. Everyone else does it."

3. Being "friendly and merry at a wedding" refers to going along with worldly practices
in wedding ceremonies and their receptions, which often involved dancing and excessive
drinking. The Dutch Second Reformation divines condemned these practices.

4. In Teellinck's day, most Reformed families prepared simple meals for the Lord's Day
on Saturday. Those who adhered to a less strict Sabbath would, on occasion, invite relatives
for a large Sunday meal, which prevented them from attending the Sunday afternoon worship service. Teellinck is lamenting that practice.

Truly, sin has become so brazen among people because of the world's deceitful examples that they sometimes go as far as to pledge and bind themselves under oath, either by solemn promise, handshakes, or sometimes even a stiff drink, to do what is not right and proper—indeed, to do evil. This deception has filled the world with many shameless evildoers since each one is encouraged to outdo the other. Following the general trend embarrasses no one. They usually exchange words of praise, honor, and gratitude, whereas shame and embarrassment are what they really deserve. This has resulted in untold harm to true godliness. Therefore, we should be on our guard against being gored by this horn.

3. The third horn of the world: the erroneous and evil premise of reward and recompense. It is like this: The evil, fallen world, which hates godliness, works hard to aid and promote ungodliness—at least in subtle ways. So it manages affairs in such a way as to threaten and intimidate, as Saul did to his courtiers in 1 Samuel 22:7–8, those who sincerely want to openly persevere in godliness. It does this with the message that they will never be very successful in this world if they persist in their ways. Indeed, it tries to convince them that those who choose to walk that path will be made unwelcome everywhere. It tells them that they are not living in a world in which godliness should be strictly practiced in the ways we have just described. However, if the godly still persist, then it begins to openly intimidate and threaten them by saying they cannot expect to make any progress and they will never gain a promotion. Everyone will be against them, and they will be pushed aside and rejected as prudish people, whereas others will enjoy the best of everything. By contrast, the world promises everything to those who will conform and adapt to the world's ways and fashion themselves to the norms of social life and agree with all its values. They will be welcomed and loved by great and small alike. Indeed, they will be courted and helped along the way by all who have power to do so (Num. 22:7, 16–41).

That is how the wicked world goes to work. It does not stop with just threats and promises but actually carries out those threats against many people, going so far as to label those who will not conform as useless people. We find that worldly people will not cooperate with those who begin to practice true godliness in honesty and sincerity and who order and arrange their affairs according to God's service, subjecting all their matters to his will. The world brands these people as uncooperative folk when in reality they are most friendly, polite, and loving. Yet wicked, worldly people believe that whatever believers do diligently in the service of the Lord is done only to reproach them because of their lukewarmness and indolence. Therefore, worldly people cannot enjoy the presence of the godly and hate the sight of them.

On the other hand, the worldly minded reward and support those who model the worship of God after the manner of the world and who adjust and conform to its ideas. When pliable Christians have learned to tolerate such arrogance and lasciviousness and have lost concern for practical godliness, they will never rebuke others for their wrongdoing. They keep silent when they see these wretched, secular people corrupting their souls. Yes, they even encourage them with their smiles. Such people will be courted and welcomed everywhere.

Of course, worldly people will love them to the degree that these fickle people show the form of godliness. Because those who are regarded as religious and who know worldly conduct for what it is do not complain or warn them, secular people consider their lifestyle and conduct, which is totally wrong, to be good and pious. Only opinionated and intolerant characters tell them that they must be more diligent in the practice of true godliness in order to enjoy the commendation and true comfort of real godliness.

And so the practitioners of true godliness are not at all respected by worldly people. Nor are they rewarded or supported in their efforts. On the other hand, the people who would shape godliness according to the world are heartily welcomed and assisted. It is precisely by this unjust and perverse application of reward and compensation that many a soul has been greatly wounded and that true godliness has been severely suppressed. Therefore, the person who sincerely wants to practice godliness must arm himself thoroughly against these goring horns. We will say more on this when we consider the kingdom of grace.

The Devil with His Three Horns

When we refer to the devils of hell, we mean all the powerful, spiritual, evil spirits that are in the air (Eph. 6:12) and control the children of disobedience (Eph. 2:2). The head and ruler of this evil realm, named Beelzebub, is more commonly known as the devil (Matt. 12:24). This devil of hell, together with his hellish angels and spirits, is an enemy who is greatly to be feared, for he is full of venom, craftiness, and power. Moreover, he is unrelenting in his efforts. He lies in wait for us day and night. He cannot be satisfied but is like a ravenous wolf or bear; the more soul blood he has devoured, the more rabid he becomes and the more blood he craves. What makes this enemy even more dangerous and harmful is that he also has the world and our own depravity working on his side. They are his allies against our poor, naked, defenseless souls. The devil knows extremely well how to use them to ruin more and more souls. In this he is just like cruel Pharaoh. He uses our depravity and the world as his chariots and horses to hunt us down, catch, and ruin us. This furious devil of hell has three dreadful and destructive horns that are especially to be feared. Truly, he fatally injures many souls and suppresses true godliness with the horns of (1) demonic, evil, and immoral inner temptations; (2) false doctrine and its enforcement; and (3) fierce persecution and slander.

Various Evil Temptations

There are many evil inner temptations, harassments, activities, and thoughts that Satan uses as his fiery darts to assault men and miserably wound their souls. These may be grouped into three categories: (1) those that he stirs up and arouses from the impulses of a person's own depravity, (2) those that are a result of outward worldly things, (3) those that he arouses in man without using the above mentioned conditions.

1. Those that he stirs up and arouses from the impulses of a person's own depravity. The situation is as follows. Satan investigates with the greatest care to discover the sins and wrongdoings to which each man is individually most inclined because of the special circumstances of his body, education, and habits. He accordingly incites that man's depravity and increasingly entices him by means of evil suggestions, corrupt imaginations, and frightening contemplations toward that very sin to which he is already most inclined, be it meanness, sexual indecency, pomposity, or whatever. So the man begins to feel the carnal lust and desire gradually heating within him to

the boiling point. He experiences unusually strong stimulations and inclinations to that particular sin of indecency or revenge or anger. This is secretly caused by those hidden stirrings, the fiery darts and provocation of Satan.

That is why the apostle warns us against unrighteous anger by immediately adding, "Neither give place to the devil" (Eph. 4:27). He thereby teaches us that it is the devil who fans rising anger. It is the same with other sins, yet foolish man usually does not pay attention to this. If he still thinks about it at all, for the devil also tries to remove all such concerns from his mind, he thinks that his flesh is growing a little stronger, more luxuriant, or more obstinate in fighting sin. All the while, this is controlled by our spiritual enemy, who is manipulating and goading that man to do what he already is inclined to do. Satan does this in the dark, as it were, so that he is not seen, and there is neither wisdom nor power present in vulnerable man to ward off these fiery darts of the devil any more than thirsty animals, when they are untied and led to a bucket of water, have the mind to abstain from drinking. A person must pay careful attention to this if he wants to refrain from sinning and practice sincere godliness. When he feels his flesh increasingly lusting for something, particularly when he realizes that this lust is urging him on and when his passions become hot, then he should pay attention to the claws of Satan in this and leap back, seeing to it that he does not surrender lest he be thoroughly ruined. Indeed, the more he is aroused, the more he needs to be on his guard.

As we consider this point in particular, we should carefully note that Satan possesses three more fiery arrows. These are despair, conceited imagination, and laziness. Satan does not always shoot these arrows, but he does use them when he sees a person at the point of beginning to pay attention to his eternal salvation. He shoots these arrows according to the character that he observes in people he is stalking. While he waits in ambush in order to deceive them, he sees that some are pessimistic, some are optimistic, and some are in between and of an easygoing nature.

He assaults the first group, the pessimists, with desperation and disbelief. He seeks to hide the compassion of God from them. He tries to deceive them into thinking that God's righteousness is so severe and so demanding that Christ's merits are difficult to obtain. He suggests that since their sins are so many and so great, there is no hope for them (Ezek. 33:10). With these cruel torments he often terrorizes the pessimists so that they see no comfort and yield without hope. These people cannot be helped unless they begin to take notice of Satan's cunning and realize that this is only the fiery arrow of one who is a liar and a murderer from the beginning (John 8:44).

Others, whom Satan recognizes as optimists, are assaulted with presumption and conceit. Satan deceives them into thinking that it is the easiest thing in the world to get to heaven since you only have to say clearly eight words: "Lord, have mercy on me, a poor sinner!" Satan uses these words to turn God's grace into lasciviousness (Jude 4) and to persuade the lighthearted to misuse the liberty, to which they insist they have been called, as occasion to sin in the flesh. He hides God's severity toward sin from them and persuades them that God abounds in mercy and that Christ the Lord accepts all sinners. He also teaches them that their sins are not as great as preachers want them to believe. On this point, he turns himself into an angel of light and promises people a taste of the power of the future world (Heb. 6:5). They seem to have a taste of the heavenly joys and are therefore strengthened in their conceit. It makes no difference to them how much preachers may warn and preach against this. They think, "We know what we know and what we have experienced, and no one will take this from us. We know that we are just as good as the best of God's children, for have we not already felt the seal of the Spirit's comfort in our hearts?" In this state, they cannot be helped unless they are shown Satan's cunning mischief and learn to guard themselves against the fiery arrow of conceit with which he has mortally wounded many and greatly suppressed godliness.

The third group of people, who are somewhere between the other two groups, have an easygoing nature. Satan, who also assaults them according to their nature, tempts them with a calm indifference. "Well," Satan says to them, "see what fuss there is in the world concerning the salvation and damnation of people! Note how distressed some are and how happy others are, all according to their own imagination. Really, it does not matter much and does not deserve all the fuss. Certainly it is not worth racking a poor man's brain over! We know very well that a poor man cannot do much about this. These great matters of salvation and damnation have not been placed in the hands of ordinary man; they surely are 'not of him that

willeth, nor of him that runneth, but of God that sheweth mercy'
(Rom. 9:16). After all, the great God has kept the distribution of
this to himself and does with the children of men as he pleases."
The devil also says to them, "Surely the Lord God is a good God,
and you, after all, are not the worst offenders. So all will be well in
the end. What good will it do for you to worry so much? Just let
things take their course! The Lord will take care of everything. You
just take care to do the best you can in carrying out your duties as
things arise in this world, and life in the hereafter will be just as
much for you as for any others."

Truly, this is one of Satan's most awful fiery arrows. He wounds
many souls with this device and greatly suppresses godliness with
it. A man will not escape unharmed if he does not remain alert
against this arrow and realize that these words come from the devil
of hell and will lead to hell. Is it not true that the greatest wisdom
lies in being most concerned about the most vital things? Should
we then not treat these most vital things with great concern, casting off all other concerns? Surely we know that the Lord God, who
is eternal life and has eternal death in his hand, earnestly admonishes us everywhere in his Word to seek eternal life from his hand
by following his counsel in order to escape eternal death (Ezek.
18:31; Amos 5:6).

2. Those that are a result of outward worldly things. Satan shoots
so many arrows, such as evil attacks, seductions, activities, and
thoughts, that not only are in regard to but often include the external things of this life. When Satan has learned to which sins we
are most prone by nature or habit, he soon begins to act on things
that happen in the world and happen to a person, such as particular situations and the things in which that person is engaged. For
example, seasons of prosperity or adversity; times of merriment,
such as wedding days, or of grief, such as days of mourning; times
of great exertion, such as market days; or times of idleness, such as
holidays, as the world calls them. Also, situations of great gain—
of pleasure or profit—or of loss, unhappiness and shame; situations with beautiful women, fine dinners, or tasty, pleasant drinks;
situations of illness or health; and a thousand other things, such as
people's labor at home or outside the home—yes, even all external
religious matters such as churchgoing, the observance of the Lord's

Supper, or whatever else may be. In all this, Satan is lurking everywhere, seeking to shoot his venomous arrows to poison souls. He secretly pollutes everything in this life, setting one snare or another so that it is impossible for a person to escape unharmed unless one watches one's steps against the craftiness of Satan. The devil is busy setting his nets and placing his snares everywhere around us. Besides that, he is also busy with secret and underhanded evil assaults to inflame people's lusts and desires. He keeps going until he succeeds in arousing human lust and desire and wholly evil inclinations and thoughts in the worst way by means of those things that are neither good nor bad in themselves. Indeed, the good things of God are being thoroughly spoiled and poisoned for careless people because of the activities of Satan on every possible occasion. Thus, people are unmistakably harmed each time they are engaged in these things.

With regard to this point, Satan has three particular lures that he knows how to use to wreak havoc and wound many souls. They are worldly honor, worldly pleasure, and worldly gain.

This is what actually happens. As soon as this sly, spiritual enemy, the devil, gets ahold of some powerful bait that exists in pleasure, profit, or honor, he skillfully exhibits and displays it before the eyes of the careless children of men. He throws out his lures, each one designed after the individual inclination of a person's heart. Immediately, the devil is surrounded by a host of reckless birds that swallow the bait.

By means of these sly, evil attacks, Satan works so powerfully and entices people so completely that they stop at nothing to commit this evil. Satan's lures miserably wound many souls, causing many to backslide greatly in godliness. For what undermines godliness most? Is it not when careless people, having caught sight of Satan's bait of great profit, pleasure, or honor, are greatly aroused to pursue it? Does not experience teach us that in such a case no admonitions are taken seriously and a deaf ear is turned against all our warnings? Is it not true that soon all thought of living a godly life is abandoned and all holy practices are trodden underfoot in order to follow and obtain that bait? A careless person will never emerge unscathed, nor will anyone who is not on guard against this device of Satan.

3. Those that he arouses in man without using the above mentioned conditions. Concerning evil temptations and thoughts, there are several—yes, many, even beyond number—that Satan throws in by himself without the help of others. The apostle Paul was greatly plagued by these devices even after he had been caught up to the third heaven (2 Cor. 12:7). Unless great care is taken, a person's heart and mind can be greatly confused and made unfit for God's service. Someone may think too little of malicious thoughts (as the greater part of worldly people are inclined to do, feeling that these thoughts are not costly) or may take them very seriously, as many devout Christians with tender consciences do. Christians believe that God loves truth in the innermost part of the heart and hates the least and most furtive evil thought. They experience much grief as a consequence. The middle way is very difficult to find. If a person thinks little of evil thoughts, he will not resist them as he should, and his mind will become greatly corrupted and polluted. If he takes them very seriously, he may become very depressed, become greatly discouraged, and slip in his service to God.

Such thoughts, which Satan ignites in the hearts of people without any help from others, are mainly of three varieties. The first are blasphemous thoughts against God's highest majesty. The second are cruel, venomous, and unnatural thoughts against ourselves or against our neighbor. The third are loathsome and indecent thoughts with regard to the chastity of the body. All these thoughts come straight from the devil and bear his image. They are really so awful and terrible that we had better keep silent rather than specifically name them or describe them in detail. We must simply conclude that such terrible activity truly originates from the devil himself. We can see this in part by noting that such thoughts often overcome a person suddenly, when he is busy with something that is not wrong in itself or often even when he is absorbed in good and holy activities.

If Christians are not to be discouraged by these attacks of Satan or become defiled by thinking lightly of them, they should be ever vigilant and accustom themselves to regard such thoughts, which are so terrible and attack men so badly, as they truly are, for they are, without question, Satan's own attacks and sins. We must offer holy resistance to them. We must not find pleasure in them in any way but try to ward them off with all our might in order to escape being harmed. Thus did Christ the Lord when Satan hurled his evil temptations before him (Matt. 4:1–11) in order to ensnare him, but Satan was not successful (John 14:30).

False Doctrine

Satan also uses false and distorted doctrine as a fiery arrow to wound souls and suppress godliness. After all, in principle, all false and corrupt doctrine comes from Satan, who is a liar and murderer from the beginning (John 8:44). Truly, false doctrine is nothing other than a foul stench that rises from the bottomless pit where Satan rules (Rev. 9:2). It would be too much to name all these false doctrines.

We will refrain from naming all of them, but we will point out how Satan uses great ingenuity and has many ploys that he uses to confuse right doctrine. We should pay careful attention to the way the devil operates! His strategies have caused some who once confessed the true faith to fall prey to false doctrine. Because of this, some have become lost even amid God's true church and under sound doctrine. These crafty, yet entirely false schemes generally include the following:

1. A false front. Satan tries to cover horrible sins under a veneer of obvious virtues. He fools many people with the following: Shameless conceit is called "a strong and secure faith," indolence and fear are called "Christian discretion and prudence," and awful meanness is called "faithfully caring for the family." These are only a few of thousands of examples that might be cited to show how the spirit of darkness changes itself into an angel of light (2 Cor. 11:14).

2. A smearing of sin. Satan tries to besmirch glorious Christian virtues with the filth of sin. A good conscience that guards itself against small and great sins is thus regarded as fussy preciseness. Similarly, a good, orderly Christian home in which God's Word is read with members of the family, in which the name of the Lord is called upon morning and evening, and in which the catechism is taught is called sheer hypocrisy and pretence. The holy zeal that is expressed when we speak frankly about God and his Word, even in large meetings, is denounced as spiritual pride. There are a thousand other sit-

uations in which Satan tries to hide an angel of light with a spirit
of darkness.

3. Drawing false conclusions. With this scheme, Satan tries to
draw false and venomous conclusions from true doctrine and uses
that to corrupt us. He does this in the following ways.

First, from the true teaching that even the most holy saints stumble in many things and that all men are sinners, he draws the false
conclusion that it does not matter much if one falls into sin or yields
to a darling sin to which the heart clings and thinks most desirable,
provided one takes care not to belong to the worst class of offenders. After all, the devil says, "Everyone has his own peculiar sins. It
would be too severe to label everyone as bad and mark their favorite
sins as evil. Surely, if judged in this way, no one could be saved."
Everyone has his own sins, and all are tarred with the same brush.
If someone wants to dispute this, followers will soon cry out, "He
that is without sin among you, let him first cast a stone at her" (John
8:7). Satan tells us, "You should not be so concerned whether you
live with some particular sin, for you simply have this sin, and someone else has another sin; there is no one without fault. It will be just
as well with you in the end as it will be for anyone else, provided
you make sure that you are not the worst offender."

This is Satan's conclusion, but it is a totally wrong, false, and
deceitful deduction. It makes a great difference whether you are
without sin or whether you love sin, whether you coddle some darling sin (as worldly people do) or fight against it (as the saints have
always done), for one person is a worker of unrighteousness whom
God will not regard in grace (Matt. 7:21), and the other who practices righteousness is one whom the Lord surely will regard in mercy
(Ps. 103:13). Clearly, the difference between the two is so great that
one will enter heaven and the other will go to hell. It is certain that
a person does not have to be one of the worst sinners who ever lived
in order to be lost in the end. It is enough to damn a person forever
when he remains what he is by nature, unconverted, and when he
is no different from the great majority in the world. That and that
alone is sufficient to see him damned forever (Luke 13:5). We have
already seen that, of all our sins, our favorite sins are the ones that
the Lord God demands that we part with and hate. Yet this hell-

ish and false conclusion would have us believe that everyone may yield to his favorite sin.

The right and true conclusion, of which other profitable consequences flow, is that since all men, even the best, are sinful, no one should think that he is made righteous by his works. Rather, each person should seek his salvation in Christ alone, after the counsel of Christ himself, and diligently follow the whole counsel of the Lord. In that, he will be blessed and led to salvation.

Second, Satan falsely concludes from this true doctrine that we are made righteous not by our works but by faith in Christ, so we should not be at all concerned with good works. Yes, we have seen some that are deceived into thinking that the worse they are in practicing good works, the more assured they may become because they are made righteous before God by faith in Christ alone. Thus, their faith is much stronger and secure without any good works (Rom. 3:8). This is completely wrong! God's Word teaches us that although our good works do not have priority in God's judgment to justify us since righteousness is granted to us solely on account of Christ's merits (Rom. 3:25–28), yet our good works will appear before God, not to justify us but to witness of our faith and show that it has indeed been true faith (Matt. 25:35; Rev. 14:13). Faith that has not been proved by good works on earth will not be accepted at the judgment seat of God (James 2:18). Thus, the right conclusion from this doctrine is that since our works cannot make us righteous, we should acknowledge and confess after we have done all we can do that we are still unprofitable servants (Luke 17:10). We should reject any idea of our merits and expect to receive salvation only by grace from the Lord Jesus Christ (Acts 15:11).

Third, Satan falsely concludes from the true doctrine that all men are liars (Rom. 3:4) and that great men also err sometimes (Ps. 62:9) that we therefore should not be so deeply committed to the things that servants of the Word daily teach us to intensify true godliness. Instead, each person is free to follow his own understanding and make his own choices. Satan tells us not only that the simple and unlearned can make mistakes and fall short but also that great people and preachers do too. And when someone is sternly told to take things more seriously, Satan urges him to protest, "The more one learns, the more one errs!"

Because of these false conclusions, many people turn a deaf ear to the good advice and faithful admonitions of true theologians. They follow their own ideas and make their own evil and warped opinions a sort of bible. Indeed, crafty Satan knows how to take advantage of this. The result is that people become bold in choosing to accept and practice only what is agreeable and pleasing in what men of God preach and teach them. They take only what they like and what seems agreeable to them, while neglecting and completely ignoring the rest (Ezek. 33:31–32). This results in contempt and backsliding in the spiritual life. Once a person reaches the point of daring to accept one part of what is faithfully preached while ignoring another, then almost all sermons and diligent work of the men of God become of no use to him (Matt. 11:17). Truly, this will only bring upon him a more severe judgment because, like the wicked servant, he has known the will of God but chosen not to do it. The outcome is inevitable. He will be beaten with double stripes (Luke 12:48).

The correct conclusion that should be drawn from this doctrine is that each person must deny his own opinions and subject all his thoughts to God's Word (2 Cor. 10:5). No one may reject or ignore what men of God have taught on the basis of their own views or opinions but must diligently compare the teaching of the servants of God's Word with the Holy Word, not their own understanding. That is what the Bereans did (Acts 17:11). If a messenger from the legislature or a servant from the court of the prince were to announce something in the name of the court, we would seriously consider it. We would be afraid of falling into disfavor with the court (providing the herald had such a commission) if we had not taken the trouble to thoroughly consider it. Since people deceived by Satan do not take a serious attitude toward the servants and messengers of the Most High God (2 Cor. 5:19), they must fall from the almighty God's grace and find themselves on the wrong path that leads to their destruction. Add to this that everyone knows their own trade best, so in regard to doubtful issues and difficult matters we should follow the opinion of men of God rather than follow our own understanding. That is especially so when men who have been appointed to search God's Word appear to be diligent and conscientious and try to practice what they preach (1 Tim. 4:12). After all, does not Scripture declare that the "secret of the LORD is with them that fear him; and he will shew them his covenant" (Ps. 25:14)?

Observe how craftily Satan goes to work in presenting false doctrine, even in the midst of God's true church, where sound doctrine is preached and confessed. The Christian who is not on guard will not escape unscathed if he does not notice that such conclusions, just as other false teachings, originate from the devil and from the pit of the abyss, with the intent of dimming godliness and leading the believer to eternal damnation.

Fierce Persecution

This vicious devil uses fierce and terrible persecution to injure souls and oppress godliness. When he can have his way, he produces the gallows, wheel, sword, noose, and stake; indeed, he has all kinds of deadly and terrible weapons to destroy that small number of the righteous who still desire to lead many to conversion (Rev. 2:10). When he is unable to do this and is bound, as it were, by the chains of God's providence, Satan foams at the mouth and vomits a whole stream of slander and serious insults against his opponents, seeking to persecute them with a lashing of the tongue (Rev. 12:15). Truly, he always uses this wickedness, even when he is able to use the stake, noose, or sword. That is why he is called the devil, that is, a slanderer and "the accuser of our brethren" (Rev. 12:10). All vilification and evil smearing really originate from him. He directs these slanders in mainly three ways: against sound doctrine itself, against its confessors in general, and against some particular defenders of true doctrine.

1. Against sound doctrine. Satan heaps all kinds of lies and distortions upon sound doctrine, never ceasing to misrepresent and slander it. For example, he charges it with being a novel kind of teaching, or a doctrine that causes men to sin, or a doctrine that makes God the author of sin or something of that nature (Rom. 3:8; 6:1). The doctrine then is hated and opposed by people before they ever understand what kind of teaching it is and of what it actually consists (Acts 21:21–25).

2. Against its confessors. With those who not only confess this doctrine with their mouths but also express its power in their lives,

it is remarkable how the devil persecutes them with slander. That was what Ishmael did to Isaac. Everywhere, good people are made out to be impostors, hypocrites, narrow-minded, bigoted, stiff-necked, extremists, and anything else that this embittered spiritual enemy spews out against them (1 Peter 4:4).

It would not be so bad if this happened only among worldly people, but (and here we really notice Satan's craftiness) these scurrilous lies even circulate among those who confess the same holy doctrine (2 Cor. 11:12–14). Indeed, among so-called Christians, there are many who dare to slander truly godly people and to ridicule those who not only confess the Christian faith with their mouths but also strive to practice it. The apostle clearly refers to this when he emphasizes that it happens now as it did in the time of Abraham, when Ishmael, who was born after the flesh, persecuted Isaac, who was born after the Spirit (Gal. 4:29). The same is still true now. All hypocrites and deceivers, all the unregenerate, all who are born only after the flesh still remain persecutors of true Christians, who are genuinely born of the Spirit, even if they join the church of God and profess to believe.

So shameless is this great slanderer, the devil, that he even incites some who confess true faith to ridicule, slander, and abuse those who are in deed and in truth the genuine Christians they profess to be. It becomes a cause for ridicule that a believer is no longer satisfied with just the outward name of Christian or with mere idle confession but only with living a life that is truly Christian, just as God demands in his Word.

Truly, by this Satan mortally wounds many souls and greatly suppresses godliness. A Christian will never rise above this if he does not recognize that these crafty, unnerving devices originate with Satan. He will not be unscathed unless he clearly understands the entirely hellish nature of those professing to be Christians, who, like Agrippa of old, are only "almost persuaded" Christians and ridicule others for wanting to be totally committed Christians like Paul (Acts 26:28).

Of course, the most serious defenders of the true doctrine of godliness become the devil's chief targets. He knows that they do him the most damage (Revelation 11; 12:4), so he rouses the most awful and bitter slander against them. Satan had Tertullus say that this man Paul was a "pestilent fellow, and a mover of sedition" (Acts

24:5). He also made Diotrephes prattle against the apostle John "with malicious words" (3 John 10). Indeed, Christ the Lord, the unspotted Lamb of God, did not escape slander. He was called a glutton, a winebibber, a friend of publicans (Matt. 11:19), someone possessed with a devil, a Samaritan (John 8:48), and everything cruel. See how much evil the devil has also spoken in our times against outstanding defenders of the holy gospel! He neither spared Christian rulers nor the most devout teachers but sought to malign them with every conceivable insult to make them objects of hatred. Satan continues this practice. This wounds many careless souls, especially those who are shallow and receptive to all kinds of rumors and slanderous talk. They think that a doctrine cannot be right when its most important defenders are alleged to be so entirely corrupt. However, they should have realized that it is an old trick of Satan to tarnish the best with the worst slander. They should also consider that the doctrine Judas the hypocrite taught did not cease to be true, despite his evil character. We give the devil too much honor when we reject holy doctrine because Satan slanders it. We should realize that such slanders come from the devil and are only inspired in order to obscure the holy truth.

To summarize, Satan directs all his fiery arrows in the following manner. First, at some opportunity, he injects exactly the wrong thoughts that lead to a specific evil deed, false doctrine, or persecution. In this way, the devil implanted his evil thoughts into Judas: Betray your master! The text in John 13:2 specifically says that the devil "put into the heart of Judas Iscariot" the idea to betray his master. Satan similarly deceived the woman Eve after he had prepared her by saying, "Yea, hath God said, Ye shall not eat of every tree of the garden?" (Gen. 3:1).

Second, Satan encourages people to adopt this depraved thought and carry it into action, urging it on with every deceptive reason he can muster. Thus, he said to the woman that if she ate of the tree of the knowledge of good and evil, "Ye shall be as gods" (Gen. 3:5).

Third, he urges man on by repeatedly badgering him. He excites our evil depravity as much as he can or uses whatever he is able to get hold of in us to deceive us into committing those evil sins that he avidly wants us to commit. He was a "thorn in the flesh" for Paul (2 Cor. 12:7), using that thorn to goad and excite the apostle (as much as he could) to make him sin. The Lord tempts no one in this way.

Yet in all this, Satan is only a challenger; he can never force our compliance. He causes us to sin only if we consent. Otherwise, this whole matter is nothing other than his own sin. It was no sin in Christ the Lord that the devil suggested that Christ turn stones into bread, that he throw himself down from the temple and worship Satan (Matthew 4); it was the devil's own sin that he dared to suggest this to Christ the Lord. Similarly, a virtuous girl does not sin when she hears an indecent person in the street spewing out obscene language that she detests. It is different when wrong stirrings arise from our own flesh, however, and we feel ourselves somewhat excited by them. We know that the devil can only tempt us, not force us. Therefore, let us always be armed in the fear of the Lord with the intention that we will never consent to the devil's evil inspirations and suggestions. Then we will overcome his temptations and not be harmed.

The Conclusion: We Should Guard against the Kingdom of Darkness and Satan's Activity

Take note, this is the real situation with regard to the kingdom of darkness and the perverse powers that resist the practice of true godliness. We must pay close attention to this in every respect. Those who truly desire to live godly lives must keep a strict vigil. If you do so and have learned to watch vigilantly and to consider habitually this unending warfare, then whenever you experience an uneasiness or inner opposition in the practice of godliness, you will soon see that it originates from the kingdom of darkness—yes, even from the pit of the abyss itself—and that it leads to perdition. The knowledge of this strengthens you to resist it, especially when you thoroughly understand and always remember that the devil of hell entices you to sin at every opportunity. He tries to outwit you so that you sin and enter the paths of destruction.

Of course, worldly people do not like to hear such talk. They can barely tolerate a conversation about the devil. So he makes every effort to ensure that he is mentioned very little, unless it is in swearing and other bad language, so that he is better able to deceive men from, as it were, under the cover of darkness, just as he deceived our first mother Eve when she was not even thinking of him (Gen. 3:1–6). Truly, he would prefer that he is not discussed or noticed or given any attention until the moment when his victims see themselves, as a result of his devices, sinking with him into eternal ruin. Satan seeks to crush and destroy many this way.

But praise God, the Holy Scripture tells us about greater grace, which helps us fully understand that Satan is the great dragon, the "old serpent," who is called the devil and who deceives the whole world (Rev. 12:9). Scripture teaches us clearly that Satan constantly works in all our circumstances to lead us into sin. Indeed, he is the most important instigator to sin by his own activity in the things of the world and by our own debased lusts. He is, therefore, called the tempter (1 Thess. 3:5).

When we read how David, lulled into a mood of overconfidence, decided to count the people of Israel (2 Samuel 24), Scripture goes on to explain that it was really Satan who inspired David to do this (1 Chron. 21:1). When we read that the false prophets wrongly advised Ahab to go up against Ramoth in Gilead (1 Kings 22:12), Scripture adds that this happened by the inspiration of lying spirits (v. 22) who deceived Ahab's prophets. When we read that the Chaldeans and Sabeans robbed Job of his goods, Scripture again confirms that it was the devil who inspired them (Job 1). When pagans opposed the building of the temple of the Lord (Ezra 4:1–3), Scripture tells us that it was really Satan who put them up to it (Zech. 3:1).

When Judas decided to betray Christ the Lord, Scripture also affirms that the idea came from Satan, who had entered into him (Luke 22:3). When Ananias and Sapphira agreed to keep back part of the price for their land and said they had given all of it to the poor (Acts 5:1–2), Peter assures us that this thought came from Satan, who had filled their hearts to lie to the Holy Ghost (v. 3). When false teachers deceived the Corinthians, Paul says that the devil used them to do it (2 Cor. 4:4). When some young widows became wealthy, the apostle declares that they "turned aside after Satan" (1 Tim. 5:15). When some resisted sound doctrine (2 Tim. 2:25), the apostle testifies that they fell into the snares of the devil (v. 26). When some became unrighteously angry (Eph. 4:26), the apostle says that they thereby were giving place to the devil (v. 27). When the incestuous person who was disciplined by the church at Corinth fell into despair through too much sorrow (2 Cor. 2:7), the apostle makes it plain that the thoughts of Satan were at work in him (v. 11). When a servant girl of the high priest and others strongly pressed the apostle Peter to deny his Lord, the Lord Christ testifies that the devil intended this to sift him as wheat (Luke 22:31). Indeed, when Peter wrongly advised the Lord, Christ the Lord rebukes him, saying, "Get thee behind me, Satan: thou art an offence unto me" (Matt. 16:23).

There are many such testimonies in Scripture. In them, the Holy Spirit takes great pains to make us understand that the devil is the great tempter (Matt. 4:3) and has a large part in all occasions of sin. Therefore, all good Christians who want to live a godly life must let themselves be warned and welcome any reminder that Satan is often a part in our thoughts or inclinations, devising ways to harm them, for he is the most important warrior in the kingdom of darkness. Therefore, that kingdom is called Satan's kingdom (Matt. 12:26). If we truly know this through and through, it will help us to be tirelessly vigilant. It should strongly prevent us from yielding to the devil's schemes and from having anything to do with the crafty devices that originate in the kingdom of darkness, out of which Satan works, so that we will not become entangled in his snares and brought to ruin.

BOOK
3

The Kingdom of Grace
Promotes Godliness

Introduction to the Kingdom of Grace

It is necessary to earnestly warn slothful, inattentive, careless people that there is an antagonistic power, a united realm of darkness, that opposes those who walk in true godliness and works incessantly to ruin souls and stifle godliness. It is just as necessary for the encouragement of godly people that we do not neglect to point out that there is a divine power, the united kingdom of grace, that is on the side of all who sincerely surrender their hearts and souls to practice true godliness (2 Peter 1:3). Although cruel and evil horns are out to destroy the godly, the Lord has prepared courageous blacksmiths to scare away these detestable horns (Zech. 1:19–21). In accordance with this kingdom of grace, all who eagerly want to practice godliness should properly ponder this matter, since the realm of darkness stands directly opposed to the kingdom of grace (Rom. 5:21).

The kingdom of light uncovers every secret of the realm of darkness; it reveals every sly, dark deceit as well as the great pitfalls and crafty schemes of this wicked realm. Not only does the kingdom of grace as a kingdom of light disclose every black and dark deception of the realm of darkness (Acts 16:18), but it also offers true, godly, and sincere Christians assistance and strength to resist and overcome the ploys of the realm of darkness.

Our spiritual enemy seeks to hide the united kingdom of grace from those who sincerely desire true godliness. Satan greatly succeeds in this effort because many people do not realize how much assistance is available to those who sincerely want to live a godly life. It is easy to understand why they accomplish little in the practice of godliness, since they never progress beyond an appearance of godliness and never know its power (2 Tim. 3:5).

These people trust in their own wisdom, strength, and good intentions when they try to practice godliness. We can understand how the wisdom, strength, and good intentions of a poor, feeble, and sinful man, as we all are by nature, are a poor foundation for constructing the splendid edifice of a godly life, especially when we remember this united realm of darkness. This powerful and crafty realm is loaded with fraud and deception and teems with tireless, villainous, skillful, and deceitful spirits who incessantly seek to ruin souls. These spirits seek to tempt poor, feeble, and careless people to ensnare them in sins and divert them from godliness and lead them to hypocritical godliness, if not open godlessness. If we take this into account, we soon realize that none of these people (and there are many everywhere) are able to succeed because they seek to practice true godliness through their own wisdom, power, and good intentions, without any knowledge of the kingdom of grace and the divine power that is found there for the benefit of the saints (2 Peter 1:3). Such people will inevitably be misled by crafty spiritual enemies from the realm of darkness into embracing a phantom, an empty hallucination, instead of true godliness.

In ancient times, the philosophers were such people. In our days, they are the heretics who depart from the Christian faith and never gain a true and right insight into the kingdom of grace. They also include those who are living under the light of the gospel, perhaps having made a profession of true faith, but who do not diligently search the Scripture for a faithful revelation of the natures of the realm of darkness and the kingdom of grace.

The Three Powers in the Kingdom of Grace: The New Creature, the Church of God, and the Spirit of God

Since a special knowledge of grace is necessary and profitable for living a godly life, we will now clarify its character. We need to know that just as there are three fierce spiritual enemies in the kingdom of darkness—the flesh, the world, and the devil—which constantly oppose true godliness and its practitioners, so there are three powers in the kingdom of grace that fight against the demonic enemies. These are the new creature, the church of God, and the Spirit of God.

The new creature, or the renewed spirit, fights against the flesh (Gal. 5:17); the church of God fights against the world (John 15:19–25); and the Spirit of God fights against the devil (1 John 4:4).

These three powers also join forces to fight against the evil three so that the new creature fights against the flesh as well as against the world and the devil. If we can get the kingdom of grace completely on our side, we will be more than conquerors through Jesus Christ our Lord, despite the great ingenuity and tirelessness of our evil enemies in the realm of darkness. The three powers in the kingdom of grace are composed in such a way that a Christian who wants to take the matter seriously must come out victoriously. We will now study these excellent powers in greater detail.

The Three Gifts of the New Creature

In 2 Corinthians 5:17, the apostle Paul speaks of the new creature as that excellent workmanship of God that is "created in Christ Jesus unto good works, which God hath before ordained that we should walk in them" (Eph. 2:10). He also refers to this creature as "the spirit," in contrast to "the old man" (Eph. 4:22), or "the flesh." The new creature is created to fight against the old man, the evil world, and crafty Satan (Eph. 6:10–12) but especially to bring the old nature into subjection, to crucify (Gal. 5:24) and mortify it (Rom. 8:13; Eph. 4:22; Col. 3:5).

A person who has been brought into the kingdom of grace by the wonderful work of the Almighty is like one born anew (John 3:3). He receives youthful vigor and strength that enable him to act in true godliness. He receives a reverent fear of God, true knowledge of God (Col. 3:10), righteousness, and holiness (Eph. 4:23–24). He receives faith, love, and hope and partakes of the divine nature by regeneration. He receives new life (Rom. 6:4) so that Christ now lives in him (Gal. 2:20). This makes him able to express new obedience in daily living.

Many professing Christians do not pay attention to this renewal, so it is completely hidden from their eyes. That does great harm to the practice of godliness, for it is impossible for anyone to lead a godly life unless he strives to obtain this new creation. If someone claims that he already possesses this new creation, he must persistently stimulate it and use it to oppose the flesh. Just as it is impossible for anyone who does not have life to act as if he does, so it is impossible for anyone who has not yet received new life to produce the works of the new and godly life. This is true of everyone who has not yet become a new creature.

We should thus make it our first priority to be born anew. When a man has received this new creation, this true rebirth, he has a new spirit within him (Ezek. 36:25f.). This spirit is alive and active in promoting the activities that belong to that life (v. 27), including, as the apostle tells us (Gal. 5:17), working out true godliness and striving against the old man, the flesh, and all evil lusts and desires. This also includes striving against the world and the devil, since they are allied with the old man to ruin souls and stifle godliness.

A new creature also possesses gifts that oppose the destructive horns of the old nature. We have already learned that the corrupt flesh, or the old man, has three horns. These horns wound many souls and choke godliness. These horns are the natural mind, evil desires, and a corrupt conscience. The new creature receives special gifts to break the power of these horns. They are an enlightened mind, which opposes the natural mind; holy desires, which resist the evil desires of the flesh; and a tender conscience, which opposes a hardened conscience. Let us now discuss each one.

An Enlightened Mind

The true Christian who has been born again by God's Spirit and made a new creature receives an enlightened mind from God with which he clearly sees that his natural mind is a blind guide in spiritual things (1 Cor. 2:4). He also sees that if he were to be led by his natural mind, he would fall into the pit of ruin, for, as Christ says, "If the blind lead the blind, both shall fall into the ditch" (Matt. 15:14). The regenerate person also sees that man's wisdom is pure foolishness to God and that we are mere children in the things of salvation. When our natural mind is not led by the Holy Spirit, it provides us only with wisdom that is earthly, sensual, and devilish, as James 3:15 declares.

In order to be saved, then, we should deny our natural mind and let ourselves be guided by the Spirit. We will not be happy and blessed unless we follow the Lord's counsel, for a true spiritual life cannot be modeled after our own insight but, rather, must be formed according to God's Word (Ps. 119:6). We see that the only true measure of diligent and godly exercises is not derived from worldly sources or from our imagination but is found in the Word of the Lord. We see the futility of all earthly things—riches, pleasures, and splendors—which so lamentably bewitch the worldly.

We also see the glorious bliss of a peaceful conscience, the living hope, and the excellence of heavenly treasures, which are completely hidden from the eyes of worldly people. These considerations will greatly fortify us against our natural mind, which would otherwise tend to mislead us.

Holy Desires

The true believer, who has been transferred by regeneration into the kingdom of grace and has been made a new creature, also receives new and holy desires. He gets a taste, so to speak, for spiritual riches. While his heart was once inclined to the lusts of the flesh, the delights of the eyes, or the pride of life (1 John 2:16), he now fervently desires spiritual gifts (1 Cor. 14:1). Above all, he wants to be zealous in keeping God's statutes (see Ps. 119:5). He has the Spirit of prayer working within him whereby he cries, "Abba, Father!" (Rom. 8:15), which helps him obtain many good things.

On the other hand, worldly people, who are still in the realm of darkness, stifle all longings for spiritual blessings and the true knowledge of God, righteousness, holiness, faith, love, and hope. They are carried away by their desires and chase after things that are not appropriate and are contrary to reason and against which their natural minds even warn them.

How different, then, is the new creature, who is infused with holy desires after heavenly things. Holy desires subdue or at least restrict and weaken intemperate desires for money, property, pleasures, and worldly splendor. They restrain the Christian from surrendering to wrong desires and stimulate him to resist evil desires with all his might. He now realizes they can cost him his life (1 Peter 2:11), no matter how friendly and flattering they appear. The fervent love for spiritual riches gradually consumes the regenerate person and puts to death his love for earthly things and fleshly desires that have marred and imperiled many a noble soul.

A Tender Conscience

The true Christian, who has been transferred into the kingdom of grace by regeneration and has become a new creature, also receives a tender conscience. This makes him sensitive to spiritual and heavenly things (Psalm 119). Worldly people commit gross sins without feeling pain or sorrow (Prov. 30:20) because their consciences are debased and numbed (1 Tim. 4:2). The souls of such people can become so miserably foolish, confused, and injured that they can commit even murder without remorse.

By contrast, the truly regenerated have such sensitive consciences that they feel sorrow over any sin. The smallest sin distresses them; their souls are bruised by it. A tender conscience is what made David cry out, "Lord . . . heal my soul; for I have sinned against thee" (Ps. 41:4; cf. Prov. 8:36). True Christians are spared from carelessly and callously continuing in sin. When they have fallen into some sin, they have no rest until they are delivered from it. Their conscience is so clear and tender that they cannot bear even the smallest sin.

A tender conscience also allows the believer to experience the deep peace, comfort, and joy that can be found only in working for the Lord and in the development of true godliness. Just as a godly man feels grief and sorrow when he is overcome by sin, so he feels joy and comfort when he has been careful not to sin. For example, he is happy when he has not overindulged at meals, was not frivolous in company, or was not deceitful in business. Rather, he has diligently applied himself to the practice of godliness, praying fervently, visiting the sick, giving gifts to the poor, or lovingly admonishing his friends to obey God rather than the world. A truly regenerated person is never happier than when he is serving the Lord. While the natural person callously wallows in sin or carelessly disregards his spiritual state, the regenerated person is drawn away from evil toward good.

The new nature, by its very character, fights against the old man and the flesh. Those who truly want to practice godliness need to understand that they are made partakers of the divine nature through regeneration (2 Peter 1:4). They have been given the power and gifts of this regeneration for the rest of their lives. That allows them to break the power of the old man and the flesh in order to develop godliness. We will show how this happens later and in more detail.

Many people do not realize this and thus fail to make a true effort toward a new heart and a new spirit. They try to practice godliness in their better moments, but they soon tire of the effort and quit trying. They fall short of reaching the power of true godliness and come no farther than the appearance of it. They miss the most important element needed to produce godly works: new life itself. We must understand this and take it seriously so we may develop genuine godliness.

God's Church and Her Three Gifts

We know the church of God as the assembly of those who have been born anew and who share all the privileges and powers that God has given them (Matt. 16:18f.). God's church stands against the old man, the world, and the devil, who, as we have seen, are the principal allies of the realm of darkness in opposing and suppressing godliness. Scripture says that God's church stands against the realm of darkness, "terrible as an army with banners" (Song of Sol. 6:4).

Although God's regenerated children find themselves greatly strengthened by the new spirit that helps them resist their spiritual enemy, they soon become aware that they need the "communion of saints" and all its privileges to overcome their spiritual enemies (Rom. 1:11–12; 1 Peter 5:9), for when those who are occupied with the practice of godliness fail to pay attention to their need for the church, matters do not go well. They do not make use of what God considers essential for his children to stand in the day of evil. Those who want to make progress in godliness will not neglect this much-needed help.

Although God's church fights against its spiritual enemies—the old man, the world, and the devil—it also combats the three horns of the world that destroy so many souls and greatly hinder godliness. These include wrong habits and customs, today's bad examples, and a faulty application of rewards and compensation. God's church breaks the power of these goring horns with the following three things: the Word of God, which opposes bad customs; the examples of the saints, in contrast to the bad examples of the world; and the keys of the kingdom of heaven, which oppose sinful desires for payment and compensation.

The Word of God

The Lord God gave this precious treasure to his people to reveal his godly wisdom and teach them everything that is essential for salvation (2 Tim. 3:15–17). Holy Scripture contradicts all evil customs, bad habits, and poor morals of the world in order to abolish them, no matter how respected they may be. God's Word is older than anything else and contains the law of the God of Jacob, against which no defense is possible (Ezek. 20:13–19). Therefore, we may apply the precious Word of God just as the prophet Jeremiah did (Jer. 44:28–29), showing those who cling to bad habits that they are completely wrong and without excuse, for God's Word is older than any of their traditions and institutions.

Those who insist on following their old customs, even though they know that God's Word is against them, clearly are worldly people who do not share in the inheritance of God's children. No matter how beautifully they act, these worldly people offer no more than a pretense of godliness. A person who acts this way cannot fool others. We can see what is in his heart when he chooses to cling to the bad customs of this condemned world rather than subject himself to the holy ordinances of the Most High God. He shows intolerable pride in despising God's law and its divine wisdom while clinging to the bad habits and inane customs of the world, which are earthly, carnal, and demonically evil (James 3:15).

The church helps God's true children and all saints to oppose habits and customs that are in opposition to God's Word. When God's children personally reflect on God's Word and when they have a hold on an appropriate text in God's Word that speaks against the evil customs of this world, they are empowered to fiercely attack these practices (Jer. 15:19–21). They will not ignore God's will in the situation nor accept the customs of the world for any reason— not to gain love, to avoid grief, to get approval from their friends, or to ward off threats. As David testifies, "Thy word have I hid in mine heart, that I might not sin against thee" (Ps. 119:11).

God's Word strengthens us in our godly walk because this Word is sealed to us by baptism, the Lord's Supper, and by our own frequently renewed promise that we will live out our allotted time in harmony with the revealed will of God and not according to our own opinions. We want to repudiate our carnal nature, the world, and the devil and try to observe everything that the Lord has commanded us in his Word (Matt. 28:20). We no longer belong to ourselves but pledge to live in accordance with God's Word. The Word of God, that precious jewel of the holy church of God, is a mighty help against the customs of the world and against our spiritual enemies.

The Examples of the Saints

The life and conduct of God's saints oppose the bad examples we see around us every day in the world. With their lives, the saints convict those who habitually do what is inappropriate or neglect what should be done with the excuse that that's the way people are used to doing it. While the world follows worldly examples, God's church convinces those who are not completely worldly of the necessity of leading a different kind of life. The church of God offers examples of more excellent people than the world will ever be able to produce.

When the world, for example, quotes the example of a prominent citizen who lives a luxurious life, the church of God challenges this with the examples of Abraham and Sarah, a most superior couple, who were modest (1 Peter 3:4) in clothing and food (Genesis 18).

When the world cites the examples of people who are celebrities but who pay little attention to their families, fail to instruct them in the fear of the Lord, and do not pray with them or walk with them in holiness, the church of God counters them with the examples of King David, the man after God's heart (Psalm 110); Abraham, the father of believers (Genesis 18); and Cornelius, the centurion who was devout, God-fearing, and generous (Acts 10). The world may provide examples of people who are prominent but who do not observe the Lord's weekly day of rest, who do not love Zion's dwellings, and who do not regularly attend the assembly of believers. In their eating and drinking, these men keep themselves, their hired help, and their guests from going to church on the Lord's Day. They thus deprive their souls of food while they stuff their physical bodies.

Against that example, the church of God presents the patriarchs, prophets, and apostles throughout the ages who observed the Sabbath day of rest and loved the assembly of believers above all of Jacob's dwellings (Psalms 42; 122). The church of God cites the examples of devout rulers of God's people who kept their consciences pure because they habitually went into the temple of the Lord on the Sabbath with the people of God (Ezek. 46:10).

God's church offers examples of pious and godly persons in every age who regarded the ways of godliness seriously and, like Zachariah and Elizabeth, walked blamelessly in the commandments of the Lord (Luke 1:6). With God's help, they lived undefiled in the world (James 1:27), even though, as far as the world was concerned, they have gone unrecognized.

A small number of prominent and famous people, by the light of the gospel, have also set a good example for others. Clearly, their examples should mean something more to those who do not want to deceive themselves in the matter of salvation than the examples of people who follow the course of the world. The apostle Paul warns us (Rom. 12:2) that our souls will not fare well if we walk in worldly ways.

The greatest example of all, however, is our Savior and sanctifier, Jesus Christ, who, by his conduct and activity in the days of his
flesh, provided a perfect example of true godliness that we are called
to follow (1 Peter 2:21). His example should be more important to
us than those of every other learned and prominent person. We
ought to keep this in mind when the world tries to mislead us with
wrong examples.

For example, if we are at a banquet and are tempted by others to
join in rough joking (something that Paul condemns in Ephesians
5:4) and drinking too much (which Peter condemns in 1 Peter 4:3),
we should ask how the Lord Jesus Christ would have acted had he
been at that banquet. Would he have acted like everyone else and
joined in every toast? Would he have joined in the dancing, singing,
kissing, and other inane activities like everyone else? Our hearts tell
us that the Lord Jesus would never have conformed to such behavior. Rather, in all modesty, he would have spoken out against such
improper behavior.

When we are in similar circumstances and are tempted to sin,
let us remember that Christ's example should have more effect on
us than the example of people around us who keep such sinful practices alive. For it is said, not of those who are now on earth but of
Christ: "He that saith he abideth in him ought himself also so to
walk, even as he walked" (1 John 2:6). This should help us shun
overindulgences, even when we see prominent people forgetting
moderation.

We should give special attention to the example of Christ because
it shows us perfectly what we should be doing. It also helps us to
do it (Heb. 4:2), for a certain power goes out from the Lord Christ
to those who seek to follow his example, strengthening and quali-
fying them. In this way, God's church is supported by the examples
of the saints in the ongoing battle against the bad examples of the
world.

The Keys of the Kingdom of Heaven

This is the spiritual authority that Christ has given to his church,
through which it may extend comfort and encouragement to people who are diligent in their godly walk. It does this through the
proclamation and application of God's Word to their spiritual con-

dition. It also uses God's Word to admonish and alarm those who do not walk in holiness. Accordingly, each godly heart in the church must conform and submit to the Word so that each person's conduct will attract and help others and will also shun those whose conduct is sinful (Ps. 15:4; Matt. 18:17; 2 Thess. 3:14). The Lord God Almighty does the same in the highest heaven (Matt. 16:19; John 20:21).

This power of God's church also challenges the world's system of rewards and compensation. It strongly convicts those who are misled by the evil system of rewards that is customary in the world. Just look at the lengths to which the world goes to keep people in its service. The church of God also presents powerful reasons to lead a person into the service of God. But if a believer wants to obey the commandments of God, submit his possessions to the service of God, and make the practice of godliness his most important activity, the world may threaten him with loss of popularity. It may treat him like a nobody. It may revile him, insult him, despise him, and deny him success.

Even if the world succeeds in this, the church of God has an effective countermeasure. The church assures the believer that, as much as the world despises and rejects him because he serves God diligently and lives a godly life, so much more will the true children and saints of God love him. What's more, the Lord God himself will take note of what the believer has suffered and bless him according to what he has endured (Matt. 5:12; 2 Cor. 6:4). In such a case, the church of God may use the keys of the kingdom to open the rich treasury of our great God and show how believers will receive a hundred times more from God than the world can take away from them (Mark 10:29–30).

The world promises advancement, riches, pleasure, and happiness to those who follow its ways. The world deceives many by granting these things, but the church of God says that all these worldly things are temporary and will one day cause only grief for those who strive after them (Rev. 18:7). Those who turn away from the Lord God and cling to the world will face eternal poverty, shame, and pain. The Lord God, his holy angels, and all the saints will be against them. God's church, in such a case, can close heaven with the keys of the kingdom by rightly applying the Word of God. That means withholding spiritual comfort from souls who walk in evil paths and who demonstrate by their example that they are slaves to their sins and are entirely worldly.

The church of God also has something to say about worldly offers of rewards and compensation. The church makes abundantly clear to the Christian that, whatever trouble or difficulties the world threatens him with for serving God, serving the world will result in trouble a hundred times worse, for if serving God makes worldly people despise us, serving the world brings upon us the contempt of God and all his saints. If serving God brings troubles upon us in this world, serving the world will bring us a thousand times more trouble in the age to come, including everlasting shame and unendurable pain.

The world promises us favors if we serve it. But the church of God promises us the loving-kindness of God and all his saints if we serve the Lord and practice godliness. If the world rewards us now when we conform to it, the church of God assures us that we will receive, even in this life, a hundred times more from God when we cling to him, and in eternity, immeasurable benefits and blessings.

Here we see how God's holy church helps believers fight the temptations of the world. If we are to demonstrate true godliness, we must take hold of this. True believers strongly desire to meet with other believers in godly activity in order to be strengthened against the world (Heb. 10:24–25). Those who live outside the bonds of the church rob themselves of its precious means and fail to be strengthened in their quest for true godliness.

The Gifts the Spirit Offers to Promote Godliness

We are not speaking here of the Spirit of God as the divine nature (2 Peter 1:4) that we received at our new birth and that Scripture sometimes calls being "spiritually minded" (Rom. 8:6) or having the "new spirit" (Ezek. 36:26). Rather, what we mean here is the Holy Spirit, who together with the Father and the Son is the only true God (1 John 5:7) and our sanctifier (1 Peter 1:3). He is the One through whom we are able to conquer the flesh, the world, the devil, and death. He empowers us to be more than conquerors over everything (Rom. 8:37). We should pay special attention to the work of this Spirit.

All our attempts to resist and overcome the power of the kingdom of darkness would be of no avail without the Holy Spirit. Through his powerful and victorious operation, the Holy Spirit defeats our spiritual enemies, breaks their power, shames their cunning attacks, and makes them a footstool for his feet. Through the Spirit, the saints are comforted, knowing that he who is in them is greater than he who is in the world (1 John 4:4). The good Spirit of God, who is all in all, is almighty in the battle against our spiritual enemies. That is why Scripture says that where the Spirit is, there is liberty (Ps. 51:12; 2 Cor. 1:3). We must make it our priority to seek the help of God's Spirit.

Though the Holy Spirit helps us battle all our spiritual enemies, he uses specific weapons against the destructive horns of Satan. Those horns of the devil that injure many souls and stifle godliness include inward assaults and enticements, false doctrine and influences, fierce persecution and slander. God's Spirit opposes these horns with three weapons: heavenly operations and suggestions against devilish assaults, the truth of God against false doctrine, and God's comforting operations against persecution.

Holy and Heavenly Operations

The Holy Spirit, who is Lord of our hearts, has taken it upon himself to keep our hearts and minds in the peace of Christ, which passes all understanding (Phil. 4:7). With his powerful grace, he evokes holy, sweet, and lovely thoughts in the hearts of his children on every possible occasion, sometimes without preceding inclinations on our part. The Holy Spirit knows how to create light out of darkness, which is far greater than creating thousands of opportunities for good thoughts. Triggered by our natural depravity and the evil that flows from it, he stirs our hearts to humbly, and with deep sighs, ask the Lord for help. This, in turn, greatly annoys the devil, who then intensifies various temptations and accusations against God's children. This stirs their hearts once more to humbly and urgently cry out to God for help against wrong motives prompted by the natural depravity remaining in their hearts.

The Holy Spirit uses these occasions to bring God's children to more fervently forsake the world and live with the Lord. Through his holy, powerful grace, he stirs up good and holy thoughts. However, there are three specific ways in which God's Spirit stimulates holy, spiritual, and Christian activities:

1. He shows us the power of Christ's death. Because of the relationship we have with Christ, the Spirit helps us experience the power of Christ's death. That mortifies our earthly lusts (Phil. 3:10; 1 Peter 4:1) and breaks the power of the evil operations and temptations of Satan.

The death of Christ benefits us by paying for our sins (for which we deserved death), but it also is effective in putting to death the old man (Rom. 8:13) in us and in all who have their lot in Christ. Because Christ our Lord, the second Adam, died, our old man died in him, just as our first innocent nature died with Adam (see Romans 5; 6:2–4). In fellowship with Christ the Lord and from the death of the crucified one, true believers receive power to increasingly put to death the old man and his deeds. That strengthens them in many ways against the evil temptations of Satan.

2. He shows us the power of Christ's resurrection (Phil. 3:10). Through the Holy Spirit, the resurrection stirs up in us many good and holy activities that are related to newness of life (Rom. 6:3–4). Just as various physical functions were reawakened in Lazarus when he was raised from death to life, so we are awakened by the Spirit from sin's death to new life through Christ's resurrection. That new life prompts many spiritual changes in us, which break the force of Satan's vicious assaults. Take note: If we want to practice godliness, we must make use of this help. Sharing in Christ's death and resurrection comes through the activity of the Holy Spirit.

3. He prompts in us the spirit of prayer (Rom. 8:26). In this spirit of prayer, we may go to the Lord our God on every occasion and receive great power from him against all Satan's assaults, whatever they are (Eph. 6:11–18).

With these holy exercises that the Spirit rouses within us, the Lord offers us tremendous help against the vicious assaults of Satan. We should pay attention to this and make it a habit to discern the presence of God when we feel these good impulses stirring in our hearts. We should also use each occasion to stimulate these gifts from God. Even more, we should cling to the presence of our good God and wrestle with him in spontaneous prayers, as Jacob did, to obtain even greater blessing. This will be tremendously useful in helping us increase and grow in godliness.

God's Holy Truth

God's holy truth, which counters the devil's false doctrine, is sound doctrine (2 Tim. 1:13; Titus 1:1), by which the Spirit of God powerfully and gladly leads those who walk in godliness into truth (John 16:13).

Like many other people, you may say, "I would gladly serve God with all my heart and live a godly life, but there are so many different doctrines and faiths in the world that I have no idea where to turn." Do not fear. If you have a genuine desire to live a godly life, then you already have come a long way. Don't be discouraged. Start with serving God as sincerely as you can. Seek after God; sigh, pray, and beg for guidance from his good Spirit (Luke 11:13). Once you have made him your guide, he will guard you against false doctrine (Prov. 2:10–12). Even if there are a thousand sects and heresies, he will show you the way to go, teaching you what you need to know and directing you in the way you should go (Isa. 48:17).

As the Holy Spirit leads believers into truth, he offers three distinct works of grace:

1. Rules that help distinguish between truth and lies. If we have any doubt about what is presented to us, we can find help from these rules:

Sound doctrine glorifies God. Scripture says, "He that glorieth, let him glory in the Lord" (1 Cor. 1:31; cf. Jer. 9:23). The Lord God created heaven and earth and everything in them for his glory. He gave sacred Scripture to instruct us in sound doctrine so we would exalt his name and increase his glory (John 5:39). The Holy Spirit teaches believers to use this rule to test what they hear. It protects them against many deceptions that may sound pious but are snares of wickedness.

For example, someone may attend a dinner at which people call those who would witness for God and his grace "stiff-necked hypocrites." A godly person will immediately recognize these name callers as ungodly, for someone who testifies of God and his loving-kindness brings only more glory to God. This rule may be applied to a thousand other situations in life.

Walking in divine truth promotes godliness. Faithful teaching and divine truth avert the evil deeds and wiles of the old man (2 Tim. 3:16) and stimulate every holy gift in us. True faith acknowledges the truth that seeks after godliness (Titus 1:1). Only those who put off the old man and the walk that yearns after falsehood have rightly learned to know Christ. They have put on the new man, which is created after God for true righteousness and holiness (Eph. 4:20–23).

The grace of God that brings us salvation teaches us that we should forsake ungodliness and worldly lusts and "live soberly, righteously, and godly, in this present world" (Titus 2:11–12). The Holy Spirit shows us how to test for truth with this rule and preserves us from much that would mislead us in the practice of godliness.

For example, when debating whether to maintain Lenten Eve (Fat Tuesday), Epiphany (when the wise men saw the Christ child), and other Roman Catholic holidays or to radically abolish them, some people may say yes and others no. However, the godly immediately know the right way, for they understand that Roman Catholic holidays have no basis in Holy Scripture and that regular observance of them offers occasion for much sin.[1] These celebrations cause great disorder in the places or homes where they are observed and become a stumbling block to real holiness as they strengthen the old man. The godly swiftly conclude that Reformed Christians who would gladly abolish or ignore the feast days have the truth on their side. Again, this rule may be applied to countless other situations in life.

The practice of sound doctrine brings comfort (Rom. 15:4). This is the promise for this life and the life to come (1 Tim. 4:8), for in

---

1. Teellinck took the position of many of the Reformers and the Puritans, who held that the "holy days" of the pre-Reformation church calendar should be abolished because (1) they were not divine but human institutions; (2) they detracted from the importance of the Lord's Day as the Christian Sabbath; and (3) they gave occasion to licentious and heathen festivities (K. DeGier, *Explanation of the Church Order of Dordt in Questions and Answers* [Grand Rapids: Netherlands Reformed Book and Publishing, 2000], 97).

keeping God's commandments there is great reward (Ps. 19:11). That is why Christ clearly declares, "If ye know these things, happy are ye if ye do them" (John 13:17). James also says that those who not only hear but also do God's will are blessed in their deeds (James 1:25). Thus, in matters of godliness, believers are greatly comforted because their good works show the rightness of their faith (James 2:18), by which they are justified (Rom. 5:1).

The godly test the truth by this rule. Good friends might sit down at noon on the Lord's Day for a big dinner when the church bells signal that it is time for them to go to the house of the Lord. The friends discuss whether they should remain seated to enjoy the good food or modify the meal so they can still get to church in time. If one person says that they should go to church while another argues that it is not necessary to be so exact in observance, then the godly will immediately understand, by the help of this rule, on which side God's truth lies. They will remember what great comfort they have enjoyed in their hearts when they have interrupted their meal and hurried to the assembly of believers.

By contrast, they will remember their troubled conscience when they lingered over a meal while God's children gathered to be nourished in their souls by the Word of God. They decide quickly that those who want to shorten the meal to go to the assembly of believers are right. Once again, this rule may be applied to many other situations in life.

2. Love for the truth (Ps. 119:97). This, too, is an excellent work of the Spirit. Sometimes people see the truth but fail to love it (2 Thess. 2:10). They may even hate the truth, just as evildoers hate the light that exposes their evil deeds (John 3:19f.; Gal. 4:16). However, the Holy Spirit keeps cultivating the hearts of the godly. Just as he reveals truth to them, he also brings them to love the truth. He uses divine revelations to teach the godly to love and practice the truth of God with all their heart. He particularly teaches these truths:

The grievousness of resisting and rejecting the truth. He opens their eyes so that they see how unrighteous it is to suppress God's truth in unrighteousness (Rom. 1:18), what misery it brings with it (Jer. 2:19), and what an expense this will cost in the final judgment. It

will certainly result in great damnation, for the servant who knows
the will of the Lord but does not do it will be beaten with double
stripes (Luke 12:48). So the Holy Spirit wins the hearts of the godly
to forsake sin and love the truth.

The beauty of obeying God (1 Peter 1:22). How joyful is the creature who obeys his Creator, and the redeemed his Redeemer. The
Holy Spirit opens the eyes of the godly so they see more clearly
what the Lord Jesus Christ has done for them and how willingly
they must listen to his words and obey them in every way they
possibly can (Rom. 12:1). This fills their hearts with zeal to follow truth with all their might so they cry out with David, "What
shall I render unto the LORD for all his benefits toward me?" (Ps.
116:12).

The vanity of earthly things. These are things that make worldly
people, like Demas, love the present world so much (2 Tim. 4:10)
that they forsake the truth. The Spirit shows believers that the riches
of this world, for which worldly people commit many sins, are vain
and uncertain and often fly from one person to another (Prov. 23:5).
Likewise, the respect of the world, which many value so highly, will
fly away like a bird (Hosea 9:11). What's more, all the foolishness
of this world, with which many people suffocate their souls, is nothing more than the crackling of burning thorns under an earthen-
ware pot (Eccles. 7:6)! They make noise for a while but soon leave
nothing but the ashes of gnawing remorse.

Truly, the Holy Spirit shows that worldly things pass away with
use (1 Cor. 7:31). They may be quickly taken from man, or man
himself may be quickly taken from them by death (Luke 12:20).
The Holy Spirit so persuades believers of this that they do not consider any worldly thing worthy, no matter how beautiful it seems.
They do not forsake truth for it either or hold on to sin. They realize that God's truth is a thousand times better than anything the
world promises.

3. Drawing the right conclusions. The Holy Spirit strengthens
the godly by teaching them how to use basic principles to promote
true godliness and to edify and build themselves up in the faith
(Phil. 1:9–11). Some scholars may be experienced in religious
debates but may not know how to explain Scripture passages to
defend God's truth and to uncover errors as well as those who have

studied these passages and have become personally aware of the contents of such verses and how they apply to everyday life. So it is with godly people, whom the Holy Spirit graciously encourages to live a godly life. Their upright hearts and minds are like a commentary for the correct understanding and right application of many Scripture texts.

The Lord Jesus says in John 8:12, "I am the light of the world: he that followeth me shall not walk in darkness, but shall have the light of life." We may find that simple and humble people who practice godliness with all their hearts are able to instruct others in many areas of Christian life better and more clearly than others who have ten times more intelligence and education but are not as experienced in practicing godliness. The apostle Paul says to the saints in Rome, "And I myself also am persuaded of you, my brethren, that ye also are full of goodness, filled with all knowledge, able also to admonish one another" (Rom. 15:14). John likewise persuades us that this knowledge flows from the Holy Spirit into those who by His grace are "full of goodness" when he says, "But ye have an unction from the Holy One, and ye know all things" (1 John 2:20).

I cannot say how many edifying conclusions the godly, with the help of the Holy Spirit, may draw from the many circumstances of their lives, but they draw those conclusions by applying the three sound rules to distinguish truth from falsehood. In summary, the practice of healthy doctrine and divine truth:

Exalts God. The godly conclude that God will not acknowledge as genuine confessors of true faith those who do not glorify God, such as the pagans, Jews, Roman Catholics, and hypocritical saints among heretics such as the Anabaptists and radical mystics (Matt. 5:20). Therefore, they are pushed to show their zeal for the Lord in countless circumstances and to spread the glory of God as best they can.

Encourages the progress of holiness. The godly realize that the greatest disgrace is to boast of possessing and agreeing with the purest doctrine yet failing to show the power of godliness and to avoid evil in their lives. This makes them walk carefully and live a modest life so that their lives are more righteous than those of the pagan moralist philosophers of yesterday and the legalistic sectarians of today.

We read in 1 Corinthians 9:25–27, 2 Corinthians 11:12, and Philippians 4:8 that such was the practice of the godly Paul.

Comforts and benefits those who practice it. The saints realize the foolishness of setting aside God's truth to gain worldly profit, favor, or reward by following lies and sin. Because the Holy Spirit helps them with truth that is deeply engraved on their hearts, they know that the Lord God, who cannot lie, declares that godliness is the greatest gain (1 Tim. 6:6). Therefore, anything they might chase after at the cost of godliness will result only in loss and ruin. This mightily arms them against occasions to sin, which plague the worldly and lead them astray because they are not trained by the Spirit to draw specific conclusions from sound principles and use them to progress in godliness.

In such ways, godly people receive the Holy Spirit's good help in applying God's truth against the devil's false doctrine and malicious schemes, by which he misleads many heedless people. Those who would practice true godliness should be mindful of the Spirit's help so they may make progress in living a godly life.

Certain Special Operations

Let us now consider the gracious workings of the Holy Spirit by which he opposes the vicious assaults of Satan. Just as the wicked devil of hell, besides his evil assaults and misleading activities, raises his hand to wound the godly and stifle godliness, so the Lord God, who has accomplished such a great work to save souls—in sending his own Son into the world, even to the point of delivering him to death—gladly stretches out his mighty arm and promotes godly blessedness by special activity. God does this in direct connection with the fierce persecution, difficulties, and problems with which Satan afflicts us in this world. To combat such tribulation, the Holy Spirit grants special gifts to the saints.

Holy Wisdom

The Spirit gives divine wisdom to believers who are persecuted or oppressed so they may benefit from the tribulation. Although God punishes the ungodly without any benefit to them, this is not his way with the godly, for while he allows the godly to suffer tribulation, he teaches them by his Spirit so they benefit from their tribulations (Ps. 94:12; Rom. 5:3–4). He shows them how they may gain wisdom and experience during times of tribulation (James 1:2–5) that helps them endure further tribulation. The Spirit produces this divine wisdom in the godly in times of tribulation by means of hidden instruction. He reveals things that they must pay attention to in order to obtain this divine wisdom. There are many rules for this, but these three are the most important ones:

1. He tells them the source of this trouble. The Holy Spirit tells the godly that this trouble really comes from the Lord, the almighty God, who has taken it upon himself to make "all things work together for good" (Rom. 8:28). For "affliction cometh not forth of the dust, neither doth trouble spring out of the ground" (Job 5:6) but comes from heaven. Yes, the God of heaven visits his people on earth with various chastisements (Leviticus 26; Deuteronomy 28), even people who are called by his name (2 Chron. 7:14). Though wicked people or the devil of hell may persecute the godly and afflict them, this does not occur outside the providence of the Almighty (Job 1; Lam. 3:37), for these persecutors are a rod in the hand of God (Isa. 10:5). In this sense, "shall there be evil in a city, and the LORD hath not done it?" (Amos 3:6).

Take careful note, for this is an important part of the Spirit's wisdom. Worldly people do not see the fatherly hand of God in the good things they enjoy every day. Just as they fail to see that the Lord gives these things (Ps. 145:11) with his gracious hand (Ps. 5:12; Acts 14:17), they also fail to recognize the punishing hand of God in their afflictions (Isa. 1:6; Jer. 5:3). They fail to see that, even though they were taught from the time they began to teethe that both prosperity and adversity come from God. The godly, on the other hand, are taught by the Holy Spirit to recognize that all the hardships they endure come from God's hand, and those who cause them trouble are merely rods in God's hand for chastising them. This great insight helps God's children in these ways when they suffer oppression:

They do not focus on the means and agents of their troubles, nor are they irritable or impatient in their affliction. Because God himself mixes their cup of sorrow, the godly do not assign their troubles to chance. They understand that it is foolish to get upset over the means that cause this affliction. They know that God is chastising them by using these means. This keeps them from fiercely reacting against those whom God uses as instruments to cause them grief. We laugh at a dog that chases and bites a stone without being aware of the hand that threw it. The godly avoid such foolishness, thanks to knowing that God is the one who afflicts them, no matter what the means may be.

We do not read anywhere in the Book of Job that Job lashed out against the devil or the Sabeans and Chaldeans, though all inflicted misery on him. Rather, he continued to look to God. Likewise, David looked to God when Absalom rebelled against him and when Shimei cursed him. And in Kings, we see great nobles bow their necks before the sword, understanding that God had sent the executioner (1 Kings 2). The godly do not behave foolishly or in great anger when anyone afflicts them, for they know that it is done by the Lord. It is vain to struggle against God, for he is too strong for them (Rom. 9:19–20).

They expect blessings through afflictions. Once the godly understand that afflictions do not happen by chance or merely from ungodly or merciless enemies but rather come only with the permission of their good, wise, and omnipotent God, they will discover that their afflictions will lead to much good. The Lord, our good God, does not delight in tormenting his children but chastens them when they need it (1 Peter 1:6). The Holy Spirit teaches the godly that God tempers the cup of sorrow they are given to drink, mixing it with blessed spices so that they can benefit from their chastisements. They thus have no reason to fear lasting harm from these afflictions.

They expect deliverance from God. He who afflicted them will also heal them; he who wounded them will also bandage them to help them (Hosea 6:1). When the Lord God wants to chasten the godly, no one may interfere with this; likewise, when he wants to deliver them from affliction, no one can prevent it (Job 9:12f.). The godly who know this see no need to consult magicians or fortune-tellers (1 Sam. 28:7), to put their trust in men, or to win over princes with smooth and flattering words to gain their help. In short, they do not use wrong means to be delivered from affliction, for they know that tribulation comes from God and can be relieved only by God, who curses all evil means and blesses good means (Ps. 34:15–22).

2. He helps them understand the role of sin in affliction. The Holy Spirit teaches the godly what causes affliction and why it happens. He shows them that it is usually their own sin that causes all kinds of difficulties (Deuteronomy 28; Leviticus 26). "If we had no sins, we would have no wounds"—how true that old saying is. Yet it is also true that the ungodly generally persecute the godly, not because of their sins but because of their virtues (Matt. 5:12). Yet God would not permit the ungodly to persecute the godly if the godly had no sin, anymore than he would allow his angels to be harassed by evil angels or the spirits of saints who have died to be troubled by the ungodly (Rev. 21:27).

The Holy Spirit teaches the godly that they are oppressed because of remaining, indwelling sin. We cannot conclude from this that the most afflicted are the most sinful (Luke 13:1–5) or that every affliction of a believer is due to a specific sin (Job 1; John 9). Yet sin is the cause of much affliction. The Lord Jesus himself was afflicted because he was made sin for us (2 Cor. 5:21). It is important that we clearly understand that our troubles come from sin. Worldly people who are not taught by the Spirit generally pay no attention to this. They have grown up saying, "If we did everything we should, we would have everything we wanted," but they pay no attention to the consequences of their sin. Only those taught by the Spirit of God have the wisdom to profit from such consequences, mainly in three ways:

They humble themselves before God and admit guilt for all their grief. They realize that they deserve chastisement a thousand times more than what they receive (Lam. 3:42). They admit that sin is the reason for their sorrow. They conclude that if God had done what they had deserved, they would have been sentenced to eternal death. In this life, only one part of a person suffers, whether bearable or not, but the godly know they deserve to be thrown into the pit of hell to endlessly suffer unbearable pain. That is why they realize that their chastisement in this life in no way equals their offenses.

They recognize the foolishness of trying to save themselves, since their own sinful actions are what brought grief upon them. Once we realize how sin causes every possible trouble, we know that we cannot be helped out of our difficulties by more sinful acts anymore than we can gather grapes from thorns or figs from thistles (Matt. 7:16).

Even if sin brought us temporary benefits, that relief would only compound our problems and difficulties in the end. Those who would save themselves from difficulty by sinning are asking the devil for help. Woe unto the patient whose physician is Satan!

They see that the best way to be delivered from trouble is to be delivered first from sin. Urged on by their problems, the godly begin to examine themselves thoroughly to find out what sins lay hidden in them and need to be dealt with so they may escape tribulation and find help and healing or at least find some easing of their pain and grief. Once the cause is found, the suffering can be taken away (cf. book 1).

3. He helps them understand God's purpose for their affliction. Affliction comes to the godly because of their sin, not to destroy them but to save them (Rom. 8:28). God allows his children to suffer because he loves them (Rev. 3:19). Part of the Spirit's gift of wisdom is clearly understanding why our wise God allows us to be oppressed. Worldly people have little or no understanding of this. They may be accustomed to say that the Lord God chastens them for their good, yet they have no real grasp of what that includes. The Holy Spirit teaches the godly at least three ways in which affliction may benefit them:

It humbles them by showing them shortcomings that still remain in them. A glass of liquid may seem clear enough when it stands still, but when stirred it soon reveals sediment that is in the bottom. This happens to many children of God. They seem to have very calm hearts until affliction empties them "vessel to vessel" (Jer. 48:11). When this happens, problems come to light, such as testiness, lack of faith, love of worldly things, and many other faults. That was what happened when the servant girl of the high priest confronted Peter, stirring up his fears and doubts (Matt. 26:69). The Lord sends affliction upon the godly to bring their shortcomings to light so they will deal with them.

It builds them up by showing them virtues that God has placed in them. We do not know how strong a person is until a heavy burden is laid on him. A cowardly soldier and a courageous soldier may look the same when first recruited, but their true nature is revealed when they confront the enemy. Likewise, in a stack of wheat bound in sheaves, it is not easy to see which sheaf contains more wheat. But when the sheaves are threshed separately, we can clearly see which yields more grain. So it is with the wheat of Christ; it must be threshed separately to yield its grain. Many expensive spices contain very sweet aromas but do not spread that fragrance until they are crushed. It is the same with many virtues of the godly. Who would have known that Abraham had such great faith in God if he had not been tested by the command to sacrifice Isaac (Genesis 22)? Who would have thought that the faith of past saints was so great if they had not been persecuted by the pagans (Rev. 13:10)?

Any virtue, any faith, any patience that is in a person will be revealed in a time of oppression. We have seen that depravity, which is still present in the Christian, is revealed in suffering. But oppression stimulates virtues in the Christian to defeat that depravity. Any virtue will be forced to reveal itself in suffering. Affliction showed that Job served the Lord his God with all his heart, not just because God had blessed him (Job 1–2). In order to reveal their virtues and to comfort the godly with them, the Lord God allows the godly to be afflicted.

It motivates the godly to correct their faults (Rev. 3:19). A fierce enemy unexpectedly attacks a town in which people have lived peacefully for a long time. In this attack, the town discovers the strengths and weaknesses of its defenses. The inhabitants set about to strengthen the weak areas and fortify the strong ones by keeping them in good condition. The Lord tests us so that we may do the same.

Truly, these teachings are beneficial to the saints. They help them to patiently endure their afflictions without being overcome by sorrow. The worldly people are overcome by difficulties because they do not pay attention to God's reasons for affliction, nor do they know from whom it comes.

Patience and Endurance

God grants patience and endurance to saints who are persecuted or abused by their spiritual enemies. The Holy Spirit is the God of patience (Rom. 15:5), the Father of mercies, and the God of all comfort (2 Cor. 1:3). He is given to believers to comfort them in their tribulations (John 14:16). He works patience in them in times of trouble, and his all-sustaining blessings of comfort and power

(Rom. 15:13) offer a solid ground of encouragement. In particular, the Spirit offers suffering believers these three assurances:

1. They are precious in God's sight. No matter how much they are persecuted, slandered, reviled, or oppressed, the godly are not one hair less precious, less important, or less esteemed in the sight of God. The apostle Peter says that Christians are actually blessed when they are reviled and insulted. When saints are greatly humiliated or slandered, that is when the Spirit of God truly rests upon them (1 Peter 4:14). Even when the godly are persecuted with fire and water and everything that hurts, they are more precious and honorable in the eyes of God (Isa. 43:2–4). What prince or king would not love his servants more than when they are mistreated by enemies for his sake (2 Samuel 10)?

God loved his servant David just as much in his sorrow as in his joy. David was just as precious and important to God when Saul persecuted him as when Saul appreciated him. Truly, David was as precious to God when he was fleeing as in the time of his glory (Psalm 56). God considers himself persecuted when the godly are persecuted (Acts 9:4), for in all our afflictions, he is afflicted (Isa. 63:8f.). God's affection for the godly does not change when their outward situation changes. Even though evil men revile and despise Christians, the Lord does not take the side of evil men, for he has no fellowship with them (Ps. 94:20). He will not despise the godly. Far be it from God that he would do that!

The affliction of the godly is no proof of God's displeasure. It rather proves that they are sure partakers of God's great favor and are his children (Heb. 12:7). The apostle Peter testifies that when we endure God's chastisements, God most identifies us as his children. When two children are fighting in the street and a passerby takes one by the arm to punish him but lets the other go, do we not conclude that the punished child is his own child? The one whom he chastises is his child; the other goes unpunished because he is a stranger.

Although we may notice God's anger toward us (Ps. 85:5) in the suffering that our sins have brought on us, we also see in it God's love and faithfulness toward us. A loving father shows anger and displeasure toward his child, but he still dearly loves the child, even when he is punishing him for his sins. He loves his son dearly and values him more than all the goods he owns. This is what the Lord says: "As many as I love, I rebuke and chasten: be zealous therefore, and repent" (Rev. 3:19; cf. Heb. 12:5–11). The Holy Spirit reminds the saints of more ways in which the Lord's affection for them never changes, even when their prosperity changes into adversity:

The sting of oppression has been removed. Just as death has its sting, tribulation has a venomous sting that sorely wounds ungodly people. But as Christ took the sting out of death for the saints (1 Cor. 15:55–57), he has also removed the sting from the affliction he sends to the godly. All oppression is a sign of God's wrath, but Christ changed its character and made it a sign of God's love (Rev. 3:19). As a result, the oppression of the godly is not punishment for sin but fatherly chastisement for their preservation (1 Cor. 11:32). Thus, the godly know that even though the Lord sorely chastens them, he is always well disposed toward them. He visits them with affliction only for their benefit.

Suffering seasons us for the journey. From the beginning of time, when sin came into the world, God has used tribulation to mature and train the godly as they have progressed in their journey toward heaven (Ps. 34:20–22; Acts 14:22). Look at how Adam, Noah, Abraham, Isaac, Jacob, Job, Moses, David, Paul, and Peter were seasoned by suffering. Pay attention to all the saintly patriarchs, prophets, and apostles, yes, to all God's beloved, and see how they were trained by tribulation. Above all, look at Jesus Christ, God's dear Son (Col. 1:13). He was made sin for us and became a man of sorrows who knew the deepest grief (Psalm 22; Isaiah 53). This certainly shows how we can both be loved by God and painfully afflicted in the world. This should also prompt great perseverance. If we reflect on those superior men of God, who were much better than we are, and consider how much sorrow they endured with great patience and in silence (Ps. 39:9), we too should curb and silence our rebellious flesh.

We might conclude here that there is not a single reason for us to be exempt from the suffering that is the portion of all God's children. If we had bodies of steel that could not be subjected to pain, sorrow, or sickness, or if we were only saints with earthly property that could not be taken from us, we might be exempt. But do we really think that we should be the only ones with unchangeable friends or the only ones with respect and fame that cannot be wounded by an evil tongue? Do we think that we alone should have a conscience or reputation that is safe from attack? Surely, it would be quite unreasonable to rejoice with all God's saints above when we have not suffered with the saints below.

If we look to Jesus Christ, who for our sake was like a worm on earth (Ps. 22:6), we should be convinced of the necessity to be servants like our Lord (Matt. 10:24). Would it be right for Christ the Lord to have suffered so much on earth and for us to suffer so little? What would that prove except that we are dead members who do not belong to Christ, the head? Meditating on this helps the godly to be patient in their afflictions. It helps them regard it joy not only to trust in Christ but also to suffer with him (Phil. 1:29; James 1:2). In this respect, believers rank above the angels in being conformed to the image of God's Son (Rom. 8:29). Imagine that there were two ways to heaven. One is a little difficult, but it has been trodden by holy patriarchs, prophets, apostles, and all God's beloved, yes, even by Christ the Lord. The other is a little easier, but it has been shunned by the godly. Wouldn't you choose the more difficult road, which is so highly praised by so many excellent travelers, such as the holy patriarchs, prophets, and God's beloved who are now in heaven?

We will persevere through this. There hasn't been a single godly person who has totally succumbed to affliction. All believers eventually are delivered from their troubles (Ps. 34:20; James 5:10; Rev. 7:14–17). Although the Lord visits the godly with the rod and chastises them with affliction, he does not deprive them of his grace (Ps. 89:33–37). Rather, he loves his own just as much when they are in great affliction as when they are in great joy. That should greatly strengthen perseverance in the godly, for they know that no matter how harsh the beginning of affliction may be, deliverance from it will be joyous.

All this nurtures perseverance, for the godly are assured that God is favorable toward them even if the whole world is against them or when they encounter many tribulations (2 Tim. 1:12). When a king looks favorably upon a soldier who receives the heavy blows of his enemies, how valiant the soldier becomes!

2. They will greatly benefit from their afflictions. The Spirit teaches us that all things work together for good to those who love

God (Rom. 8:28). That applies as well to their tribulations and persecutions. The apostle Paul says that all his sufferings served to advance the holy gospel. It also applies to the tribulations of the saints. What is more, the Holy Spirit helps the godly understand that they will enjoy the following fruits of tribulations:

Sanctification. Though the outward man may perish through affliction, the inward man, which is by far the more important and more precious part, is renewed day by day (2 Cor. 4:16). Holiness is worked in us when we are most afflicted (Isa. 27:9).

Preservation. The saints will be saved from the condemnation and destruction that awaits the evil world (1 Cor. 11:32). When the world smiles on us and favors us, it has enormous power to draw our hearts away from God toward worldly things (2 Tim. 4:10). We are so worldly minded by nature that when the world is well disposed toward us, we can hardly restrain ourselves from loving it in return. The Lord turns the world against us by means of tribulations and difficulties. He lets us experience these trials so that we will not be condemned with the world. When believers are admonished by God, remember that the painful road of tribulation leads them away from damnation and the fire of hell that will eternally torment the ungodly after their short time on earth (Luke 16:25). That should help the godly person patiently take the narrow way of tribulation, knowing that it leads away from everlasting torment.

Eternal glory (Acts 14:22; 1 Peter 1:6–9). As 2 Corinthians 4:17 says, "Our light affliction, which is but for a moment, worketh for us a far more exceeding and eternal weight of glory." This means that no matter how much the godly are oppressed on earth, they will be glorified many times over in heaven. Every hour of tribulation that we endure now will result in ten thousand years of joy. Therefore, these temporary pains and insults that we suffer here are only the seeds of everlasting bliss. The godly person who considers this will be encouraged to gladly bear his cross. He will despise the shame here on earth for the joy that is set before him in heaven (Heb. 12:2) and will gladly take the difficult road of tribulation, knowing that it leads to eternal rest and joy.

Look at all the benefits that the godly receive from their afflictions. This is what the Holy Spirit teaches the godly. As a result, they are encouraged to patiently endure all kinds of unpleasantness.

Men gladly endure trouble for the hope of gain. Doesn't a man work happily all day in the hope of receiving wages at the end of the day? Likewise, though our work may seem grievous instead of joyous, we may endure it patiently because it will yield the peaceable fruit of righteousness (Heb. 12:11). When we are sick, we take bitter medicine in order to get better. We thank the doctor for seeing us and pay him for the medicine. Likewise, shouldn't we drink the cup our heavenly Father gives us to drink (John 18:11) to give us eternal life?

3. They will not be given more than they can bear (1 Cor. 10:13). The cup of suffering, which God mixes for their good, will never be stronger than the godly are able to take. It will be prepared, not according to their merits but according to their strength. The Lord will give them comfort and strength in proportion to their afflictions so they will be able to bear them (John 16:33; 2 Cor. 1:4). The Holy Spirit also assures believers that he will abide with them to strengthen them in their troubles. A more beautiful thing cannot be hoped for. What should we fear when we have the Holy Spirit to comfort and encourage us (John 14:16)? The Holy Spirit also ensures the godly that they will not be afflicted too hard, not only when they become sick or have some other trouble that comes directly from the hand of God but also when they are persecuted by their worst enemies, for even their enemies are instruments of God's wrath (Isa. 10:6). Their enemies are still in God's hand and are directed for the benefit of his children, for it is God's gracious, wise, and omnipotent hand that holds the rod with which we are lashed. Although a loving father uses a stinging switch to bring his child to his senses, he does not wear the rod out on the back of his child or beat him mercilessly but uses it with restraint. God's children would lose all courage if they saw a sharp rod such as Assur, or the Spaniard, or the devil assault them unless they knew that God's hand was holding the rod. Knowing that consoles them and gives them hope.

The Holy Spirit offers the following three things regarding the affliction, tribulation, or persecution that the godly may have to endure:

The amount of affliction is limited. No more than necessary will be given to correct the infirmity that the Lord wants to heal. In other words, he will not make the affliction harsher than what is required. Doctors sometimes make mistakes in evaluating a patient. They may prescribe medicine that is too strong and initially makes the patient feel worse. But God, who created and formed us, knows our frame better than we do. He remembers that we are dust (Ps. 103:14). He knows how weak we are and how little we are able to bear. He wants to help his children by afflicting them, not to destroy them but to save them (Rev. 3:19). Therefore, he restrains the affliction and makes sure that it does not weigh too heavily on the patient.

The Holy Spirit assures the godly of this so that they may develop endurance in affliction. Do we not voluntarily take medicine if we know that it does not contain a single grain of bitterness more than is necessary for our well-being? Listen to how the Lord encourages his children in their afflictions: "Fear thou not, O my servant Jacob, saith the LORD; . . . for I am with thee; . . . I make a full end of all nations whither I have scattered thee, yet will I not make a full end of thee: but I will correct thee in measure, and will not leave thee altogether unpunished" (Jer. 30:10–11).

The duration of affliction is limited. The apostle Peter says that the godly will be afflicted for only a short time (1 Peter 1:6). Even our life span, after which all affliction ends, is only a short time compared with eternity (Psalm 90). Therefore, our affliction will not last a long time. The psalmist also declares that God's anger endures but for a moment, and in his favor is life; weeping may endure for a night, but joy cometh in the morning (Ps. 30:5). A surgeon may leave a bandage on a wound longer than is necessary, but our God will not. He sits as a refiner above the oven of affliction to purify his children and purge them as gold. As soon as he sees that patience has done its perfect work, he takes his children out of the fire (Zech. 13:9; Mal. 3:3; James 1:4).

The rod of affliction is most appropriate. The Lord is like a skillful farmer who knows the type of soil in which he sows and the quality of the seed he uses (Isa. 28:24). We may be assured that the Lord knows us better than we know ourselves and allows us to be afflicted only so that we bear more fruit (Heb. 12:9). He carefully sees that we are plowed and sown in a way that enhances our fruitfulness (Psalm 129). The apostle Peter confirms this when he says, "Beloved, think it not strange concerning the fiery trial which is to try you, as though some strange thing happened unto you" (1 Peter 4:12). Sometimes the godly are troubled that they are afflicted in a particular way. They think they would gladly suffer other afflictions. Many thus become impatient. But the Holy Spirit teaches us that the Lord who formed us and best knows the condition of our hearts also knows how we should be plowed and sown with the seed of affliction so that we may produce good fruit.

Knowing that we will not be too heavily afflicted strengthens us to be patient and obedient. When a man loses courage, his patience wears thin. By contrast, when a man knows that no matter how much he is afflicted, he will never be destroyed, he will patiently wait for deliverance from the Lord his God, who will help him.

Holiness

The Spirit grants holiness to the godly when they are persecuted and oppressed (Heb. 12:9), mainly by scouring away the rust of sin in them (Job 33:15–17; Isa. 27:9) so that they will increase in obedience to God (Ps. 119:71). Affliction is a kind of heavenly soap that removes the filthiness of sin from the hearts of God's children and makes them clean (Dan. 11:35). Affliction is also like the fire of the goldsmith that purges the scum and filth of sin from the godly so they may become beautiful vessels of honor. Affliction may vex us for a while, causing our depravity to object, just as wholesome medicine may make a patient a little worse for a time. In the end, however, affliction produces the fruit of righteousness (Heb. 12:11). Peace is sowed for those who practice righteousness (Ps. 97:11), but it takes time for the seed to sprout.

The godly have a great advantage over the worldly, who do not forsake their folly (Prov. 27:22) and who are crushed as wheat in the mortar of affliction because they do not pay attention to the operations of the Spirit that can change them for the better. The godly, led by the Spirit of God in all their ways, enjoy great benefits from their troubles. They find that the days of affliction are days of plowing and sowing that eventually produce beautiful fruits of righteousness. The beautiful fruits of holiness are countless, but the most important ones are faith, love, and hope (1 Thess. 1:3). Notice that the Holy Spirit stimulates these glorious virtues in the godly in times of affliction. So we may truthfully say that we are never better off than when we are afflicted. Here are some of the fruits of affliction:

1. Our faith increases. All the fiery darts of Satan cannot pierce the shield of faith but are destroyed when they touch it (Eph. 6:16). Affliction stimulates our faith in many ways, but especially in three ways:

It prompts self-examination. When we are struck by oppression, persecution, or some other trouble, the devil tries to weaken our trust in God, to undermine our holy faith, and to convince us that we are not true believers. He tries to persuade us that we are not the beloved of God and that the Lord has taken his eyes from us in our affliction (Psalm 73). Yes, believers should examine themselves to see if they have true faith and that Christ is truly in them so they may not be found reprobate (2 Cor. 13:5). Yes, they should examine the ground on which they stand, what evidences they have and how they are sealed. If their faith is genuine, then the more it is tested, the more secure it will be. We know that the more a ship's log is examined, the more its authenticity is confirmed. We also know that when a substantial inheritance comes our way, we do not check the accuracy of the will and testament as intensely as an opponent might. Likewise Job, after carefully examining the news of his losses, was moved to say, "Though he slay me, yet will I trust in him" (Job 13:15). Surely, worldly people who try to reassure themselves with false reports of God's grace toward them are in a lamentable state. The more they examine themselves, the more they lose confidence. They soon discover that they have been deceived.

It weakens our desire for worldly things. When persecution, affliction, or other trouble weighs heavily upon us, we become vividly aware of the vanity of earthly things, for those things let us down when we most need help. We then become even more aware that everything depends on God and that all wisdom, understanding, or counsel against the Lord is vain (Prov. 21:30). As a result, we are led to withdraw our trust from earthly things and put our trust in the Lord our God, who alone is rock solid. We say with the psalmist, "It is better to trust in the LORD than to put confidence in man. It is better to trust in the LORD than to put confidence in princes" (Ps.

118:8–9) or anything else in the world. Their help is only vanity; only the Lord can help us (Isa. 63:5–9).

By nature, we can hardly resist relying on earthly things that are at hand. Only when they fail us and we have nothing else to depend on, though our soul still seeks support, do we look to God and seek rest in him. The apostle Paul welcomes the sentence of death in himself so that he no longer trusts in himself but in God, who gives life to the dead (2 Cor. 1:9). Likewise, the Lord humbled the children of Israel in the desert. He let them be afflicted by famine so that they might learn that man does not live by bread alone but by every word that proceeds out of the mouth of God (Deut. 8:3). We see how the travelers called upon God (Ps. 107:23–30) when they were at their wit's end. Likewise believers, such as Jehoshaphat, honed their faith in God, saying at the moment of most urgent need, Lord, "neither know we what to do: but our eyes are upon thee" (2 Chron. 20:12).

It brings us closer to God. When persecution, affliction, or difficulty distresses us, we tend to study God's Word more often and we more earnestly examine his promises and his blessings to his children (Psalm 119). When the psalmist was attacked, he was moved to examine God's attributes (Ps. 77:7). Likewise, our faith is nourished and strengthened by the promises of God, as revealed in his Word, as a newborn baby grows on his mother's milk.

Our faith gets stronger. God's promises are the best nourishment for faith. God's Word is thus called "the word of faith" (Rom. 10:8). Every beautiful and comforting verse that we find in Scripture that applies to our situation is like a letter from heaven, sent to us by the almighty God to strengthen our faith. So affliction greatly strengthens our most holy faith.

2. We increase in love. The Holy Spirit strengthens us in times of affliction so that, truly, all the waters of affliction cannot quench love (Song of Sol. 8:7). We see this in three ways:

We reach out to God in love. When we are afflicted, we become keenly aware that the Lord our God is still our best friend and that he alone sustains us when everything and everyone else fail us (Ps. 27:10). He is the strength and comfort of our hearts (Ps. 94:19). Words cannot express how much we are touched when someone shows favor to us when we are troubled and in great need. When David meditated on how God had sustained him in his flights from Saul, he burst forth in praise: "I will love thee, O LORD, my strength. The LORD is my rock, and my fortress, and my deliverer; my God, my strength, in whom I will trust; my buckler, and the horn of my salvation, and my high tower. I will call upon the LORD, who is worthy to be praised: so shall I be saved from mine enemies" (Ps. 18:1–3).

This especially happens when we suffer and we contemplate the bitter sufferings of Christ, when we consider that the Lord did not spare his Son because of his great love for us (John 3:16) so that we would find comfort here on earth in all our troubles and later in everlasting glory. When we meditate on this, we will have deeper love for Christ the Lord, even in our own suffering, for only when we become aware of how much the Lord has suffered for us will we begin to realize how great a love we owe to God and his Son.

We reach out to others in love. When we suffer through affliction, we are better able to sympathize with those in trouble. The Lord tells us, "Thou shalt not oppress a stranger: for ye know the heart of a stranger, seeing ye were strangers in the land of Egypt" (Exod. 23:9). Affliction fills us with compassion for our neighbors who are in distress. It also teaches us to remember those who are afflicted when we come to days of prosperity and our love for them is likely to cool (Heb. 13:3). We must pray for the sweet increase of Christian love.

We grasp the love of God's Word. We have already seen that when we are afflicted, we tend to study the Word of God more. God's Word is the word of love. Every verse exhales true Christian love. All the law is fulfilled in the word *love* (Rom. 13:8; Gal. 4:15). The more suffering makes us search the Word of God, the more we will increase in love. This especially happens when we examine God's Word with a heart that is prepared by suffering to love God and our neighbor.

3. Our hope increases. No affliction is so sharp that it can pierce the helmet of salvation, which the Lord equips his saints with in the day of affliction (1 Thess. 5:8). The Holy Spirit strengthens our hope in these times:

When we sincerely seek God. When we undergo affliction or distress, we seek the Lord our God with all our heart. We see worldly people prosper and become wealthy, but the Holy Spirit, our Comforter, teaches us to realize that in due time there will be an accounting. As 2 Thessalonians 1:6–7 says, "Seeing it is a righteous thing with God to recompense tribulation to them that trouble you: And to you who are troubled rest with us, when the Lord Jesus shall be revealed from heaven." When they connect this with the persecution that believers now suffer, this greatly encourages and strengthens them in the hope and expectation of eternal blessedness that will be revealed at the last day (1 Peter 1:5). This provides them with a strong intimation that God's justice and righteousness are aimed at arranging eternal salvation for them. This greatly strengthens them by the "helmet of salvation" (Eph. 6:17), which is the hope that God's righteousness now offers them in the everlasting glory in Christ Jesus.

When God helps us. When the godly are in distress, they experience a strong sense of God's faithfulness, help, and the genuineness of their faith. The apostle says that suffering produces hope (Rom. 5:4). David was strengthened by realizing how God helped him slay the lion and the bear. That assured him that he would also defeat the uncircumcised Philistine Goliath (1 Sam. 17:34–37). So will it be with the saints who suffer affliction; the Lord will not forsake them in their trouble but will be gracious to them and help them. They will grow in confidence that the Lord God will continue to help them and finally deliver them from all their troubles. Thus, the psalmist prays, "Thou hast forgiven the iniquity of thy people, thou hast covered all their sin. Thou has taken away all thy wrath: thou hast turned thyself from the fierceness of thine anger." Because of this, the psalmist may say, "Turn us, O God of our salvation, and cause thine anger toward us to cease" (Ps. 85:2–4). Experiencing God's grace in our affliction strengthens our hope now and allows us to expect further graces on the principle that having loved his own, God loves them unto the end (John 13:1; Rom. 8:38–39).

When we realize our hope in Christ. We have shown that the godly who experience affliction tend to study God's Word more diligently. The apostle Paul says that the Word of God has also been given so that we might have hope (Rom. 15:4). The Word of God is full of glorious and encouraging words that powerfully work together to strengthen the hope of the saints. One of a thousand similar declarations proclaims, "For the needy shall not always be forgotten: the expectation of the poor shall not perish for ever" (Ps. 9:18). Truly, the Word of God leads us always to Christ (2 Cor. 3:16), our hope (1 Tim. 1:1). Hope, the anchor of our souls (Heb. 6:18–20), is more and more secured to Christ. Therefore, the more we study God's Word, the more we are strengthened in Christian hope.

Look how these precious privileges are given to believers in their afflictions. Experience teaches us this is the truth about affliction. Hear it, and know it for yourself (Job 5:27). You will see that even though days of affliction are sad, dark, and unwelcome, they nevertheless will become the most fruitful days of your life.

We become more aware of this when we compare our days of prosperity with our days of adversity. When we see that the days of our affliction are our most profitable days, we may say with Solomon, "Sorrow is better than laughter: for by the sadness of the countenance the heart is made better" (Eccles. 7:3). The devil and the world may set themselves against us, but time will show that while they thought they had done us much harm with so much suffering, they have served only to cleanse us. All they did was scrub away the filthiness and rust of our sins, making us shine more brilliantly as vessels for the house of the Lord. How gladly then we should bear our persecution (1 Peter 3:17) for the sake of the saints (2 Tim. 3:12), seeing that persecution produces so much fruit.

We have extensively treated this work of God's Spirit in the heart of the godly in times of affliction so that the godly may know that though they have been called to endure so much suffering, the comforts of the Lord are also great (2 Cor. 1:4). When they have seen the blessing and comfort the Lord has prepared for them in times of affliction, they should take care not to be taken in by the devil's wiles or let their lack of faith deprive them of these gifts. Faintness of heart could easily overwhelm those who do not know what privileges may be theirs in times of affliction, when the Lord seems to be punishing them.

Some prosperous people may not find much tasty material in this section because they lack the seasoning of affliction to make such a subject desirable. Some people might find this section too detailed. Yet we are confident that those who are now undergoing affliction will appreciate the material in this section, even if it is somewhat drawn out, and not wish it were shorter, since each part offers them new ways to turn their sufferings to good use.

The Kingdom of Grace against the Realm of Darkness

We have shown you the kingdom of grace that battles the realm of darkness. This discussion reminds us of Elijah's words to his servant: "They that be with us are more than they that be with them" (2 Kings 6:16). He who is on the side of the saints is stronger than he who is on the side of worldly people. He who clings to God with all his heart will obtain the victory and, like Judah, will rule with God in righteous holy service (Hosea 11:12). As John declares, "Greater is he that is in you, than he that is in the world" (1 John 4:4). These words are right, for:

What does the vile devil amount to when compared to the Holy Spirit of God?

What does the condemned world amount to when compared to God's holy church?

What does the old man matter when compared to the new creature?

Anyone who sees these comparisons immediately realizes which side will be victorious. The inevitable destiny of the realm of darkness is to be overthrown, for its ruler's head has already been bruised. Blessed are those who are on the Lord's side, for that is the side that will obtain overwhelming victory in this battle and eternal bliss afterward (Psalm 110).

Even those who do not want to begin the Christian life and the godly walk should pay attention. Some cite the depravity of believers, the corruption of the world, and the craftiness of the devil for excuses, as if there were no help available from the Lord our God and the kingdom of his grace. They give up and lie down in despair between their burdens like lazy Issachar (Gen. 49:14–15), without making the slightest effort to strive after godliness. Their damnation will surely be harsher, since they know that God has established a kingdom of grace to help them against the devil, the world, and their flesh. They refuse to place themselves under the kingdom that could have strengthened and saved them.

In any event, let all who earnestly intend to practice true godliness take courage and, realizing how great their help will be, devoutly engage in the blessed work they have begun. Let them continue to seek this helping power so that they may go forth in victory with the One who sat on the white horse and went forth to final victory (Rev. 6:2).

BOOK 4

Godly Living
Is the True Goal of Life

Three Things We Should Do in General to Resist the Power of the Kingdom of Darkness and to Lay Hold of the Kingdom of Grace

Now that we understand and have paid careful attention to the character and nature of the kingdom of darkness and the kingdom of grace, which are necessary to advance the practice of godliness, we must move on to consider our daily conduct, for if we wish to live truly godly lives, we must consider our behavior so that, on the one hand, we may increasingly tear down the kingdom of darkness and, on the other hand, progressively build up the kingdom of grace within us.

If ever a subject needed a thorough approach, it is this one, for this matter is vitally important and touches the crowns, so to speak, of the two most powerful kingdoms in the entire world. Many people are indifferent to this reality because both of these kingdoms are spiritual and therefore cannot be seen with the physical eye. That is why many regard these things only superficially and make so little effort to practice godliness. Clearly, we will never lead godly lives if we neglect to pay careful attention to the kingdom of darkness and the kingdom of grace and have insight into each.

The following three things in particular are very necessary—indeed, I may say they are indispensable:

- First, we should understand the proper goal of our lives and keep before us the true purpose of life.
- Second, we must correctly apply all the legitimate means that God has provided for attaining that goal.
- Third, we must conduct ourselves wisely in using and applying the means that God has provided for attaining our goal.

We will consider these points in the following three books, starting with the first one in book 4.

A General Discussion about the Right Goal and Object of Our Lives

First, and above all, it is essential that the Christian, who now has a discriminating knowledge of the characteristics of both the kingdom of darkness and the kingdom of grace, should have worked out in his mind what it means to be godly. Above all, he should now fully comprehend what the true purpose of life should be in order to be able to live in a truly godly way. He must order and regulate his entire life and conduct and make it his most important task to direct all his affairs in such a way that they never distract him from this goal. Being careful not to pursue the wrong goal in life, he should seriously consider the direction of his life—where it is leading and what he needs to achieve—for the human tendency is to strive most for the things we desire most. If we want to become rich and powerful in this world, then all our efforts will be directed toward that end. If we have some other aspiration in life, we will equally strive to attain that one. It is therefore very essential that we direct ourselves to attain the right goal in life, which is to practice true godliness and to live a godly life. Other-

wise we are like archers without a definite target, aimlessly shoot-
ing arrows into the air.

It is undeniably true that many people casually occupy themselves with the practice of godliness but do not have much success
because they fail to aim at the right target with their lives and only
carelessly shoot somewhere in the general direction. They have good
intentions, but that is about all. These people are erratic in their
pursuit of godliness; they are sometimes on track and sometimes
off. The apostle Paul did not wish this to happen. He did not want
to run uncertainly or fight as one who beats the air (1 Cor. 9:26),
but, forgetting those things that are behind, he reached forth unto
those things that are before, to the prize of the high calling in Jesus
Christ (Phil. 3:13).

It is therefore right that we move on to consider these three questions in more detail: (1) What are the characteristics of our life's
true purpose? (2) What is the nature of the Christian who pursues
this goal? (3) What scheming, cunning tricks will the kingdom of
darkness use to keep this true purpose of life hidden from us?

We know that worldly people are engaged in many things, but
we also know that only one thing is truly necessary (Luke 10:42).
Our real purpose in life is to do all things for God's glory, for the
progress of our soul's salvation, and to win others so that they may
be saved. The apostle Paul declares this in 1 Corinthians 10:31–33:
"Whether therefore ye eat, or drink, or whatsoever ye do, do all to
the glory of God. Give none offence, neither to the Jews, nor to the
Gentiles, nor to the church of God: even as I please all men in all
things, not seeking mine own profit, but the profit of many, that
they may be saved."

Clearly, the glory of God is the most important purpose and goal
of our life. We were created and re-created for that purpose (Isa.
43:7, 21). The only way we can accomplish this is by following God's
counsel and his Word (Jer. 23:22). In this, we will win many souls
and further the salvation of our own souls. Our gracious Lord has
united these things in such a way that we cannot seek God's glory
with all our hearts by keeping his commandments without edifying our neighbor. Our own blessedness then flows from this. Since
this is indisputable, we will briefly show what constitutes the true
glorification of God's honor, the furthering of our own salvation
and that of our neighbor.

The Most Important Purpose of Our Lives: To Exalt and Glorify God

All Christians agree that exalting God is the most important purpose of their lives. David therefore says, "While I live will I praise the LORD: I will sing praises unto my God while I have any being" (Ps. 146:2). What is more reasonable than to glorify and praise the Lord God, who created and formed us? Yet not everyone understands how the Lord may be glorified. In general, we should realize that glorifying God includes observing his commandments and demonstrating true godliness, as we briefly explained in book 1. Yet we need to say a little more about this for the benefit of ordinary folk.[1] We should understand that we Christians exalt God's glory in three particular ways:

1. In confessing his name. We exalt God's glory when we boldly confess his holy name and truth. Peter teaches us this (1 Peter 3:15), and God's holy martyrs set a shining example in this because they "loved not their lives unto the death" (Rev. 12:11). They confessed God's holy name and his holy truth, even when it would have made death by a horrible execution inevitable (Daniel 3).

All those who live morally unrestrained lives, those who are worldly, and hypocrites who insist that they serve the Lord their God with all their heart and spirit fall far short of this. We live in such times of ease and comfort that we do not have to fight for our lives in the interest of truth (Heb. 12:3) and are not daily counted as sheep for the slaughter for the gospel's sake (Ps. 44:11; Rom. 8:36)—which has been the case throughout our country's history.[2] Nevertheless, we should exalt God's glory every day by making it our habit to greatly praise, glorify, and magnify him for all the blessings, benefits, and mighty deeds he does on our behalf every day. We should also praise and exalt his holy decrees, ordinances, and

---

1. Literally, "simple people," by which Teellinck means "every believer who has no leadership position in government or the church" (book 5).

2. Teellinck has in mind the history of the Reformed Church. The Reformation in the Low Countries was marked by intense persecution by the Roman Catholic hierarchy and the Spanish government in a determined effort to repress what they regarded as heresy. By the mid-1560s, tens of thousands had been put to death for their beliefs. Many were burned alive, strangled, or beheaded. Dutch Reformed churches were deeply impacted by the experience of living "under the cross"—that is, under a regime of persecution.

laws and defend and publicize them at every meal or meeting and on every occasion that provides an opportunity to magnify God's name. We should persevere in this even when people do not appreciate it or it makes us unpopular (Ps. 119:46–48).

2. In living out our faith. We exalt God's glory when we are always prepared and ready, in accordance with our holy confession, to serve God above all else and to show the whole world that we are people who seek first the kingdom of God. We make serving him our most important duty (Matt. 6:33), always observing the commands of the first table of the law and performing, above all other duties, those spiritual duties that concern God's majesty, love, fear, and praise. Furthermore, by being ready and prepared for his service, we are available as we are and with whatever we have: our mind, courage, strength, and beauty; our eyes, ears, mouth, tongue, hands, feet, senses, and members; our authority, riches, and income. Indeed, all that we have to serve him is being prepared for service at every hour, day, month, and year, at short notice or not (Rev. 9:15). Thus, when the Word of the Lord, which is like a pillar of fire or a pillar of cloud (Num. 9:17), commands, "Go," we go; or "Come!" we come; or "Stand still," we stand still.

We do this not just when it is convenient or when it suits us to do God's work; we do it even when we see no good reasons for doing it, when it is very inconvenient for our flesh, when it is unreasonable to our natural mind, and even when we see many reasons to do just the opposite. We still do it even when it seems painful, harmful, or shameful, simply because God demands it. And so we show that we prefer God's pure Word and will more than our own reasoning and insight, saying like the apostle Peter to his master, "At thy word I will let down the net" (Luke 5:5). Those who act like this will surely exalt God's glory!

3. In using all our gifts for him. We exalt God's glory when we seek, by all we have mentioned, to express the glorious splendor of all those spiritual gifts with which God by his grace has adorned us (1 Peter 2:9). We try to do everything we wish to accomplish, whether spiritually or temporally, with modesty, humility, discipline, and such evidence of spiritual gifts that our eyes shine with the fear of God. Everyone will see how greatly and highly we esteem and

revere the Lord God so that even the world is forced to acknowledge that the Lord God is in our midst (1 Cor. 14:25) and that the Lord, the almighty God, surely works powerfully in our hearts.

When we act like this, we exalt God's glory, and our light so shines before men that they will see our good works and glorify our God, as Christ commanded us to do. So we will be like shining lamps full of heavenly light, in whom the life of Christ is revealed and through whom the glory and excellence of the Christian life is radiated.

This humble conduct and manifestation of spiritual gifts reveal the Lord our God in us, who is otherwise a hidden God (Isa. 45:15). Truly, by this we ensure that the Lord our God, who is otherwise unseen in the world, is seen by all who know us or notice our spiritual walk. Then the world takes note of him and discovers that there is an almighty power that makes us, though very frail and weak, walk in fear of him. Through him we deny ourselves and submit to his holy desire and will, even against our natural will, passions, and inclinations. And so we most glorify and magnify the Lord our God.

The Second Purpose of Our Life: To Promote the Salvation of Our Souls

The salvation of our souls is indeed a true and excellent goal for our lives. We all acknowledge that the soul is the most important part of man and that the image of God is especially found in our soul. If we care for our hands, feet, eyes, and ears in this life to keep them healthy and in good order, then should we not care for our souls, which are a thousand times more valuable than all our physical members? The Lord Jesus Christ, who knows the value of things best, therefore counsels us to be prepared to pluck out our eyes and cut off our feet if that is necessary to save our souls (Matt. 5:29–30). Jesus assures us that the greatest gain in the world cannot be weighed against the slightest harm that we do to our souls (Matt. 16:26). Therefore, the one thing we need to seek above all else in this life is the salvation of our souls. We must make the well-being of our souls our goal and work toward this goal in all we do. That is why we are taught in this life to work out our own salvation with fear and trembling (Phil. 2:12).

We have shown that we increase the prosperity of our souls by living godly lives and by everything that exalts God's glory. However, ordinary people also need to know that the salvation of our souls is advanced especially in three ways:

1. When our faith is strengthened. Our spiritual life grows as we increasingly arouse and strengthen our Christian faith (Jude 20). Clearly, we should be leading the Christian life with the faith by which we work out the salvation of our souls (Heb. 10:39). Without faith, it is impossible to please God (Heb. 11:6), but whoever really believes in Christ the Lord has everlasting life (John 3:16). By this Christian faith, a person is converted and returns to the shepherd and bishop of his soul (1 Peter 2:25), who took it upon himself to make sure that no one who comes to him in true faith will be lost. He has plainly stated that the end of our faith is the salvation of our souls (1 Peter 1:9).

This is how it is. Whoever wants to promote the salvation of his soul should take care of the very root of Christian life, which is true faith, for in the measure that we cherish and encourage our faith to grow and increase it, in that same measure the Christian life is strengthened within us. Our spiritual life grows in the same measure as we are confirmed in the faith to our greatest comfort and joy and assurance. Read about this in Hebrews 11.

2. When our souls are committed to Christ. We increase the blessedness of our souls when, as Peter urges us to do in 1 Peter 4:19, we commit their keeping to the faithful shepherd. Clearly, when we do evil, we depart from the ways of the Lord, which are the ways of salvation, and so leave the protection of the Almighty. We fly from under the wings of the Almighty to abide under the wings of a hellish vulture, the devil, who hovers in the air to ambush our souls (Ps. 91:1). We thus put our souls into a thousand dangers of becoming lost—that is, as far as what we ourselves do is concerned. But if we are active in doing well, we keep ourselves in God's ways, which are the ways of salvation. Then we abide under the wings of the Almighty, who gives us an escort of holy angels to protect us in all our ways (Ps. 91:11). We are then protected in every way from the fiery darts of Satan and against everything that attacks our soul or might harm it.

Anyone who wants to advance the salvation of his soul needs to pay attention to this and act upon it. Each person must have a clear conscience before God and men, avoid what is evil, and do what is good so that he will dwell in security. For it is written in 1 Peter 3:10–13, "For he that will love life, and see good days, let him refrain his tongue from evil, and his lips that they speak no guile: Let him eschew evil, and do good; let him seek peace, and ensue it. For the eyes of the Lord are over the righteous, and his ears are open unto their prayers: but the face of the Lord is against them that do evil. And who is he that will harm you, if ye be followers of that which is good?"

3. When we remain faithful. We greatly advance our spiritual life when we pay attention to whether we are progressively growing and increasing in the grace and knowledge of our Lord and Savior Jesus Christ (2 Peter 3:18). That, in turn, keeps us from failing in stead-fastness (2 Peter 3:17). If we seek to use our talents and gifts, which God has already given us, well and sincerely, we show that we are faithful servants of Christ the Lord. Christ's promise then applies to us, namely, that having been faithful in little, we will have authority over more (Luke 19:17). Clearly, to the degree that we grow in grace and in spiritual gifts, we make our salvation more sure, to our everlasting comfort. And the apostle Peter assures us that the gates of heaven will open wide for us to enter the everlasting kingdom of our Lord and Savior Jesus Christ (2 Peter 1:11).

Consider that the more you grow and increase in spiritual gifts, the more you will be assured of the salvation of your soul. Put these into practice so that you may obtain the true goal of your life.

The Third Purpose of Our Lives: To Promote Our Neighbor's Salvation

To win souls and by this to edify God's church is unquestionably another great purpose of our life. The apostle Paul zealously sought to be attractive to all men in all things so that he might win some for Christ. He twisted himself into all kinds of shapes to do this. He labored tirelessly, not in his own interest but to be a help to many so that they might be saved. Listen to what else he has to say: "For though I be free from all men, yet have I made myself servant unto all, that I might gain the more. And unto the Jews I became as a Jew, that I might gain the Jews; to them that are under the law, as under the law, that I might gain them that are under the law; to them that are without law, as without law, (being not without law to God, but under the law to Christ,) that I might gain them that are without law. To the weak became I as weak, that I might gain the weak: I am made all things to all men, that I might by all means save some" (1 Cor. 9:19–22).

Holy Scripture declares that whoever wins souls is wise (Prov. 11:30). We know very well what the purpose was of the Lord Jesus Christ's coming in the flesh, why he suffered, and why he died a cursed death on the cross. Did he not bear all of his suffering to win souls and to save that which was lost (Isa. 53:11; Matt. 18:11)? Should we then not walk in the footsteps of Christ and follow him and under his leading and through him also seek to win souls whenever we find an opportunity (1 Tim. 4:16)?

Besides knowing how to live a godly life (as described in book 1) and seeking to advance God's glory and our spiritual life so that we may improve the condition of our neighbor's soul (as we described), we should realize that we can serve God's honor and the well-being of our neighbor's soul in the following three ways:

1. When we are not stumbling blocks. We advance the spiritual well-being of our neighbor when we scrupulously and carefully avoid giving the slightest cause of offense or causing occasion for any scandal to those within or outside the church. That was Paul's admonition (1 Cor. 10:32–33). It was his own daily practice (Acts 24:16) and his desire for all believers (Phil. 1:10). Hardly anything hinders the salvation of men more than when those who profess to be Reformed Christians lead an offensive and depraved life. When devout people notice this, it grieves them. It confuses and shakes the weak, and it strengthens every worldly person in how they live, in their carelessness, their indifferent lukewarmness, indeed, in everything that is damnable.

That is why the apostle Paul earnestly and tearfully declares that such people are enemies of the cross of Christ (Phil. 3:18), no matter how much they profess and boast in the name of Christ. It means that even eating certain food, though allowed as a Christian, can become a stumbling block and destroy the soul for whom Christ died (Rom. 14:15). Paul took this so seriously that he said he would rather refrain from eating meat for the rest of his life than offend a brother (1 Cor. 8:13). He would rather keep himself from such a grievous and offensive and contemptuous sin, for a Christian is never free to commit that. Clearly, he knew that those who profess to be true Christians should be as lights set on a hill (Matt. 5:14) and as a lighthouse to aid navigation at sea. Clearly, if Christians point sailors in the wrong direction, they would deceive many and cause many a shipwreck. That is why Christ pronounces terrible judgments on such people and declares that it would be better for those who are stumbling blocks to the weak and unwary in God's church to have a millstone hung about their necks and to be cast into the sea (Luke 17:1–2).

We must guard against these offenses and take the greatest care to approve things that are excellent so that we may be without offense until the day of Jesus Christ (Phil. 1:10). If we are really serious about winning and caring for our neighbor's soul, we should also zealously remove all stumbling blocks from God's people, as God commands us to do (Isa. 57:14) and as much as is in our power. So much is gained by removing these offenses, since it will encourage everyone to be more diligent in following their calling for the well-being of their souls.

2. When we live godly lives. We encourage the salvation of our neighbor's soul, not only when we are careful not to offend him or shock him by doing wrong but also when we offer him a good and godly example in every situation. Then we can say with Paul, "Be ye followers of me, even as I also am of Christ" (1 Cor. 11:1; cf. 2 Tim. 3:10). You see, people who are yet to be won for Christ or are very weak in the faith are much better led by example than by rules. It is much better for us to lead them by good conduct than by other means.

The apostle Paul valued this principle so highly that he relied on the good example of wives to attract husbands to the faith who had no desire for the Word. An unbelieving husband might begin to take notice of his wife's exemplary behavior, then begin to heed the Word, and so come to faith through the wife's exemplary life, which invited favorable attention. Clearly, we have no better method than setting a good example and living a godly life before those who profess true faith but often fail in godliness. Sometimes people become suspicious and begin to hate true doctrine that has been poorly represented. They defiantly reject the faith even without a hearing! We can offer no better remedy against this than the godly walk of those who profess true faith.

Is it not true that ordinary folk who have little knowledge of doctrine do not really pay as much attention to the doctrine itself as to the lives of those who follow that doctrine? They would find it hard to reconcile true doctrine with those who profess it but are good for nothing. Thus, Peter says to true Christians, "Dearly beloved, I beseech you as strangers and pilgrims, abstain from fleshly lusts, which war against the soul; having your conversation honest among the Gentiles: that, whereas they speak against you as evildoers, they may by your good works, which they shall behold, glorify God in the day of visitation" (1 Peter 2:11–12).

3. When we present God's Word. We encourage the salvation of our neighbor's soul not only when we set a good example but also when we discuss God's Word with him so that he can begin to understand his condition. You see, the Word of God is the seed of salvation (Luke 8) and is powerful to save our soul (James 1:22). Therefore, we should take up the Word and apply it if we really intend to edify our neighbor and win him to salvation.

Have you noticed how worldly people attract others to join them in their worldly business and carnal matters? Do they not use mutual discussions and support to do that? Does the apostle not say that evil communication corrupts good manners? Did not the crafty devil deceive Eve by his clever conversation (Genesis 3)? May we not say, on the other hand, that good communication corrects bad manners? So also, the holy conversation of God's people may have drawn many a child of God to true faith and correcting his ways (1 Thess. 5:14).

We must seek to use all our abilities in this work. In practice, that means to consider one another and to provoke one another to love and do good works, as the apostle teaches us (Heb. 10:24), and to build one another up in the "most holy faith" (Jude 20). It also means that we admonish those who are undisciplined, comfort the fainthearted, teach the ignorant, and show people everywhere we go that our tongue is a tree of life. Is not the tongue of a dog a useful member (Luke 16:21)? Should not the tongue of a Christian then even more have this useful quality?

Let us take note and apply this principle: Those who live godly lives and carry on holy conversations may win many a neighbor's soul. Surely this goes together: A person who holds a holy conversation should also live a holy life. Is it not conceivable that a weak hand is more likely to miss a target than a strong one, even though both use the same bow and arrow? In the same way, the quality of the person who does the speaking is an important matter. Edifying words that come from an offensive person's mouth do little good, but edifying words on holy subjects from truly godly people are like the arrows of a mighty man. They are "as goads, and as nails fastened by the masters of assemblies" so that godliness takes strong root in the heart of people (Eccles. 12:11).

In sum, the true purpose of life is followed correctly only when we earnestly apply the above three things and seek to promote them. We will now move on to consider the special characteristics of true Christians who should earnestly be engaged in pursuing the real purpose of life.

The Defining Characteristics of Little Children in Christ

God's children who pursue the true purpose of the Christian life belong in one of three categories. The apostle tells us they are little children, young men, or fathers in spiritual life (1 John 2:12–14). We will now examine these three categories in relation to their true purpose in life and explain their attitude toward it. We will first speak about the condition of little children in Christ.

Little children in Christ have been born again. In accordance with the nature of spiritual rebirth, they have experienced forgiveness of their sins (1 John 2:12). They have also, to some extent, received the gift of knowing the Father—that he is their Father and they may thus address him, saying, "Abba, Father" (Rom. 8:15). Since they have experienced the goodness of the Father, they desire to behave like obedient children of such a good Father and very earnestly seek to pursue their true purpose in life. However, they have little insight into the special nature and demands of the Christian life. They are either very exceedingly comforted by God or intensely sorrowful before him, depending on if they see their most recent conduct toward God as either right or wrong. Their particular spiritual condition generally expresses itself in these three ways.

1. They know little about what's expected of them. Because they have little insight into the mystery of the kingdoms of grace and of darkness and sometimes fail to distinguish between them, these little children fail to understand God's special ways with his children. They do not understand what he normally expects from them. They do not know what the duties of the godly life are or what is required of them in order to walk righteously in everything. They do not know how to serve the Lord God to please him. They are not yet aware of how much it will profit them by constantly following the Lord, nor do they realize what it may cost them. They do not know which lusts and desires they need to deny, which habits to forsake, which difficulties to endure, and which obligations and activities to undertake and maintain. They have so little knowledge and insight into these things that they really do not know how to perform godly duties.

More particularly, they are not aware of how to practice and carry out religious duties. They lack understanding of the depths of Satan and his methods and schemes to deceive, ensnare, and tempt the simple. In short, because they are still little children, they have not had enough experience in discerning both good and evil (Heb. 5:14) to make progress in true godliness.

2. They are hungry and thirsty to know more. These little children in Christ have very good intentions. They sincerely want to walk uprightly in everything and be pleasing to God. There is no deceit, fraud, or pretense found in them, even though they are ignorant and unsophisticated in the things of their heavenly Father. They mean to do well. We know that little children who are beginning to know their parents are usually well inclined toward them because they expect many good things from them. So also are these little children disposed toward their loving, heavenly Father. Although they often stumble in many things, just like little children who are learning to walk but often fall, they nevertheless want to continue trying to walk well in every respect. They are eager to

be instructed in the ways of the Lord so that, having come to know and understand them, they will also walk in them. They desire to learn and understand these ways. Just like newborn babes, they eagerly seek the sincere milk of God's Word so that they may grow (1 Peter 2:2). That is how the apostle Peter describes them. These little children in Christ want to learn more and more in order to live better and better. And so they hang on to every word of the godly; they are constantly in church, in catechism, at Bible study, or in discussion of the pastor's sermons after the church service.

They ask many questions because everything is so new to them. They thirstily drink in the words of those who instruct them. They listen intently to those who teach them well. They do this because they sincerely want to pursue the true purpose of life. They want to keep this goal continuously before their eyes because it concerns them the most. They want to direct everything toward that purpose.

3. They are easily discouraged. Little children in Christ can quickly shift from joy to sorrow. When they notice that they have been enabled to manage their affairs fairly well and to walk righteously in the ways of the Lord, they become wonderfully encouraged. They find precious joy in the Spirit and have great confidence in God. They are like little children who joyfully and exuberantly look at their parents when they think they have behaved well. Conversely, they are extremely disturbed when they have behaved badly or realize that they have fallen far short in some spiritual gifts that other children of God possess. When that happens, these children in the faith may even doubt whether they really are God's children and whether God is their merciful Father. This especially happens when the Lord God hides his loving face from them. When that happens, these children often fall into despair. They call out in great distress as if they were completely forsaken by God and were lost for all eternity.

As we know, little ones can lose all courage when they realize that they have done something wrong. They may also despair when they are unable to get from their parents what their own sisters and brothers or other children get from their parents. They become despondent, particularly when their parents seem to be somewhat strict and a little brusque with them. So little children in Christ are also easily disturbed in their hearts. They begin to ask whether they are truly God's children. When they notice that they have fallen short in something and do not feel the grace of God flowing through their hearts as before, they say with Zion, "The LORD hath forsaken me, and my LORD hath forgotten me" (Isa. 49:14).

The Defining Characteristics of Young Men in Christ

Young men in Christ are those who, through their study and profitable times spent in the Word of God, understand reasonably well the situation regarding the kingdoms of grace and of darkness and the ways in which God leads his children. They understand what is required of them and how to perform their duties. They also know more about Satan's intentions toward the godly.

They have greater insight into these things than little children in Christ do, but they also have stronger and more stubborn lusts within them than these little ones. To combat this, they have more power to overcome the devil. They are strong, and the Word of God abides in them, says the apostle (1 John 2:14). The following three things in particular characterize the spiritual condition of young men in Christ.

1. They are more knowledgeable about what's expected of them. Young men in Christ are more mature than little children when it comes to being able to distinguish between good and evil (Heb. 5:14). They are more attentive, not only to what the Lord demands of them but also to what they fall short in and how the devil lies in wait for them. These are things that little children in Christ hardly seem to notice. They often assume that they have done their duty well when it is really only superficially done. They feel great satisfaction in having done their task even when that work was childish. When young men with their greater insight see what they lack and how great the power of darkness is that sets itself against them and seeks to hide the true purpose of life from them, they grow increasingly concerned. With their years these young men grow in discernment and increasingly notice these concerns.

2. They struggle harder against ungodliness. Young men in Christ have more inner conflicts when they practice godliness than little children or fathers in Christ tend to have. That is why the apostle calls them overcomers who take off their gloves and use their bare hands to fight the devil (1 John 2:13). That is not the case with younger children, who are not so aware of what is lacking in them. They have so recently gone through the anxieties of conversion that their fleshly lusts are temporarily somewhat deadened and numbed. They will soon regain life, however, and become like the young men who have had time to grow and now encounter more difficulties and conflicts.

Young men see that many things are wrong that they did not recognize as wrong before. Compared to when they were babes in Christ, they have much better knowledge. They thus experience more trouble and conflict than little children. Fathers in Christ are less troubled than young men because they have subdued their lusts more and have better learned to control their feelings to practice their holy duties as best they can. We will explain this more as we go on.

3. They have great courage. Young men in Christ are bolder and have more courage than little children or even the fathers in their struggles. They have the youthful confidence that the kingdom of grace will help them in all circumstances and in all their struggles against the efforts of the kingdom of darkness. The apostle says these young men are "strong" (1 John 2:14), compared to how weak they were before as children in grace. Because these young men do not easily give up or become discouraged, as little children in Christ do, they generally do not lose the assurance of their salvation in their spiritual battle. They are not often surprised and deceived by Satan either, as little children are, although they may still feel defeated at times. John declares that they thus have overcome the wicked one (1 John 2:14). These young men pursue the true purpose of life, although this does not happen without great conflict and difficulty and sometimes means that they will be severely wounded or maimed.

The Defining Characteristics of Fathers in Christ

Fathers in Christ are well informed about the characteristics of the kingdom of grace and the realm of darkness. They are not ignorant, as little children, and have even better understanding than young men about their sinful lusts and their godly duties. Generally, they do not have as much conflict, difficulty, or trouble with their lusts as others do in their efforts to live a godly life. They are more steadfast and faithful in all holy duties, although they have not yet reached perfection and are deficient at times in some aspects. Their specific condition reveals itself predominantly in these three things:

1. They have a mature understanding of the ways of godliness. Fathers in Christ have thoroughly learned to exercise their senses to discern between good and evil (Heb. 5:14). One result of this is that they have greatly increased in grace and in the knowledge of our Savior, Jesus Christ (2 Peter 3:17). The apostle John acknowledges this when he says that they have known him who was from the beginning (1 John 2:13). These fathers in Christ have entered into the deep mysteries of the kingdom and understand the works of God. They see not only the end of his works, as in conversion and salvation, which are elementary principles (Heb. 6:1–2), but also the principles in which God began them, such as his eternal love and election, which he exercised on our behalf from the beginning, even from before the foundation of the world (Rom. 8:28–30; Eph. 1:4). They also understand and observe how God deals with them and has dealt with his children since the beginning of creation. They have gained much spiritual experience from this. It has helped them greatly increase in steadfastness in their daily practice of godly living (1 John 2:14).

2. They are more equipped to practice godliness. Fathers in Christ practice godliness more successfully, experience fewer conflicts and difficulties, and succeed more in the Christian life than little ones or young men in Christ. Because of their long experience, they have become wise and careful. They are therefore better able to guard against and avoid those attacks and temptations that often fiercely attack the hearts of the young men or little children in Christ. They have progressed so much that they now exercise great control over themselves and their own hearts (1 Cor. 6:12). They have learned to mortify and subdue their passions and lusts. By long experience and diligent practice of the Christian life, they have obtained the

grace that enables them to practice godliness in a more orderly, better guided, and more faithful and steadfast way. Fathers in Christ do not have as much trouble and difficulty as young men do in controlling their desires and in carrying out Christian duties to their own assurance. Unlike young men, fathers in Christ have made the control of their lusts and the practice of the Christian life easier for themselves, thanks to the experience of controlling their desires and their lengthy practice of godliness (1 Cor. 9:25–27; Phil. 3:12f.).

3. They press on toward perfection. Although fathers in Christ have come a long way, they have not yet reached perfection. Even the godly lives of the fathers in this present world are not so perfect that we can say they have completely attained the status of a perfect man, measuring up to "the stature of the fulness of Christ" (Eph. 4:13). That perfection will be achieved only in the world to come. In comparison with little children and young men in Christ, who are far short of this assured and secure state, the fathers are called and esteemed as "perfect" (Phil. 3:15). However, we may be sure that even the godly life of the most excellent father in God's church is still imperfect and deficient with regard to God's demands, as revealed in his Word and when compared to what God's children will be in heavenly glory (Phil. 3:13). Indeed, we cannot deny that in some cases, the best of the most excellent fathers among God's people seem to be as weak as the frailest babes in Christ. They are attacked just as fiercely by their lusts as young men are, and sometimes these overwhelm them completely. Sometimes they are even sorely wounded by moral disasters, which is what happened to David (2 Samuel 11; Psalm 51), who was a father in Israel (Zech. 12:8).

The Lord God lets such things happen not only to humble every Christian but also to encourage many a weak and feeble child. Some believers would find it difficult to think that they were true children of God if such excellent men of God, who are presented to us as examples of godliness, no longer struggled with such faults.

We cannot deny that even the best and most godly life of the most experienced Christian in the world lacks something. Nevertheless, it is also certain that all who are true believers, even though they are little children in Christ, do not conduct themselves so badly in their Christian life that there is no longer a great difference between them and worldly people who do not have this Christian life within them. We can easily deduce this from our discussion in book 1, particularly where we dealt with the practice of godliness and especially with those failings of the godly wherein they become completely like worldly people.

We have already said much about the true purpose of life and the special state of true Christians who pursue that purpose. We need to move on now to show you briefly which devices the kingdom of darkness uses to lead many Christians astray so that they might fail to achieve the true purpose of their lives.

The Scheme of the Kingdom of Darkness to Lead All Believers Away from the True Purpose of Life

We need to know next that our spiritual enemies seek to distract us from the true purpose of life whenever possible, indeed, even from the time of our earliest development, and even more when we reach the years when we start to use our minds. They know very well that when we travel out of town and turn onto the wrong road, that the farther we go and the faster we walk, the farther we will get from our intended destination. That is why our spiritual enemies try so hard to hide the true purpose of our life from our eyes and why they seek to keep us busy with other things. They do that so we will be without a specific purpose in life at all, or will be without the true purpose, or else will fail to understand thoroughly the true purpose of life. We will look briefly at these three crafty attacks in order to uncover them and to warn people against them.

1. To live without ever knowing the true purpose of life. Our spiritual enemy persuades many people to live in total wantonness, just as they please, without ever knowing the purpose of life. We find such people in droves among nominal Christians. They give no thought to why they are in this world or to any goal in life except to live as they please and do whatever they want. Such people are a long way from salvation. They will never be saved if they do not repent. How sad that such people give no thought at all to the purpose of life. Such people never come to themselves and ask, "What have I done? Will this lead me to blessedness, to salvation? Am I

doing what I was placed in this world to do and for which God gave me a living soul?" (cf. Jer. 8:6; Luke 15:17). No, these people never think like that but go on walking thoughtlessly or rushing on like an impetuous horse rushing into the battle, despite the prophet's reproach (Jer. 8:6). It will be a fearful day for them when they have to give an account before God!

2. To pursue the wrong purpose in life. Satan holds a wrong goal before some people's eyes and minds, and they will not be moved from it. For example, they want to build their own house, increase in wealth, leave their children a rich inheritance, and, if they live long enough, marry off their children well. Truly, this is the greatest goal that most good and respectable citizens pursue in this world. They focus all their energies on this goal and are so busy pursuing it that it becomes their most important occupation. The work of the Lord is nothing to them but a daily drag; they perform it only when it suits them and when it does not interfere with their own agenda, which is what really matters to them. When these people have to give an account before God's judgment, they will tremble in fear because of their choices in life.

Truly, when the Lord comes to judge, he will not ask people how much money and how many belongings and properties they have accumulated, how many jobs and appointments they managed to get, or whether they managed to enrich themselves or their children by marrying into the right families. Those are things that people often imperil their souls to obtain, but such things will not count at all before the judgment seat. Clearly, these things will not even come into consideration then.

It will surely be a poor defense for a man to say, "Lord, I have lived thirty or forty years in the world. I entered this world naked, my parents did not leave me much, yet I managed to accumulate hundreds of thousands of dollars, and so I have left my children a good inheritance." None of this will count for anything. In the last judgment and in the last day, the focus will be on whether a man has radiated the glory of God during his life and taken care of his own and his neighbor's soul and did them some good. People who have neglected this, even if they made a lot of money, show that they have missed the true purpose of life. Since what occupied their hearts fell far short of knowing God's grace and the power of his salvation, they will be ashamed on the day of judgment, unless they repent in time.

3. To halfheartedly pursue the right purpose. Although these people seem to make the glory of God their priority in life, they fail to do it with the firm conviction and commitment that they should. As long as they can accomplish this purpose with ease and as long as circumstances are favorable for their flesh, they are fine. But they back out whenever putting God first conflicts with their own profit or popularity or something else they cherish. They will hardly succeed in the practice of godliness. They too will tremble in fear when they have to give an account before the judgment of God.

Truly, these people have an ungodly goal in life because they have a purpose in this life that fails to look sincerely to God and does not end in God. Their purpose is solely their own gain, reputation, enjoyment, or passions and ends in man alone. Surely, they will have only a poor account to give to the Lord our God on the day of judgment. Remember that the nature of the Lord our God is such that he does not glorify anything other than his own majesty. He hates everything that deviates from this and regards it as an abomination to him. The Lord our God is worthy of all things focusing on and ending in him. All creatures gifted with mind and will must sincerely perform all their works for his great majesty. These must end in him. "For of him, and through him, and to him, are all things: to whom be glory for ever. Amen" (Rom. 11:36).

Whosoever sincerely seeks to serve God and seeks to guard himself against the kingdom of darkness and the schemes of Satan with the help of the kingdom of grace should keep the true purpose of life before his eyes. He must establish this goal with a firm decision and commitment so that nothing in the world will deter him. He must do so with such determination that he would rather die than dishonor his God and hinder his own soul's salvation or that of his neighbor. Every Christian should be persuaded to do this when he sincerely considers what an affront it is to the Lord when professing Christians miss their true purpose in life or pursue the wrong goal.

Think how terrible and monstrous it would be if the sun, created to give light to the world, were to spread thick darkness instead. What terror this would cause! How horrible it would be for us! Or if fire, created to give heat, were to discharge fierce frigid cold. Would that not astound us? Consider further what it means when a Christian, created and regenerated to let his spiritual light shine and so glorify God, misses the purpose of his life and, in place of letting his light shine by his godly walk in the midst of a crooked and sinful generation, exudes the foul fumes of an offensive life and conduct. He would dishonor the Lord his God and at the same time impede the salvation of his own soul and that of his neighbor. Consider this sincerely and shrink back from ever becoming known as such a hideous earthly monster. Always keep the true purpose of life before your eyes, and strive after it with all your might so that it will always and eternally be well with you.

BOOK
5

The Means to Attain
the True Purpose of Life

The Necessity of Using God-Given Means

It is natural that as soon as man has chosen a particular goal, he considers the means that will enable him to attain that goal. We see this even in toddlers who are just starting to walk. They are very resourceful when they want something that is just outside their reach and will climb on a small chair or stool to reach the desired object. Even a thirsty bird knows that by filling a bucket with little stones it can make the water level rise until the water, previously out of range, can be reached. The bird then can quench its thirst.

People who are forever talking about wanting something but never use the means available to obtain it clearly show that they do not really desire it with all their heart. They are like the man who tells us how he longs to visit The Hague but makes no effort to go there, although he is in good health and has the opportunity and the means to travel there. We would conclude from this that he was never really in earnest about going there. This is also true of people who seek to convince us of their fervent desire to spread the glory of God and of their aspirations to attain the true purpose of life. How many do this but all the while neglect to take advantage of the means that would enable them to spread God's glory? Doesn't this clearly show that they are not at all sincere in the first place?

Anyone who earnestly desires to spread God's glory and to seek to advance his and his neighbor's spiritual welfare must rightfully use all the means God has provided to promote those great ends. How important it is that we give heed to these matters! How can we, frail creatures, advance God's glory as well as our spiritual prosperity and that of our neighbor as we ought if we do not find encouragement in the help and the counsel of God? What do God's counsel and help mean to us? How can we ever succeed if we neglect and ignore the means God has prescribed in his Word to enable us to glorify him and further our own spiritual welfare and that of our neighbor? It may help us to look at these matters in more detail and consider the following three things:

- the nature of the means we can use to reach our desired purpose in life
- the types of Christians who should make use of these means
- the devices that the kingdom of darkness uses to confuse Christians when they apply these means of godliness.

We will consider each one, looking first at the nature of these means of grace.

The Means for Advancing the True Purpose of Life

By God's providence, we have many means that will help us to advance the glory of God, our own spiritual welfare, and that of our neighbor. God has provided us with these means in the manner we described above. All the Lord's counsel and all his commandments to us as well as everything in the kingdom of grace, of which we have already spoken at length, are appropriate means for us. Among the means of the kingdom of grace, what is most essential and indispensable for us to attain true godliness and blessedness is, first of all, a renewed heart.

We must pay close attention to this, for whatever we do for God will not please him unless we do it with all our heart (Col. 3:23). The heart is the specific instrument we must use to glorify God and to exercise true godliness. We should always keep it ready and prepared, as it has been renewed and regenerated by God's grace in our rebirth. We have already spoken of this extensively when we considered the kingdom of grace. However, we need to look at this matter more closely and consider three means in particular that strengthen us to glorify God and to exercise true godliness. These three means are God's holy institutes and ordinances, God's works, and God's promises. We will now move on to discuss each one.

God's Holy Ordinances

God's holy ordinances and institutes include those general means, such as the practices, duties, and activities that the Lord God has revealed in his Word, that will help us glorify his name, edify our neighbor, comfort our souls, and stir up true godliness. These include public or private exercises, whether civic efforts or acts of charity. There are so many general means that they can be divided into categories. Some are simply spiritual exercises, some the daily duties of our calling, and some works of love, charity, and friendship. We will discuss each one.

1. Spiritual activities. These include diligently and eagerly listening to God's Word, reading it, discussing it, and using it to teach, comfort, and admonish others. We should also reflect and meditate on the Word.

We should watch and pray as well. We should be much in prayer, in praising, and in thanking God. We should be joyfully singing the Lord's praise. We should be rightly observing his holy day of rest. And we should be good soldiers of Jesus Christ, standing watch, fighting devoutly, putting on the Christian armor, and using it correctly. We should remember to increasingly stir up this gift within us to stimulate the power of the kingdom of grace. We should not forget our holy baptism and the Lord's Supper but keep observing these sacraments. We must also humble ourselves by means of fasting and praying and, if necessary, bind ourselves to God's service by vows.

2. The daily duties of our calling. This is what we are expected to do daily in our work, whatever our calling is, whether we are involved in the affairs of our country or at home, whether we are businessmen, tradesmen, shopkeepers, lawyers, soldiers, fishermen, sailors, farmers, shepherds, or workers in any other lawful occupation.

When people work hard at their jobs and do what is expected of them with skill and diligence, it is a significant help toward attaining the true purpose of life and stirring up godliness. That is why the Lord required work from man before as well as after the fall (Gen. 2:15; 3:19). The apostle Paul therefore exhorts every Christian to walk as he is called (1 Cor. 7:17).

We know that the Lord is pleased when the children of men are honest and diligent in their work. He has shown this by giving his children special grace when they performed well, not only when they were engaged in spiritual exercises, as in Acts 4:31, but also when they were engaged in a secular profession (Luke 2:8; 5:2; John 21:3). For example, we know that Peter and Andrew were called when they were casting their nets into the sea, while James and John were called while they were mending their nets by the seaside (Matt. 4:18, 21).

Note this well, for it was in his great wisdom and grace that God commanded the children of men to work in their daily employment for six days of the week. Clearly, this is no obstacle to the practice of true godliness; rather, it is just as profitable as all other holy ordinances of God. It is certainly only a human idea, then, for someone to hide in a monastery or convent and separate from the world in order to live a godly life. The Lord Jesus Christ prayed for his own, not that they would be taken out of the world but that they should be kept in this world from the evil one (John 17:15). Rendering pure and undefiled service to God does not mean cutting ourselves off from all worldly things but making use of them and walking uprightly so that we may keep ourselves unspotted from the world (James 1:27).

3. Works of charity. These include showing compassion, mercy, and friendship to others as well as ourselves. Giving money, visit-

ing the sick, speaking kindly to our friends or inviting them to our homes, and also taking time for ourselves to rest and relax after work are very beneficial in promoting godliness if they are done well— that is to say, when we keep our true purpose before our eyes and pursue everything with a sanctified and affectionate heart to the glory of God. As the apostle Paul says, "Whether therefore ye eat, or drink, or whatsoever ye do, do all to the glory of God" (1 Cor. 10:31). When we seek to serve God in this way, we will be successful in all our affairs, for there is absolutely nothing in the world that we can be honestly engaged in that will not contribute to our desired purpose and stir up godliness in us.

The Lord our God, whom we serve, is so wonderful that we may serve him in all permissible ways if our hearts are attentive and ready to serve him. Clearly, the Lord does not ask for our service because he needs it, for he can make and bring into being all things, including whatever he desires from us or others. The Lord God desires our service because he requires our obedience to be tested. We can show our obedience in the smallest things and, indeed, mostly in these. When we do even small things with a sincere heart, we are encouraged to live more godly. The loving-kindness of God is so great that to those who are faithful in little he will give charge over much. Those who by faith cheerfully observe God's ordinances and statutes in the holy liberty that he has mercifully given and conduct themselves properly in eating, drinking, sleeping, and all other daily affairs will then experience God's blessing in those things. And so we are helped and encouraged in the love and fear of God and in spiritual gifts.

Observe that the Lord ordains all his commands to us and all that he permits serves as suitable helps to us. These negative and positive commands come from a wise God by his Word in order to help us realize our purpose and to quicken true godliness in us.

In all his means, the Lord, the almighty and wise God, provides marvelous assistance to benefit his children and to quicken godliness in them. Therefore, we should try to make use of his means, each according to its own nature and character, for they offer us the greatest possible expectation that they will be truly profitable. Indeed, we should recognize that they are the means ordained by the almighty God himself to destroy the kingdom of darkness and to establish the kingdom of grace in order to spread his glory, build up his church, and increase our godliness.

Is there any greater and more important purpose than this one? Should we not then most diligently use these means and expect them to be greatly beneficial to us? Truly, we should apply these means with all our strength and ability and expect great benefit from them in every way. We should expect great encouragement, strength, comfort, and assurance because God has given them to us in his great grace and for his purposes. This golden rule should not be despised. Yet many do so by ignoring it, especially ignoring the use of the means of grace such as reading and hearing God's Word or praying. They work hard but ineffectively and accomplish nothing because they do not do these things from the heart and they expect little benefit from them. All those who long to obtain God's blessings through these means should adopt the habit of using them in all sincerity and with the greatest possible expectation of great blessing (Eccles. 9:10).

God's Works

In particular, God's holy and glorious works are the activities of his daily rule and reign over the children of men. Thus, the psalmist cries out, "O LORD, how great are thy works! and thy thoughts are very deep. A brutish man knoweth not; neither doth a fool understand this" (Ps. 92:5–6). Here we should define and understand God's works as God's activity and guidance in our lives. We should note in particular how he blesses us, how he chastises us, and what activities his actions prompt in our hearts. We will briefly review each one.

1. How he blesses us. Consider the many good things the Lord our God gives us in our lives. He grants us many healthy days, a good income, honor and respect with our fellow men. Truly, he loads us with his benefits (Ps. 68:19).

These gracious benefits of God contain a hidden spiritual blessing. They promote true godliness and salvation, as long as we pay careful attention to and properly understand their purpose, for these benefits incline our hearts to love God more and more, and rightly so, and also prompt us to obey him more diligently, especially when we discover that the Lord our good God continues to speak kindly to us.

If we fall short in our service to him and forget to serve him wholeheartedly, he does not forget to care for us with lavish tenderness. Listen to what the psalmist has to say: "And he brought forth his people with joy, and his chosen with gladness: and gave them the lands of the heathen: and they inherited the labour of the people; that they might observe his statutes, and keep his laws. Praise ye the Lord" (Ps. 105:43–45).

Should not a grateful child seek to obey God more diligently because of his grace and loving-kindness?

Although Satan, the evil abuser of power, may seek to use prosperity to turn the careless children of men increasingly away from God, whose blessings they themselves confess, so that they will love the world with all its license, debauchery, vanity, and attractions, the blessings of the Lord God to his children are really meant to encourage them to do good (Rom. 12:1).

2. How he chastises us. From time to time, the Lord tries his people, or more specifically, each godly person, with many afflictions. He uses evil men to perplex them or sends upon them serious illness, harm, or loss, or whatever other adversity he may choose. Nevertheless, a blessing is still included in all of this adversity, for adversity is given to increase true godliness and bless us, but only if we are wise enough to discover it. The Lord our God, who tests us, is so wonderfully glorious and loving that even his lashes are therapeutic and serve us for good. That is why, as Moses testifies, the Lord God humbled the people of Israel to do them good in the end (Deut. 8:16).

The godly have often experienced this. When they have rightly regarded God's trials, they have increasingly died to the world. They were humbled because of their sins and relied on the comfort of the Holy Spirit. By their trials they were refined as gold through fire. Thus, the Word of the Lord tells us that the godly often confessed that it was good for them to have been afflicted by the Lord (Ps. 119:67, 71). Our spiritual enemy tries to use the great afflictions that the godly sometimes undergo to frighten us away from serving God and stir us up to murmur and wrongly respond, but God wants his children to benefit from their afflictions so that they might increasingly partake of his holiness (Book of Job; Heb. 12:9).

3. What activities his actions prompt in our hearts. This work is highly necessary to help people live godly lives, but only if we are wise and understanding enough to note this thoughtfully, for through these good and holy activities, which the Lord God awakens in our hearts, he knocks, as it were, at our hearts so that we will invite him to enter in and bless us (Rev. 3:20). The Lord may permit other more troublesome and disturbing activities or thoughts to rise up in our hearts, or the devil may awaken or stir them in us. The Lord permits those to serve us by humbling us and showing us how weak and insignificant we really are so that we might look up ever more to the Lord our God and seek shelter under the wings of the Almighty. We will then be governed and guided by him (2 Cor. 12:7–9).

In ancient times, the Lord God often used dreams to instruct his people and to teach them how to know themselves better. We know that he still does this daily through those inner activities and promptings that he generates in our hearts. As Elihu testifies, God often uses such means to dissuade men from their purpose and check their pride in various circumstances (Job 33:15–17).

Godly people should note this well. Although our spiritual enemy may try to use various shameful thoughts that rise up in our hearts to unsettle, frighten, and discourage us, we should remember that the Lord God has a mightier hand in all of this. We should therefore seek to discover some benefit from such trial. We will then advance in godliness in every way, thanks to all that the Lord does in us or permits to be done in us.

Observe that these are very important actions that God works in us. We should pay careful attention to them and their character so we will advance in godliness. Godly souls should consider with a wise and teachable heart whatever the Lord sends them or allows to happen to them, whether prosperity or adversity. How many healthy days has he granted us? How many illnesses, pains, losses of goods or friends? What other afflictions has he permitted, and how did he deliver us from them? From what great tragedies has he spared us and why (Psalm 107)?

We should also take note of the good activities and holy prompt-ings that our good God sometimes produces in our hearts. What troublesome and melancholy thoughts does he allow to enter our hearts, and how do we react to those and use them for our benefit? You see, if we use all this with a wise and teachable heart to awaken our hearts more, to fear and love God more, and to rely and trust in him more, then it, too, becomes a precious means to attain the real purpose of life and to practice true godliness. If we are wise and understanding enough to see what wonderful assistance and aid we have in all of God's glorious and excellent operations, then we will find wonderful help and support for his holy service. We must be wise to see and keen to obtain whatever God has included.

But what so often happens? Our spiritual enemy tries to hide this from our eyes. He goes to such great lengths to conceal this that we find masses of people who take no notice of God's activi-ties and do not make the least effort to stir themselves up to under-stand the purpose of God in such situations. Thus, they miss the blessings God would like them to have.

The Lord God expects them to note his operations. Although they know when they prosper and when they do not and rejoice or complain accordingly—just like the animals in the field do—they fail to take notice of God's finger in those circumstances. They do not lift their hearts above their circumstances but notice only their situations. What a foolish attitude! They should know better.

We expect that as our own children get to know us better they will become increasingly more thankful for all the good things we give them. And we expect that as they begin to understand this they will show a different kind of gratitude for all those good things than we get from cats and dogs on the street. If we are God's children, we should pay attention to the works of his hands. Oh, how it hurts parents when a child, who they have brought up with great care and should use his head better, ignores them and acts callously and fool-ishly toward them! Well, that is the way we act toward God when we fail to take notice of his concern for us. Scripture calls such peo-ple fools, and rightly so (Ps. 92:6). Should the almighty God of heaven and earth constantly concern himself with blessing and chas-tising us when we do not keep our eyes on him? Should he deal with us to shape our hearts in a particular way, to harden it or soften it (Isa. 64:7), while we ignore him? What foolishness!

Those who want to walk in a godly way should develop the habit of diligently contemplating God's works, especially those he openly reveals to them. They should make sure not to miss the purpose of the Lord toward them but be very attentive to God's work so that they can receive the particular blessing God has intended for them and offers them in these actions. They will learn to fear and love and trust him more. This will also greatly stimulate true godliness in them (Psalm 107). You will find this explained in more detail in my book *The Balance of the Sanctuary*.

God's Promises

We understand God's promises to be the merciful and gracious commitments God makes to us in his Word. He promises he will strengthen all who commit themselves with all their hearts to him in godly living, giving them everything they need for life and godliness (2 Peter 1:3). The apostle Peter calls these promises "exceeding great and precious promises: that by these ye might be partakers of the divine nature, having escaped the corruption that is in the world through lust" (v. 4).

God's children particularly need the following things to live a good and godly life: knowledge of the godly things they observe, obedience in accordance with this knowledge, and encouragement in obedience. The Lord Jesus Christ puts these together when he says to his apostles, "If ye know these things, happy are ye if ye do them" (John 13:17). We find exceeding great and precious promises in God's Word concerning these things. We will briefly consider each one.

1. Knowledge of godly things. The Lord God has promised his children that he will put his laws into their minds and write them in their hearts (Heb. 8:10). The Lord has also promised that he will teach them useful knowledge to profit and lead them in the way they should go (Isa. 48:17). The Lord has assigned his Holy Spirit to his children with the promise that he will teach them everything (John 14:26; 1 John 2:20, 27). These exceeding great and precious promises are a part of the imperishable seed of God's Word. Whoever receives these promises into his heart by faith will, through their power, grow in the full knowledge of God.

2. Obedience in accordance with this knowledge. It is our duty to zealously render obedience to God because we know the truth. The Lord God has promised to give his Spirit to us and to make godly people of those who walk in his commandments, observe his laws, and act according to them (2 Chron. 16:9; Isa. 40:29–31; Ezek. 36:27; Hosea 14:5–7; Joel 3:16). These texts do not speak of God wanting us to have a mere intellectual knowledge but a convincing and powerful knowledge that will capture all our thoughts in obedience to Christ. Christ suggests the same thing when he says that the Holy Spirit will teach us all things (John 14:26) and guide us, actually causing us to walk in all truth (John 16:13).

So you see that these exceeding great and precious promises are the godly seed of true obedience. Whoever truly receives these promises by faith, deep in his heart, and looks to God, learning to wait for their fulfillment, will obtain encouragement and a godly strengthening to show henceforth true obedience in being faithful to God's commandments.

These promises are linked to all God's commandments in the new covenant. If we enrich our faith with them, we will receive power to do over and above what we pray or imagine. Truly, these promises will increasingly strengthen our faith. After all, God's Word commands us to believe, and faith is also one of God's commandments—indeed, a most special commandment that we must keep and observe in all our ways (1 John 3:23).

3. Encouragement in obedience. The comfort of the Holy Spirit in obedience is very essential to godly living, for if we lose courage and think that nothing we do delights or pleases God, then the ongoing work of salvation in our hearts is greatly slowed (Isa. 64:7). But when it pleases the Lord our good God to comfort us through the Holy Spirit, then we are able to walk in the way of his commandments (Ps. 119:32–35). The apostle Paul links God's comfort of the heart with the Holy Spirit strengthening us in all our good words and work (2 Thess. 2:17).

The Lord our God has given us, his children, beautiful and precious promises, of which the most important are those that strengthen us against the deficiencies of our obedience. Even our most perfect obedience is still imperfect (2 Cor. 10:6; 1 Thess. 3:10). However, God has promised his children that he will not break a bruised reed or quench a smoking flax (Isa. 42:3; Matt. 12:20), meaning that even if our obedience and faith are as weak as a bruised reed and as close to vanishing as flax that burns with a weak or smoldering flame, he will make sure that they will not go out or be completely quenched. He promises that he will have mercy on those who fear him, even as a loving father cares for his children (Ps. 103:13). Indeed, he will gather his weak lambs in his arms, carry them in his bosom, and gently lead those who are with young (Isa. 40:11). Moreover, God will be pleased with our honest attempts to obey him. He will be pleased with our hunger and thirst after righteousness (Matt. 5:6) and will forgive us our sins, iniquities, and transgressions (Exod. 34:7) when we are tired and weary and burdened with our sins. We will experience the sufficiency of his grace in times of our greatest need (2 Cor. 12:9) because of the perfect obedience of the Lord Jesus Christ (Rom. 5:19).

Our Lord therefore invites us to come unto him. He calls to us, saying, "Come unto me, all ye that labour and are heavy laden, and I will give you rest. Take my yoke upon you, and learn of me; for I am meek and lowly in heart: and ye shall find rest unto your souls" (Matt. 11:28–29). These and other exceedingly great and precious promises are seeds of true comfort to those who have a clean heart (Ps. 73:1). When these promises are thoroughly mixed with faith, they produce such comfort and strength in the hearts of God's children that we really cannot describe it.

There are thousands of such promises in the Word of the Lord. Let us mix these with faith to live a godly life and so attain and fulfill our true purpose in life. On the basis of these promises, we can be certain that the Lord, our mighty and powerful God, will extend a helping hand to us, giving us grace and enabling us to do over and above what we pray or imagine (Eph. 3:20; Phil. 4:13).

This is highly necessary if we are to live truly godly lives. You see, this is the situation: By nature we are so unfruitful in good works and so dead in ourselves that we lack any ability to bring forth something good. We are like the holy woman, Sarah, Abraham's wife, who was unable to conceive seed because she was barren by nature. Her womb was also dead because of her old age (Rom. 4:19). After Sarah received the promise that she would deliver a son in her old age, she mixed this promise with faith and received strength to conceive seed "because she judged him faithful who had promised"

(Heb. 11:11). We poor, depraved, and barren people are in the same situation. In ourselves we are not able to produce even one good thought, but we become able to do so because God has promised power and ability to live a godly life and good works to all who are joined to him with their whole heart. Only those who, like Sarah, mix these promises with faith will receive the power to bring forth good works for the glory of God and to live truly godly lives.

This is a great mystery of the kingdom of grace, of which worldly people are completely ignorant. That is why, when they occasionally have the desire to lead a godly life, they begin in their own strength, without faith and without earnestly looking at the promised help of the Lord our God, who is our strength (Joel 3:16). Because their own strength is useless to bring forth the power of true godliness, they soon tire of it and stop altogether. Or they only attain a form of godliness that satisfies them. This happens because they do not think it necessary to receive God's help by faith to live a godly life. The crafty ways of our spiritual enemy keep their need for this hidden from them.

Indeed, this matter is such an extraordinary mystery of the kingdom of grace that many children of the kingdom and true believers would have been translated much sooner into the kingdom of grace, humanly speaking, if they had taken this matter more seriously and had strengthened themselves with the promises of God's help. Then the Lord could have given them the ability to do many things that they otherwise would have regarded as unattainable. Through such neglect, they have suffered immense loss in their practice of godliness. They have been troubled a long time by all kinds of failures that they could have overcome long before by these God-given means.

Those who are so ready to say that they serve the Lord God to their utmost ability should pay particular attention to this. Clearly, their ability is not sufficient. Rather, we must serve God according to the ability of the Most High, who promises to help us so that we can do his work as we need to and to do it well. We know that we wish to do our work well. When this is understood and mixed with faith, then poor, feeble man will be fortified with power from on high (Luke 24:49) and enabled to do more than he could ever have imagined. Truly, the child of God will be increasingly freed from sin by faith in God's promises, while the unbelieving world rots and passes away in its sins. The believer will advance in newness of life by faith in God's promises, to the glory of the Lord our God, to the edification of his church, and to the inexpressible comfort of his own soul.

Note carefully that these are particular characteristics of the most important means by which we should seek to attain our true purpose of life and advance true godliness. We will go on to speak about the special traits that believers should make good use of to pursue these means.

Christians Who Should Make Use of These Means

Those who should use the above means to promote godliness in the Christian community include civil authorities, or Christians in government; church officers or overseers; and those without any particular office, either in the state or church, including men and women, young and old. Clearly, all of them should try to use the means to godliness in order to damage the kingdom of darkness and establish the kingdom of grace. They should use the general means for edification and godliness, and, as we have shown in *Zion's Trumpet*, chapters 18–20, everyone should do this according to his position. We will examine this, starting with the duty of Christian authorities in civil government.

Civil Authorities

Christian leaders who have more authority and power than other Christians should seek particularly to strengthen Christian people against the kingdom of darkness in order to promote the kingdom of grace. They should use all the means of godliness entrusted to them by God on account of their particular office and in accordance with their special nature and power. The following three ways of doing that are the most important:

1. Setting a good example. Christians in authority are to lead the way in living a devout Christian life. They should do this by diligently keeping all God's commandments and being in submission to them (Deut. 17:11–19; Job 29:7–17). They should heed the activ-

ities of God in themselves and in others and take God's exceeding great and precious promises to heart. By this they flee the corruption that is in the world because of lust and grow in the grace and knowledge of our Lord and Savior Jesus Christ. You see, when rulers seriously promote a godly life, it greatly influences people's hearts. Is it not true that "like ruler, like subjects"? The example of a leader shapes the activity of a ruler's subjects at mealtimes, at functions, and in all circumstances.

Since leaders excel in authority, their subjects pay attention to them, but what is more, nearly everyone follows their example. That is why leaders should take care that they surpass others in diligence and godliness just as much as they surpass them in authority. After all, have they not received greater blessings from God in this life than other people? Do they not have important means they can use to encourage the godly? They have the means to call on strong, godly men who are well instructed in the kingdom of heaven (Matt. 13:52). They can summon these men, just as Nebuchadnezzar and Herod could call on and make use of the pagan wise men in their kingdoms (Dan. 2:2). By the virtue of their counsel and advice, these leaders were able to carry out their affairs well.

If leaders do not excel in godliness more than others because of these greater opportunities, their account at the last day will be frightening. Indeed, since they are rulers like "gods" on the earth, they should pay particular attention to their conduct. Like Enoch, they should lead a godly life before the Lord their God (Gen. 5:24), and, like David, they should magnify their God, who has favored them (Psalm 108).

2. Punishing with discernment. These rulers are to use the sword with discernment in punishing and restraining criminals (Rom. 13:4). All of us are greatly inclined to evil. Evil springs up like weeds in the furrows of the field if we will allow it (Hosea 10:4). Moreover, we find that sin is very contagious. Although we are taught to do good, we are more inclined to follow evil (Rom. 7:23). You see the same thing in nature: A healthy person catches the serious illness of another by intimate contact more easily than a sick person catches the health of a person he lives with. We find many sins and scandalous offenses that are very obstinate and stubborn and persist in spite of all teaching and serious warning. The Lord has pro-

vided Christian leaders with the means to combat this stubborn wickedness to some degree (Rom. 13:4). Therefore, civil authorities should not passively stand by in these circumstances but use their authority. Like David, they should cut off all evildoers from the city of the Lord (Psalm 101).

3. Revering godliness. Civil authorities should also use their authority to honor the devout and keep godliness in high regard (Rom. 13:3; 1 Peter 2:14). That is not to say that Christians should not love godliness for itself, for even if all the great men of the earth were against godliness, they should still be faithfully devoted to living godly lives. But not all believers have such strength. There are many who are in the process of becoming good Christians, and they can still be won over. In any case, whatever the duty of another may be, it is still the duty of Christian leaders, in their position as "gods" (Ps. 82:1; i.e., rulers or magistrates) on earth, to follow the God of heaven and earth. They are to show greatest love to those to whom the Lord God has shown the most love. They should show the greatest favor and preference to those who most love and fear God. They should offer privileges and preferences to them so that everyone will see that the best way to get promoted in the service of the country or in some other department of Christian government is by being faithful and strict in the service of the Lord our God.[1]

Overseers of the Church

These overseers, or officers of the church, have been charged with governing Christian people who are subjects of the kingdom of grace. These overseers are to do their utmost to demolish the kingdom of darkness and promote the kingdom of grace with every possible means of godliness that the Lord God has entrusted to them. In their position, they are to do this in the following three ways.

1. Teellinck is affirming the Dutch government's decision in 1579 to establish the Reformed faith as the faith of the national church and to ban the public practice of all but the "evangelical Reformed religion." Throughout continental Europe in Reformation times, state governments were prone to be closely knit to the particular church (Roman Catholic, Lutheran, or Reformed) that was formally embraced (cf. Belgic Confession of Faith, Article 36). So, for example, the Dutch government paid the salaries of Dutch Reformed ministers, called and financed the Synod of Dort (1618–19), and sent Reformed ministers as chaplains on numerous ships.

1. In presenting God's Word. These overseers are to present God's Word well, accurately and faithfully teaching it to the people (Acts 20:20–27), each according to his calling, because the Word of God has been entrusted to each in a particular way. Truly, the Word of God is the sword of the Spirit and the means to pull down the kingdom of darkness and strengthen the kingdom of grace (Eph. 6:17). The Lord God uses his Word to perform great miracles, to rebuke and suppress sin, to stir up spiritual gifts, and to win many souls, as we saw in book 3. The overseers of the church (Acts 20:28) should therefore firmly keep in mind that the Lord God has provided them with the means that, when used properly and subjected to God's grace, may, on the one hand, cause the devil to fall as lightning from heaven and expose and disturb his kingdom of darkness (Luke 10:17–20). On the other hand, they will greatly advance the kingdom of grace. For this reason, they should not be slow in using these means, lest they bring serious charges of blame upon themselves.

2. In administering discipline. Overseers have the task of seeing that Christian discipline is correctly exercised. You see, in Scripture, true believers are called not only sons and daughters of God but also children—even little children (1 John 2:1). We know that in a well-ordered household in which God's ordinances are followed, not only are children admonished but a rod is also prepared for those who fail to heed the warnings (Prov. 2:15; 13:24). God has ordered his house in the same way (1 Tim. 3:15) and regulates matters in such a way that in addition to his Word of admonition, there is also the rod of his discipline (1 Cor. 4:21).

Discipline must be applied with discrimination and care, according to the nature of the offense and the persistence of sinning, if we wish to maintain good order in God's house and advance godliness among believers. Moses says of the law he was given that the word was not a vain thing for the people (Deut. 32:47). Likewise, we also say that the rod of discipline was not a vain thing. Our wise and good God and Savior has not instituted discipline for us for any reason other than that it is highly necessary for the welfare of his Christian flock, even under the gospel.

3. In living a godly life. Like Christians in government, church rulers are to set a good example in leading a devout, godly, and

Christian life (Phil. 3:17; Titus 2:7; 1 Peter 5:3). They are called leaders of the people because they can lead by example in all holy and godly activities and be at the forefront in their practice (Heb. 13:17). You see, there are many duties of the godly life that ordinary people generally do not understand well. They may think that these duties are useless or even dangerous. The overseers should faithfully and diligently lead in the practice of these duties in order to show the whole world that there is no danger in them and that, on the contrary, these obligations are right and in perfect harmony with the spiritual life. Indeed, they will benefit us as good pasture for our souls (John 10:9). Ordinary people, like sheep, will then gladly follow the examples of their overseers. In so doing, they will increase and advance in godliness in every respect.

Ordinary Christians

When we speak of ordinary Christians or laypeople, we do not mean only the simple and the poor but also the rich and the powerful; indeed, we mean every believer who has no leadership position in government or the church. These ordinary Christians also ought to do their part in using the God-given means to advance true godliness. Like everyone else, they have a soul to be saved or to be lost, and their souls are just as precious and valuable to God as the souls of the mightiest and greatest of men (Exodus 20). The kingdom of darkness also fights against the souls of ordinary people, and the duty to pull down that evil kingdom also rests on them so that they might advance the kingdom of grace with the means that God has entrusted to them. These means include the following three:

1. Helping one another live right. Ordinary Christians are to take good care of one another, doing good at every opportunity and helping one another to live godly lives (Jude 20). Nature teaches us that people who associate with one another must take care of one another to ensure that no one comes to any harm. If we see someone about to hurt himself or someone else, either through carelessness or for another reason, then all who are present must seek at once to prevent this. If we know that spiritual life is more precious than temporal life, then how much more should Christians take care that no one hinders anyone from living a godly life.

If everyone would put this into practice, you would see how marvelous and great their edification would be, what loss the kingdom of darkness would suffer, and how godliness would flourish! We would then see every Christian in the community become a faithful watchman and courageous overseer to frustrate and expose every device of Satan so that souls would be kept from corruption.

2. Getting people together to build their faith. Ordinary Christians should organize holy meetings in families or with their friends and acquaintances in their areas and neighborhoods for the purpose of edifying one another and building one another up in their most holy faith. Is it not true that this is Israel's way (Job 1; Jude 12)? If so, should it not also be a custom among Christian people? Do not friends and acquaintances who are affiliated with one another, either by family relationships, working in the same place or at the same trade, or living near one another, tend to meet at times and visit one another to have a good conversation? Should they not call on one another and cordially invite one another to their homes and give them a warm reception? Is it not the practice among relatives, or those who belong to the same organization, or those who live in the same neighborhood to meet one another often and on various occasions?

It is beyond description how much it would strengthen godliness if the godly were to focus in such meetings on building one another up in their most holy faith and sharing the spiritual gifts the Lord our God has given to them, for these gifts are such that no matter how much we share them with others, they do not decrease. Instead, by sharing them, these gifts are multiplied. See what the apostle Paul has to say about this (Heb. 10:24), what his practice was and what he desired. Let him speak for himself in his letter to the Romans: "For I long to see you, that I may impart unto you some spiritual gift, to the end ye may be established; that is, that I may be comforted together with you by the mutual faith both of you and me" (1:11–12). Is this not also an important part of the communion of the saints?

We have seen this practiced in some places with such great joy and success that we cannot doubt that Satan must be at work when he manages it so that groups of Christians get confused, and their meetings turn out not for the better but for the worse (1 Cor. 11:17). In so doing, he has succeeded in ravaging Christian people.

This is easy to understand if we use these meetings with couples and friends and neighbors to talk about trivialities, chattering foolishly and peppering our conversations with gossip. Instead of talking about edifying subjects, we chat about anything that happens in our town or village. Sometimes people are slandered. But if we talked about the kingdoms of God and of darkness and everything associated with these kingdoms with the purpose of building one another up in the most holy faith, would we not see that such visits might yield glorious fruits of godliness? If we invited a few friends or, for that matter, many friends to dinner and at the end of the meal sang a psalm and gave thanks on our knees in all reverence, with sincerity and true devotion, who would not immediately see that this could greatly encourage and strengthen godliness among us?

However, these kinds of meetings are neither custom nor habit among us but are unheard of. The idea of them sounds strange and somewhat odd to us. So since this precious virtue is a stranger among us, our meetings often take place entirely for the worse. Professing Christians think it is odd to promote such gatherings and find it even more strange when not every professing Christian follows them in the worldly excesses they perpetrate at meetings, dinners, or wherever they come together (1 Peter 4:4).

3. Obeying people in authority. Christians ought to set a good example for one another of loyal obedience and appropriate respect for their overseers, into whose care they have been entrusted in one way or another (Rom. 13:1–3). It is hard to say how much benefit and edification is produced by a good example. Great confusion and serious disturbances are often caused by those who live a loose, unbridled, and lawless life, behaving like Belial's sons. Such behavior tramples underfoot and makes ineffective all good works, ordinances, rules, edicts, laws, orders, or whatever is issued by the government to correct disorder in the state or ordered by the heads of households in their family. If only laypeople would make it a habit to obey and be submissive, thereby setting a good example. If they would encourage one another in this, then we would soon see a reformed republic, with fewer troubles. Evil deeds would promptly be suppressed, and duties would be faithfully performed. The outcome of all this

would be the great advancement and encouragement of true godliness by all who wholeheartedly made the effort to set so good an example.[2]

We have said enough now about the most important means to obtain the real purpose of life and to advance true godliness. We have also said enough about the special nature of Christian people who should use the means we have discussed for promoting true godliness. It follows then that we should briefly show you what devices the kingdom of darkness uses to distract people from the true means of godliness.

Devices Used by the Kingdom of Darkness to Distract Many from Godliness

We should know that our spiritual enemies are bent on preventing as many people as possible from using the means to godliness, or providing them with the wrong means, or even having them use the right means in the wrong way. They know well that just as the Lord God established order in nature, and usually advances natural things by natural means, so God also established order in the works of grace. He promotes the works of grace through the right means, which are rich in mercy, and thus encourages and advances the way of godliness. We see in everyday life that those who fail to employ any means, or employ the wrong means, or use the right means in the wrong way will never be successful. Likewise, we should be aware that those who fail to use the means of the works of grace, or use the wrong ones, or employ the right means wrongly will greatly harm their souls.

2. By hoping for a "reformed republic," Teellinck expresses a wish that the Reformed faith might prevail in the hearts and lives of all citizens, especially the ruling class. He believed that the policies and practices of a Reformed commonwealth should be consistent with the faith it confesses. The problem was that Teellinck's idea of a commonwealth in which God's law would not be flouted did not correspond to the notions of the political elite. For example, Teellinck held that a godly commonwealth was one that averted God's wrath by denying succor to the foreign enemies of God (e.g., by not allowing Dutch merchants to trade with Spain) and by enforcing the laws against Roman Catholics at home. Government leaders and many of the patrician elite, however, thought that preachers should keep out of politics (after all, permits for trading with the enemy were an important source of revenue!) and aim at unifying the commonwealth rather than causing division into warring doctrinal camps.

Our spiritual enemies are therefore particularly determined to ensnare or mislead us in one of these three ways. They are quite successful in their ploys with careless people. We will briefly consider their clever tricks in order to expose them and warn people who are unaware of them.

The Enemy's Clever Tricks

1. Preventing people from using the means. Our spiritual enemy tries to get many people to ignore or neglect any means to salvation. He persuades them to let things run their course or to leave these matters to God so that he might do as he pleases. Saying that it is "not of him that willeth, nor of him that runneth, but of God that sheweth mercy" (Rom. 9:16), they then ask, "What use is it then to wear yourself out by using these means? Is it not all of God? Is he not able to give without the use of such means?" Clearly, we need to consider this approach in more detail to see what is wrong with it.

It is a worthless proposition. To begin with, this scheme assumes that if our salvation entirely depended on us, it would be worthwhile to try to achieve the desired goal, but since it all depends on God, why should we put a lot of effort into it? Surely, this is a very evil and objectionable proposition. Is it right that frail people should use all possible means to attain salvation and blessedness and to advance their spiritual life and godliness if the result depended even partly on them? Should we not then consider it more right to use the means given at God's command in order to obtain God's blessing when we understand that it all depends on God? If salvation depends partly on us, who are evil and depraved, should we not expect better blessings if salvation depends completely on God? Are we better than God? Perish the thought; what a detestable idea!

God works through these means. We should remember that the Lord God, who is not restricted to any means and who is able to give with or without means, nevertheless established this order that he will work through means, even in the works of grace. We read everywhere in Scripture that God often affirms that everything depends on him and that he does whatever pleases him in heaven and in earth, in the seas, and in all deep places (Ps. 135:6) and that no man can come to the Son except the Father draws him (John 6:44). What is more, we are not able to think even one good thought in and of ourselves (2 Cor. 3:5). Yet God still commands us everywhere to use and apply his prescribed means to salvation and to godliness. He cries out in a loud voice, "He that hath ears to hear, let him hear" (Mark 4:9). He often says, "Call upon me in the day of trouble: I will deliver thee" (Ps. 50:15). Elsewhere we read, "Turn ye, turn ye from your evil ways; for why will ye die, O house of Israel?" (Ezek. 33:11). When the Lord God, on whom all depends, demands and commands us to use the means so that we may obtain his help in salvation, it is seriously wrong to insist that it does us no good to use them. Although the Lord God is able to give blessings without these means, he chooses not to do so.

We will be blessed by using these means. We should consider that the Lord God shows us in our temporal life that, in general, everyone will be blessed to the degree that he uses the means. Is this not our experience? Whoever does not put forth his hand to work will not succeed in his work, even in the things of this mortal life. The Lord leads us by the hand through experiences in temporal things so that we will notice his ways in spiritual things. Clearly, we know by experience that though we obtain spiritual gifts purely by his blessing, no one will receive this blessing (while the light of the gospel is here) except those who faithfully and seriously use the means God has ordained. Take notice, beloved, and see where people are won for the Christian faith. Is it in brothels? In bars? In casinos? Or is it in the assembly of believers?

Also, who are the ones who tend to increase in the grace and knowledge of our Lord Jesus Christ? Is it those who are slow and weak and careless in applying the God-given means? Or is it those who use them with steady persistence—those who with diligence, zeal, and faithfulness daily exercise their senses in searching the Word of God, in praying, and in actively and effectively partaking in the communion of saints and in the community of believers? Since it is indisputable that no one obtains God's blessing except those who use the God-given means, what a misdeed it is, then, if we were to neglect the means God offers to obtain his blessing! So we see that, however it may go with those who use the God-given means, it is still certain that those who despise or neglect the means God has given are very far from succeeding in the end.

Indeed, the apostle Paul testifies that whosoever neglects so great a salvation, which is offered by the Lord, will not escape punishment (Heb. 2:3). The Lord Christ himself testifies that it shall be more tolerable for the land of Sodom and Gomorrah in the day of judgment than for a city that had the means available to it but failed to use them. We spoke about this point at length in my first tract on perseverance. We recommend that you read it again, as it is so relevant to this subject.

2. Persuading people to use the wrong means. If Satan is unable to prevent a person from neglecting all these means to salvation and godliness, he does not leave this matter as is. Rather, he will try to get the person to at least use the wrong means. Instead of using God's ordinances, activities, and promises, the person will be persuaded to import human inventions and traditions, which supposedly will advance true godliness. Satan has been terribly successful in this, particularly with Roman Catholics. He has greatly deceived these poor people, heavily burdening them with futile and wearying toil in their efforts to advance godliness. All their toil and effort is in vain, however, because they do not use God's means but their own fancied methods and innovations.

Some of these inventions are the use of statues to arouse devotion; confession, as practiced by the Roman Catholics; all kinds of monastic and cloistered living and various disciplines associated with it, such as going barefoot, lying on hard beds, wearing coarse habits, going on pilgrimages, and so on. These are all human inventions, traditions, and devices. Thus, they cannot produce anything that really is from God, as true and precious godliness is, to which we aspire. It is impossible for them to produce true godliness, which is so precious and for which we strive. Let us now consider the failures of this approach in more detail.

Human effort cannot produce godly ends. Nature itself teaches us that all this striving means wasted effort because human devices cannot produce godly ends. Take note of what we are saying here. Can a person catch the wind in his fist or grasp the soul of his fellow man? Can you do physical therapy on someone's body with your soul or hold someone's hand and feet with it? Everyone knows that this is impossible. Physical things are treated with physical means, and spiritual things with spiritual means. The conclusion is indisputable: Human schemes, traditions, and institutions cannot help us achieve heavenly objectives, nor will they yield heavenly fruits. No matter what form of godliness it may seem to have, human effort is just mere deceit and vanity (Col. 2:23). Godly living and godliness will not be obtained or advanced without God's ordinances and statutes, which concern the body as well as the soul (1 Cor. 6:20; 1 Tim. 4:8).

God's means are sufficient. The Lord God has established precious, beautiful, powerful, and plentiful spiritual means for salvation and godliness and has explained them in his holy Word. There are more than enough for us so that we are likely to complain that there are too many of them, and, such is our weakness, we have difficulty in applying them well. We certainly do not have to design or invent other means not mentioned by God in his Word. Does this not show just how weak and depraved we are?

Just look at all the various spiritual means to salvation, as shown in God's Word, that we have already presented, simply and thoroughly, in this book. I fear that some would sooner complain about their great number than say anything about the many new, invented ones that the Lord God has not revealed and commanded and certainly never thought of, such as the many devotions that are so highly esteemed in Roman Catholicism (Jer. 19:5).

God will not honor human means. Finally, we should know that the Lord strongly affirms in Scripture that we worship him in vain if we substitute the commandments of men for God's doctrines (Matt. 15:9). Scripture further declares that the Lord will never have fellowship with the throne of iniquity that wrongly teaches the law (Isa. 29:13), or, rather, that the throne of lamentable manmade hardships, namely, the throne that commands torment and obstacles by an edict, shall have no fellowship with God. The Lord will not have fellowship with any devices, edicts, and ordinances that have been invented to burden people. Not a single blessing will result from them. It is therefore pure nonsense and completely wasted effort to think that we can advance godliness in others and ourselves by our own devices and schemes. For it is written in Jeremiah 23:22, "But if they had stood in my counsel, and had caused my people to hear my words, then they should have turned them from their evil way, and from the evil of their doings."

3. Persuading people to apply the right means in the wrong way. If our spiritual enemy is not able to persuade us to apply either wrong means or no means at all, then he goes to considerable lengths to have us use the right means in the wrong way. He takes great delight in his shrewd ploys to present God's own means and ordinances as useless and powerless. He uses all his craftiness for this, trying to steer those who use God's means toward separating what God has joined together. This may be in using only some of God's revealed means, or it may be in using all of them but doing so only out of habit and being satisfied with that. They may also seem to be using all these means but not in the special way that God intended them to be used.

You see, Satan conjures up these specific things, knowing that if he succeeds in getting us to do things Satan's way, it will keep God's blessings from us, even if these people do use some of the means God has given. Remember that it is not the mere outward or superficial use of means that God blesses but the right spiritual use of them. As the apostle Paul says on this subject, "And if a man also strive for masteries, yet is he not crowned, except he strive lawfully" (2 Tim. 2:5).

We will look at this only briefly, as we will have opportunity to consider this material in more detail in book 6. Nevertheless, we should say a little more here about Satan's tricks.

Combating Satan's Tricks

We will begin by looking at the neglect of certain means, why some of them are seldom used and practiced, and what we are to do about that.

1. Choosing some but not all of the means. Clearly, the Lord, our wise God, who knows our weaknesses best, would not have revealed his divine things so abundantly that we could take or leave these matters as we see fit. No! It is written that we must walk according to all God's commandments (Num. 15:38–41; Heb. 13:18). We are not to rule over God's commandments, for the Lord

is to prescribe and we are to comply. We read that the bride of Christ made use of all the means God gave her before she found her bridegroom (Song of Sol. 3:1–4).

We are not told this so that we have to fret and agonize every day to make absolutely sure that we observed and daily complied with every means to salvation and blessing God has revealed. Surely, we could not do that; that is impossible to achieve. Nevertheless, we should make a holy decision and resolution not to forget even one of God's given means but use them all at the appropriate time; sometimes this one, sometimes that one, depending on what our situation requires at a particular time. And we should be ever so careful that we do not act like those who wish to read the Word of God in their homes but have no intention of going to church, or those who wish to go to church but have no desire to partake of the Lord's Supper, or those who perhaps would like to partake of the Lord's Supper but do not wish to exercise Christian discipline at home. Be careful to seek for and to observe such important and well-known means. Guard yourself against any neglect or abuse of God's means. Rather, use all of them diligently and faithfully, as much as you can and as often as possible.

2. Using the means purely out of habit. It is an evil trick of Satan to tempt people to use some or even all of the means God gives purely out of habit or to keep up a custom. We should be mindful that this is a ploy of Satan that he often uses in Roman Catholicism to make people satisfied with what they themselves have done. However, instead of promising a blessing for these efforts, the Lord threatens those who practice them with severe punishment, saying, "Forasmuch as this people draw near me with their mouth, and with their lips do honour me, but have removed their heart far from me, and their fear toward me is taught by the precept of men: therefore, behold, I will proceed to do a marvellous work among this people" (Isa. 29:13–14).

God's judgment upon mere habitual devotion is just, for if we should dare to approach the Lord God with our body but without seeking him with our heart and soul, then our religion is completely dead (1 Chron. 22:19). To God, that would be as if we were dangling some rancid bait before him (Isa. 66:3). We should carefully watch that we are not controlled by using the means without zeal but out of mere habit.[3] Such superficial habit will harden our hearts rather than benefit them.

3. Overlooking the importance of the means. Even when we are on our guard against being satisfied with the progress we have made, we should not overlook the importance of these godly means. We should consider Solomon's warning that if "the soul be without knowledge, it is not good" (Prov. 19:2) and that the Lord has no pleasure in the sacrifice of fools (Eccles. 5:1). We must remember that our spiritual enemy is extremely crafty and goes to great lengths to confuse us, even when our hearts seem prepared and eager to serve God. It is necessary that we take the greatest care to obtain all the godly wisdom we can so that we may make good use of all our God-given means.

We need to cover this in more detail now. We know very well that no matter how good a person's intentions are, no matter how good the goal is that he has in mind, and no matter what means he has at hand for attaining that goal, he will still fall short of reaching that goal unless he conducts himself as he should in using those means. "Ye ask, and receive not, because ye ask amiss," says the apostle James (4:3).

We know that, although we have the material available to make a good suit, the cloth can be spoiled in the cutting so that the suit will not fit. Likewise, even though we have the best medicines, they can be wrongly prepared so a sick person will not benefit from them. And so it is necessary that we show how the Christian should conduct himself with the aid of the God-given means that we have already discussed in order to obtain his real purpose in life and to practice true godliness.

In order to attain this goal, the following things are necessary: a good, methodical, and consistent lifestyle; a keen and sincere attention to maintaining this lifestyle; and a devout fight against all that falls short of and conflicts with this disciplined lifestyle. We will talk about this very important and useful material in more detail in the next book.

---

3. Teellinck does not intend to discourage daily devotions here but mere habitual devotions. He viewed regular devotions as essential, but the believer ought never be satisfied with his devotions as long as his mind and heart are not fully engaged in them (cf. book 6).

BOOK
6

Using God-Given Means
to Practice True Godliness

If a Christian desires to practice true godliness faithfully and attain his real purpose in life, he should use the means referred to in a disciplined way. It is necessary for him to observe a good, established, firm, and regular rule of life. He must not live carelessly and haphazardly but follow this standard (Gal. 6:16). God's blessings are promised only to those who order their lives well (Ps. 50:23). Surely, it is easy to understand how fundamental this is because, as we have learned, the life of godliness involves many things of immense importance.

We all know that anyone who has important business matters that are crucial to him and demand detailed attention will have to go about his business in an orderly manner and act wisely, or he can expect little success. Can you imagine the executive of a large organization having no strategy but working haphazardly and without order? Can you imagine him starting one thing, then dropping it and flitting from one task to another without ever considering why he abandoned the task at hand? Can you imagine his failing to consider what he had achieved or to review and analyze his plan to determine its progress? Suppose he approached each task carelessly, without any objective, working one day on one project and another day on whatever might happen to turn up? Every competent businessman knows well that this man's business would soon be in shambles, and his money would rapidly disappear.

We find exactly the same thing with the daily practice of the godly life. It is impossible to live a godly life unless we begin and continue this life with direction and in a disciplined way. If we live casually, taking days as they come, paying no attention to rules or order, we will deceive ourselves, and, of course, we will inevitably fail. We will inevitably neglect something important here and forget something essential there, causing untold harm to true godliness. If we look at the reasons why many Christians who are sincere and highly value the godly life fail so badly among believers, make so little progress in holiness, and are so pitifully negligent—or at least profit so little and grow so little in the practice of godliness—we will discover that they lack a disciplined lifestyle. They live haphazardly and deal with whatever turns up and whatever suits them; thus, they forget and neglect many things that pertain to godliness. They become confused and entangle themselves in many things that cause untold harm to true godliness. Clearly, they could have prevented this if they had followed a well-regulated and ordered life. We ought to pay close attention to this.

A good, established, firm, and regular rule of life consists of three specific practices:

- establishing fixed times and hours for all our duties
- assigning priorities, or first doing those things that are most important and essential
- making it a daily practice to examine how we have conducted ourselves and how it is with our hearts

We will discuss each point, starting in this section with the first one.

Allocate Certain Times Each Day to Accomplish Our Duties

In order to lead a disciplined life, it is necessary to set aside specific times for those things that we know for certain need our attention. This will enable us to start our daily work in an orderly fashion and work at it diligently so that we will be able to accomplish these things well. We should pay close attention to our priorities at the start of the day, during the course of the day, and at the end of the day, giving all essential daily tasks their allocated time or hour. For example, Scripture tells us that it was the practice of David (Ps. 55:17) and Daniel (Dan. 6:10) to pray three times a day. Here are some of the priorities we should set.

1. Time for prayer and devotions. We should set aside a certain time at the beginning of each day to call on the name of the Lord and to read God's Word, both personally and with the family. The head of the family may choose a time that suits him and his family best. He should see that this time is strictly adhered to but with some flexibility, should circumstances demand it, to prevent it from becoming a mere ritual or superstitious observance. These set hours and times ought to be chosen as an aid, not an obstacle, to faith. If circumstances offer a justifiable reason not to follow our usual practice, then we should willingly change the time with the understanding that our regular hours remain the norm. We simply have to make sure that by changing the order, the rule is not overlooked. If possible, we should make arrangements for an hour that better suits our circumstances.

2. Regular times for daily activities. We should then plan our days, assigning the most suitable and convenient times and hours for each daily task. For example, on workdays, we should have a specific time to perform each of the ordinary duties of our occupation. We should set aside times to relax and enjoy ourselves and to have our meals. Then, too, it is a great blessing for us to set aside some free time to perform works of charity and friendship—as much as we can and not only on the Lord's Day but also on other days. These acts include visiting, comforting, and helping others as the opportunities arise. Doing these things is virtuous not only on the Lord's Day but also during the entire week.

3. Ending the day with the Lord. We should set aside time at the end of the day for devotions with God, to personally read God's Word and to pray with our families. We should set aside as much time for this as we can without tiring ourselves. It would also be good for us to spend some time examining our conduct during the day that has just ended.

In short, our first priority is to follow certain sound and established rules in life that will enable us to lead a truly godly life. We really cannot express how much serenity, assurance, blessing, and comfort this will give to those who routinely observe this.

Assign Priorities so the Most Important Things Are Done First

Another part of a godly lifestyle is wisely evaluating the true worth of all our tasks and making it a rule to perform first what is most necessary and important to complete those tasks.

God's Word teaches this everywhere, particularly in Matthew 6:33, which says, "Seek ye first the kingdom of God, and his righteousness; and all these things shall be added unto you" (see also Matt. 22:37–39). True wisdom demands and requires us to subject the insignificant and inconsequential things to those that are of greater importance. This is essential for attaining the true purpose of life and practicing true godliness. The person who follows the wrong order in this, ranking earth above heaven, pleasing men above pleasing God, and valuing earthly things higher than heavenly treasures, is apt to prefer and perform the least important tasks before the most important ones. Such a person obviously would not glorify God, let alone show even a glimmer of godliness. Therefore, we should follow the rule in every part of our lives and in all our conduct to perform the most necessary and most important things first. To do this, we must observe the following:

Rule 1: Put God first. All our earthly work, our occupation in life, our welfare, pleasures, good name, and profit must come second to serving God and doing his holy will. This means we must put all our affairs aside to make way for serving and obeying God. We may no longer cling to or pursue pleasures and enjoyment, achievements and welfare, honor and respect, and whatever else we may love or want to obtain if it means going against God's will and breaking his commandments. Instead, we may value or possess or serve these things only in accordance with the good will of the Lord our God and his holy commandments.

This is a most excellent rule to follow in our work if we are to attain our real purpose in life and achieve true godliness. Is this not a most reasonable rule? For what is more sensible than that our God, who is above all, should be honored and served above all and that all things must be subjected to the things of God?

Although this rule is most reasonable, it is, unfortunately, practiced very little. Because of the intolerable pressures we live with, almost everyone tends to give the things of God a lower priority than his own needs. Many serve God only when it does not interfere with their worldly affairs. That is why so few resolutely demonstrate true godliness in their lives.

Those who would sincerely practice true godliness should take care to observe this rule. They should make sure that they manage the daily tasks of their profession in such a way that these tasks do not become a hindrance or obstacle to the work of the Lord and the service of the almighty God. Those who want to practice true godliness should regulate their work so they do not become workaholics who are so immersed in their work that they have no time or interest for ordinary godly commitments and activities.

We must pay close attention to this essential order and priority. Experience shows that the Lord God, according to his manifold wisdom, has commanded the children of men to work to humble them and lead them to true godliness (Eccles. 1:13). However, they abuse this by not subordinating their work to his claims and hindering others in their search for true godliness. Forgetting this golden rule, they fail to place all the activities of their profession under and unto the service of God. Instead, they make the activities of their profession their most important occupation. They subject everything to their work, even the work of the Lord, and so they burden their hearts. They have ignored Christ's admonition in Luke 21:34 about being weighed down with the cares of life. In so doing, they have caused untold harm to their souls and true godliness.

All true godly people should gladly heed this warning and take care to manage and perform the work activities of their profession in such good order, measure, and fashion that these activities are no longer a hindrance but an aid to true godliness. They should make it their habit to use this world and not let it trouble them (1 Cor. 7:31). They should willingly shun everything that will take them away from their godly walk of life, just like those who fight for the prize (1 Cor. 9:24). The godly must always remember the words of Paul that no soldier in battle should entangle himself in the affairs of this life so that he may please him who has chosen him to be a soldier (2 Tim. 2:4). We should do likewise, subjecting all things to the pleasure of our commander in chief, the Lord Jesus Christ (Heb. 12:2–3).

Rule 2: Practice mercy. We ought to observe mercy in everything that pertains to godliness. That means we should not only observe the duties of the first table of the law, which contains the first and greatest commandment, placing those ahead of the requirements of the second table of the law (which was explained at length earlier), but we should also practice mercy before sacrifice, for that is the Lord's greater charge to us (Matt. 12:7). In practice, that means being willing to set aside temporarily or delay religious practices such as resting on the Lord's Day, hearing the Word of God and formally calling upon God's name, holy baptism, and the Lord's Supper—indeed, all so-called sacrifices—should there be an unexpected emergency. It means postponing those things when we or others have a crucial situation that requires our immediate, active assistance and support. We need to do so if a house is on fire, a child falls into danger, or something else comes up that needs immediate action. We may also have to do so when we are too weak or ill to go to church to join the assembly of believers. In these and a thousand other cases, it is our duty to practice mercy above sacrifice. We should postpone or interrupt the formal worship of God rather than overburden ourselves or leave our fellow men in an emergency.

We must pay close attention to this rule because it advances true godliness. Otherwise, the tender consciences of other people may become confused and troubled in such cases because they are not sure what is right to do. Should they have accepted something as good or rejected it as bad? We should familiarize ourselves with this rule of God about putting mercy before sacrifice, for it has been instituted by God.

Rule 3: Do what is most necessary. We should make the duties of our profession or position that have a special influence on our condition, occupation, or standing in the community a priority. We should take advantage of our status, making good use of it in our dealings with others with whom we have contact so we may edify them and lead them heavenward. We should avoid everything that would cause us to lose the respect of others. Godly wisdom teaches us that we should not be busy or overload our minds with all sorts of things that are neither necessary nor useful. Rather, we should apply ourselves to the one thing that is most necessary. We should concentrate on that good part that is most needed by all of us (Luke 10:42).

Clearly, many people could have done much better by obeying this rule. They could have governed the country, the church, their own family members, and others so much better if they had used their precious time more profitably and given their efforts to those things that were most needed and best served. But experience shows that through carelessness, many people wasted their time and effort on obtaining things or learning things that were not really useful or important, as they themselves discovered with time. If these people had devoted their time and effort to more needful things, they would have been more useful and influential members of the church of God and more fruitful citizens of their country.

This is a sly trick of our spiritual enemy. He likes to have us occupied with the wrong things and living lazy and idle lives. If he does not succeed in this, he tries to get us involved in all sorts of trivial or needless things that require great effort. We should be on our guard against this and give our free time to things that make us most useful for the service of God's church and our nation.

Note this well. If you desire good results in the practice of true godliness, you should also be on your guard when you study God's Word so that you do not spend more energy and time on those things that are less useful and necessary to know and understand. Be very careful! Our spiritual enemy seeks to lead astray those who search God's Word so that they fail to learn something that will enlarge their assurance of salvation and advance true godliness. He tries to distract such people from studying and applying some useful and important doctrine. Or he will engage them in some obscure controversy, the meaning of which they often never quite understand because they lack insight into the mysteries of the kingdom of God and true theology. They waste their energy, time, and effort, which results in the gross neglect of their practice of true godliness.

Had these people been more astute and remembered our rule of first studying and performing those things that are most useful to them, in accordance with their abilities and situation, they would have made infinitely greater progress in the practice of true godliness. If they had chosen to thoroughly and accurately learn the first principles of Christian religion and had built daily on this precious foundation with gold, silver, and precious, costly stones (1 Cor. 3:11–13; Hebrews 6), how great their progress would have been in true godliness! But because they were busy with things that were too deep for them and too readily engaged in high and difficult doctrine, which even professors find difficult to grasp and understand, they were distracted from the essence and power of true religion. The kind of godliness of some who have gone in that direction seems to consist of nothing more than an argumentative contest that only confuses the peaceful church of God and fills the community of the saints with confusion.

Those who would practice true godliness must pay close attention. They must not involve themselves in difficult and deep points of religious differences before they have first acquired a thoroughly good and sound foundation of knowledge and godliness in their hearts. When they have done this, the Lord may graciously lead them to understand the weighty, deep, and important matters being debated. We should not have a problem with this, for we know very well that God's Spirit works where he wills. We know that some unlearned and ordinary people, for example, craftsmen, are so full of understanding and knowledge in the ways of the Lord that they can handle the most difficult and controversial issues admirably and with great competence, even in the most difficult disputes. May the good Lord increase their number daily.

Remember, however, not everyone has been given this knowledge, so typical Christians should seriously examine their competence and not venture beyond it. They should not reach for high things but always condescend as men of low estate (Rom. 12:16). If they act in this way, they will increase in godliness because they paid attention to this good rule.

Use Self-Examination to Discover How We Have Occupied Our Days

The third and last activity that is part of a good and ordered life consists of frequent (daily, if possible) and habitual examination of our conduct to see how we have passed our days and how well it is with our hearts. The apostle Paul strongly admonishes us to do this, stating in Hebrews 3:13, "But exhort one another daily, while it is called Today; lest any of you be hardened through the deceitfulness of sin." A well-ordered life clearly demands this.

Surely, everyone knows that those who manage their business in an orderly manner and conduct their affairs well will regularly review their position to determine the success of their business. They do that to see whether they are making a profit or losing money. But it is even more essential that those who practice godliness follow this practice, since their hearts, which should always be immersed in the practice of godliness, are still of such a nature and character that, unless they carefully mind what they are doing, examine themselves often, and lift their hearts up to God's presence (Acts 7:55), they may quickly lose their love for heavenly things and cherish worldly things (Rev. 2:4). They are still worldly minded by nature. They should therefore pay close attention to this and be on constant watch. They should find opportunities to interrupt worldly affairs and raise their hearts, as it were, into the presence of God by holy self-examination in order to keep themselves continually in good order and ready for God's service. The following three things in particular will help us successfully and rightly perform this examination and supervise our hearts:

1. Review what you did that day. You should briefly review the day and think about how you did, which obligations you met and which you neglected. Furthermore, what kind of thoughts you entertained, how you spoke and acted, into which sins you fell, and which sins you courageously resisted and overcame. Also, what fortune and misfortune you experienced and what you liked and disliked. Were you praised or reprimanded, treated courteously or ungraciously? Consider how the psalmist David examined his heart and mind. He says that he thought on his ways, which means he examined himself in each day's events (Ps. 119:59).

2. Examine your heart and mind. Next, you should briefly examine what your attitude was in all these things. How did your heart and mind act and react? How did you fear and love God and your neighbor? Did you show your faith and trust? Whatever your attitude may have been, examine it. This is what the psalmist David meant when he said he thought on his ways (Ps. 119:59).

3. Ask God for help. After you have taken spiritual inventory, you should direct your attention to God. Praise and thank him for everything that went well with you, both temporally and spiritually. Blame yourself if it did not go well with you. Humble yourself before God, and seek reconciliation with him in the way we described in book 1. This is what should be practiced by truly godly people. This is what David refers to in saying he turned his feet unto God's testimonies (Ps. 119:59).

Observe, this is the essence of an established, firm, and well-ordered life, which we need to follow if we want to attain the true purpose of life and obtain true godliness. We will now discuss what it means to be constantly on our guard.

A Vigilant Christian

We have seen that it is necessary for a Christian to have a well-ordered life in order to attain the true purpose of life and to practice godliness with the help of God-given means. But the Christian must also be particularly vigilant to ensure that he rightly and properly practices everything mentioned above. This is understandable if we consider the nature of the kingdom of darkness (which we have already discussed) and how it always opposes the kingdom of grace. Just as the inhabitants of a besieged town, surrounded without by many strong and fierce enemies and troubled within by mutinous soldiers, should always be on their guard, so a Christian should always be on his guard. He should heed Christ's counsel to watch and pray so that he will not be led into temptation and destruction (Mark 13:33). Do you think it is possible for a poor, frail, weak, and sinful man to escape from the claws of the roaring lion that walks about him and continuously lies in wait to devour his soul if he were not vigilant? Could he escape if he lived without care and concern for his own poor soul (1 Peter 5:8)?

Is it not even easier for a crafty, keen, and prowling Satan to ambush a careless, inattentive, slumbering sinner and bring him to ruin? That is why we insist that it is necessary for a man to be absolutely vigilant if he wants to be saved from ruin so he can advance in the practice of true godliness with the aid of the means of grace we have mentioned. We should practice the following things if we are to succeed: We should carefully note everything against which we should be on our guard; we should be concerned for our life in all these things; and because of this concern, we should maintain a wise and cautious watch.

We will consider each point in turn, starting in this section with the first one.

A Vigilant Christian Knows What to Guard Against

It is impossible to keep proper watch if we do not know the enemies for which we should be watching and the things against which we must be on our guard. The things a Christian should watch for are explained in detail in our discussions about the kingdoms of darkness and grace. We made it clear that the believer should be on his guard against the devil, the world, and his own flesh, as well as against all their nasty and crafty devices. He should also make use of all the means available to him by the kingdom of grace, which are prepared for his well-being by the Lord his God, by his holy church, and by the new creature. For further instruction, here are three things the Christian should especially be vigilant about:

1. The sins and weaknesses we are most inclined to. We should be especially vigilant in this area, for we are very weak here. We are like a stronghold under siege. And we know that the strongest guard must be placed where fortifications in a town are the weakest (Matt. 24:42; 26:21). Are you fond of alcohol? Are you inclined to sexual immorality? Is wealth extremely important to you? Understand well your weaknesses and be on guard against these very things. There may be an occasion for great temptation, for example, at a prospective wedding or at a sensual and idolatrous feast such as a fair, car-

nival, or something of that nature that encourages wickedness. Be
especially vigilant and on your guard at such times (Eph. 5:15–16).

We should especially be on guard because of the principle of sin,
for sin is poisonous by nature. Wherever it finds a little opening in
us, it knows how to twist and turn to get all the way inside. Many
careless people fail to pay attention to this and think they have nothing to do with sin. They imagine that they can make a soft landing
but forget that they are jumping off a high tower. So they end up
completely overwhelmed.

2. The neglect of the means to salvation revealed in God's Holy
Word. We should not neglect these means but dutifully observe
every one of them at the appropriate time and in proper order (Exod.
20:8). We should take special care to practice excellent holy duties
such as hearing and reading God's Word, calling on the name of
the Lord, partaking of the Lord's Supper, praying aloud with the
family, and so on, making sure that we do not practice them out of
mere habit or to maintain a certain rule but to glorify the Lord God
genuinely and increasingly advance true godliness (Rom. 12:1). We
should be more zealous to obtain some special virtues that we need
for our edification than the beautiful women in Jeremiah 2:32
exerted to adorn their bodies.

3. The situations that may lead to sin. Certain things are not in
themselves sinful but may lead to many grievous sins if we fail to
be watchful. Because of that, Job made a covenant with his eyes not
to pay attention to a virgin (Job 31:1). We will briefly consider these
occasions in more detail, then move on to the opportunities that
strengthen true faith or obedience to faith. We should pay careful
attention to these specific situations that lead to grievous sins:

Rashness and haste in our actions. Many people become unexpectedly entangled in sin when they hastily throw themselves into
some business deal. The deal may not be wrong in itself, yet as
Solomon says, "He that hasteth with his feet sinneth" (Prov. 19:2).
An old adage says, "Look before you leap." Solomon teaches us that
we need to be prepared before we begin building a house. The Lord
Jesus tells us the same thing in Luke 14:28. Much unhappiness and
much sin result from neglecting this principle. Many people expe-

rience this cost every day. Then they complain, "Why didn't I think?" and bewail their state saying, "Look at the mess I am in!" Yet they fail to repent.

Quarrels and disputes between neighbors. Solomon says in Proverbs 17:19, "He loveth transgression that loveth strife: and he that exalteth his gate seeketh destruction." The cause of this is found in Proverbs 17:14: "The beginning of strife is as when one letteth out water: therefore leave off contention, before it be meddled with." Likewise, James cautions, "For where envying and strife is, there is confusion and every evil work" (James 3:16). Experience teaches us that when someone is involved in a dispute, his thoughts become confused and his heart hardens. He begins to notice day by day that he is not as equipped for God's service as he was before, for serving God is an exceedingly sweet and lovely affair and must be practiced with holy hands, not with ones that are occupied with wrath and quarreling (1 Tim. 2:8). A person who practices true godliness should be eager to live peaceably with all men but especially with members of his family. He should always seek after peace (1 Peter 3:8) and be willing to yield his rights in order to maintain peace. When he sincerely does this, he will be strengthened by the grace of God even if he has to occasionally rebuke unreasonable people with whom he cannot agree. Then this will not hurt him (2 Thess. 3:2).

Too much activity. We take on too many things that are difficult to perform or to complete. Whatever the reason we may have for undertaking them, whether it be out of avarice, curiosity, or meddling, this often results in our being ensnared in many sins. We poor men easily entangle ourselves in many sins, the apostle teaches us in 1 Timothy 6:9. Truly, Christ the Lord, who knows us best, has made it clear that overburdening ourselves with temporal things will burden the hearts of worldly people just as much and make them just as unfit for the service of God as drunkenness incapacitates a drunkard (Luke 21:34). You see, we are not gifted with infinite intellectual powers and abilities. When we are fully occupied with one thing, we are not able to take care of or pay attention to something else. When we occupy ourselves with what we do not have to do, inevitably we will neglect those things that we ought to do and should perform with all our strength (Eccles. 9:10). People will fall short in many obligations as they waste their time and strength with trivialities, or at least with tasks the Lord has not asked them to do. Therefore, we should be careful not to foolishly engage in things the Lord God has not called us to do and for which we are not responsible—even if we had never looked at them. Then we will not neglect those things the Lord has given us to do and for which we will have to give an account on the last day.

We ought to carefully note three excellent situations that tend to generate or strengthen true faith in us and which we should take advantage of. These are as follows:

The repentance of a friend or worldly person. At times, the Lord brings a Roman Catholic or Anabaptist to repentance and true faith.[1] Or he casts his holy fear strongly upon a foolish or very worldly person so that this person repents and completely changes and becomes a new creature. We should pay careful attention to such cases, for they may greatly strengthen our faith. We learn from the conversion of Saul (Gal. 1:23–24; 1 Tim. 1:16). We also learn from the Lord's reproach to the high priests and elders of the people. They had seen that the publicans and harlots believed John, but they failed to be convicted of this enough to repent and believe (Matt. 21:23). Does it not strengthen our faith and make us expect God's benefits more now that we have hearts that seek him and when we notice that even those who seem to be the farthest removed from true Christian faith can be brought to repentance by the powerful working of God?

Our own deliverance from difficulty. Another thing that strengthens true faith is remembering how we were delivered in the days of our own impenitence or separation from God. We should remember those times we were in peril because of illness, storms on the sea, or floods on land but were delivered so that we could benefit from them. Those occasions remind us how the Lord our good God has graciously saved us and spared us. He lengthened our days to lead us to repentance in the accepted time and in the day of salvation so that we would receive grace from him and there-

1. Following the Belgic Confession of Faith, Articles 28 and 29, Teellinck regarded both Roman Catholics and Anabaptists as not being members of the true church. Roman Catholics erred in not uniting themselves with the true church, which "all men are in duty bound to join." Anabaptists erred in separating themselves from it, something "no person of whatever state or condition he may be" ought to do. Both acted "contrary to the ordinance of God."

after inherit eternal bliss (2 Cor. 6:2). Could he not just as easily have expelled us from his countenance and cast us into the abyss of hell without any hope of mercy or salvation or grace? The apostle Paul testifies that his own sentence of death served to strengthen his faith (2 Cor. 1:9).

A personal calling to believe. Other situations that generate true faith are those beautiful occasions when we feel a desire in our hearts to believe and an awakened longing to embrace the Lord by faith. This is a beautiful situation for stimulating our faith, of which we should not fail to take advantage. At such times, the Lord comes very close to our hearts. Millions of people will never have this because they either have not heard about the things of Christ or have never had a desire for such things. When God comes near to us, we should lay hold of him in all his mercy and not let go of him until he blesses us with the most precious gift: the precious gift of faith. Clearly, God created a desire in us for it in the first place, so now we may say with the father of the demon-possessed child, "Lord, I believe; help thou mine unbelief" (Mark 9:24).

There are additional beautiful occasions that awaken and quicken us to the obedience of faith. These include:

Times when the Spirit speaks to us. There are occasions when we become especially aware of the thoughts and activities of the Spirit, either while listening to a sermon, or during an illness, in other situations, or perhaps not in any particular situation at all but because of the special prompting of God's good Spirit. You see, when the Lord God awakens good activities in us, he, as it were, breaks into our hearts. He shows us that we should do this or that or act in a certain way. This will surely affect our hearts, for it is like the disturbance of the water at Bethesda (John 5:4). Let us pay attention to this. Let us become aware of the presence of our good God in us and be assured that this power is at hand to take hold of our hearts and wonderfully change them so that they may be healed. When we respond to the prompting of the Spirit, we will make great progress in living a godly life.

Examples of other people's godliness. We should take note of exceptionally good examples of diligence that we occasionally see around us. For example, we may meet a godly person in a house of mourning or at the bedside of a very sick person. Or maybe we interact with someone at a dinner who is extraordinarily diligent and conducts his affairs with a clear indication of the power of the Holy Spirit (1 Cor. 14:24–25). We should take these examples to heart. We should try to benefit from them and warm our cold hearts by them so that we may follow that which is good and so advance the obedience of faith in us (3 John 11).

Occasions of God's judgment or blessing. We may become aware of certain remarkable workings of God in our hearts in blessings or judgments that he brings to pass in our time and in the places we live. For example, we may hear that the Lord God visited the ungodly where they lived, confused them, and destroyed them in a particular way (Luke 13:1–2). We should take this to heart and remember that the same confusion and destruction he brought upon them could happen to us if we fail to repent and make no effort to serve the Lord. We may hear, on the other hand, that the Lord has graciously gone before his little ones (Zech. 13:7), his poor and needy people (Ps. 82:4), saving them from all their troubles and prospering them. We should find such occasions and situations an incentive to seek the Lord and serve him more zealously and diligently, especially when we hear that this has happened to some of our friends (Pss. 32:7; 34:6–7).

A Vigilant Christian Watches the Deceitfulness of His Heart

To keep a good watch, a Christian should be especially vigilant in keeping an eye on himself, lest he transgress in those things we have spoken of. Otherwise, treacherous vermin will arise out of his own bosom that will deceive him and completely ruin him. Let us remind ourselves that a true Christian has two natures: a spiritual nature and a carnal one. These two are constantly at war with each other, seeking to suppress and destroy each other (Gal. 5:17). The Christian should thus be circumspect, since he still has the body of sin and death within him (Rom. 6:6; 7:24). There is no sin so grievous that he may excuse his heart from harboring it. The believer's old nature is capable of theft, adultery, murder, denying Christ— everything that is shameful. The seed of these and all other sins lies in every heart.

If you cannot believe this or will not heed our warning, you are already in great danger of grievously falling. When Christ spoke to Peter, telling him that he would desert him, Peter could not believe it. He said he would rather die than do such a thing. Yet when Peter actually got into that situation, he chose life and denied his Lord (Matthew 26). If anyone had told David when he fled from Saul that he would defile his neighbor's wife and have her husband killed, he would have fought that too. Such ideas would have been so far from him that the mere suggestion of them would have made him very angry (2 Samuel 12). If you want to do better than Peter and David, you must know your own heart better and watch it more vigilantly. Even if you find your heart somewhat tamed, you should trust it little and always think of it as a very evil and sinful nature. A believer should be as leery of his own heart as he would be of dealing with bears, wolves, or lions, which we know are voracious by nature.

All Christians—even those who pay little attention to their spiritual state—know how often they have been deceived by their own hearts (Jer. 17:9; James 1:26). Let us be like the honorable man who closely watches his wife's conduct and tries to keep her out of questionable situations because he is aware of her inclination to be frivolous and capricious and to take every opportunity to flirt.

We should have the attitude toward our own hearts that Solomon advises us to have (Prov. 4:23), for we know how our hearts have deceived and seduced us into collaborating with the world. Solomon tells us that people are most happy who always fear God (Prov. 28:14) and that the person who relies on his own heart is a fool (Prov. 28:26). No one ends up more disappointed than someone who prides himself on his own ability and least suspects his depravity. Experience teaches us that Solomon's proverb holds true, namely, that "a prudent man foreseeth the evil, and hideth himself: but the simple pass on, and are punished" (Prov. 22:3).

There are three things in particular we should pay attention to and prepare ourselves against. These include:

1. Faulty judgment and understanding. We have seen that our own understanding and wisdom is at enmity with God (Rom. 8:7). A great and evil plague resides among the children of men, urging them to follow their own understanding and insights without hes-

itation as if there were nothing wrong with them. Truly, they fail to suspect their minds or wills in eternal matters. Without looking any further, they recklessly follow their own understanding, treating their minds as if they were a Bible and acting according to their own understanding.

A theologian may be truly amazed to see how uneducated people who know they are not very bright are easily deceived by other people in eternal matters. Such simple folk will often tell you, especially when they are in the company of someone clever, that they are ignorant and uneducated and do not trust themselves to deal with important matters without the help of experts as far as temporal matters are concerned—especially when they think the person they are dealing with is more clever than they. They usually ask a person who is knowledgeable in that area to help them and advise them in such matters. Yet theologians would be truly astonished to see how impudent these ordinary people are in following their own understanding and desire in the one area that matters most—their salvation!

They turn a deaf ear when we warn them that the devil is a master deceiver and a nasty rogue who is always bent on deluding them into ruining their souls. They do not listen, even when we try to tell them that they cannot escape Satan's hellish tricks unless they are equipped with and helped by heavenly wisdom and unless they pay close attention to God's Word, which alone reveals the wisdom of God. Although they have been clearly warned against this attitude, they still become ensnared in or confused by all kinds of wrong and damaging doctrine. What is more, they brazenly respond to our warnings by saying, "I am old enough. No one has to tell me what to believe and how to live."

And so, in all these most important matters in which error will cost them eternal life without a reversal, they follow their own understanding and desires. It is amazing to hear what naïve and unsound arguments they come up with to reject the persuasive words of God's servants to make them change their minds. Remember how the idolatrous Israelites rejected the declaration of Jeremiah? They said, "But we will certainly do whatsoever thing goeth forth out of our own mouth, to burn incense unto the queen of heaven, and to pour out drink offerings unto her, as we have done, we, and our fathers, our kings, and our princes, in the cities of Judah, and in the streets of Jerusalem: for then had we plenty of victuals, and were well, and saw no evil. But since we left off to burn incense to the queen of heaven, and to pour out drink offerings unto her, we have wanted all things, and have been consumed by the sword and by the famine. And when we burned incense to the queen of heaven, and poured out drink offerings unto her, did we make her cakes to worship her, and pour out drink offerings unto her, without our men?" (Jer. 44:17–19). These impudent words were supposed to be a convincing argument against the whole plea of Jeremiah, which was so sensible. Solomon foretells the outcome when he says, "There is a way that seemeth right unto a man, but the end thereof are the ways of death" (Prov. 14:12).

Let those who would live lives of true godliness be mindful of the flaws of their own understanding and not overly trust their own judgment. Indeed, they should note how devout, godly people think differently than they do. They should gladly reconsider a matter before they dare to trust and follow their own judgment. They should remember these words of Solomon: "Seest thou a man wise in his own conceit? there is more hope of a fool than of him" (Prov. 26:12).

2. Our natural, sinful desires. We still have to contend with our passions and natural desires. As we have already seen, our hearts by nature want to go the wrong way, as the Israelites of old did (Ps. 95:10). The great and evil plague among people is that they are inclined to follow and yield to their own passions and desires. So a poor man is easily persuaded by his own mind that whatever he wants and tries hard to obtain is good, not wrong. Many are thus blinded and pitifully misled by their emotions.

When Eve desired forbidden fruit, she was soon convinced that the fruit was good for food (Gen. 3:6). This is true of all Eve's children. We should be mindful of this and take careful note of our inclinations and emotions—indeed, of those things to which we are most strongly drawn. We should consider that our nature and constitution are so evil and depraved that we are never drawn without a struggle to do what is right and to resist what is wrong. Thus, when we are strongly drawn to something, no matter how good, holy, and excellent it may appear, we still ought to be suspicious and examine our hearts to see if we are being led by a pure heart. For it is almost certain that if the matter is not right, if it appears to be noble, or even if the matter is without doubt good and heavenly, our motives in the matter may not be pure. We may have a wrong purpose, a worldly plan, or a secret carnal motive that drives us. We should pay attention to this and be on our guard if we wish to escape unscathed and if we truly desire to advance godliness.

3. Our lust for things. Finally, we need to deal with our natural lusts and passion for the things we need to live, which the Lord gives us freedom to choose. For example, in food and drink, marriage, decent and suitable clothing, sleep and relaxation, and other things of this nature, we should take care that we do not use our liberty to give way to the lusts of the flesh (Gal. 5:13). Although we generally have freedom in these things, we can still easily become ensnared in them and begin to backslide in the Christian life. We should be moderate in these things, for it is difficult to live a godly life if we do not discipline ourselves to be on guard against our own lusts and passion.

By nature, we are inclined to lack moderation in these things. Indeed, experience clearly teaches us that the permitted and ordinary things in this life have the extraordinary power to draw us away from loving God and to loving ourselves. If we do not pay attention to this and carelessly use our Christian liberty, we will soon end up being in bondage to ordinary things. We will not be satisfied until we have used them in excess (1 Cor. 6:12). Many people are slaves to their stomachs and backs and daily overindulge in luxury, laziness, and other things. They persist in this even when they are told how wrong this is and what the consequences of it will be and how they should repent of it.

Question: Where is the middle and correct way in these things?
Answer: This would require greater exposition than this space will allow. But briefly, when you notice that your use of ordinary things does not stimulate your heart to serve God but instead pulls you away from serving him, then you are indulging yourself too much in them (Luke 21:34). But when you use the things we mentioned in such a way that you do not become addicted to them, but they help you look to God in gratitude because of the enjoyment they provide so that you become more drawn to his love and ser-

vice and are strengthened in your devotion to God by means of these blessings (Acts 14:17), that, indeed, is a good sign that you have tamed your lust, denied your passion, and have not indulged your flesh.

A Vigilant Christian Wisely Keeps Watch

A vigilant Christian should not only know everything he must guard against and be mindful of his weaknesses but also conduct his watch in a wise and cautious manner. He should do the following three things to be vigilant:

1. Stay alert. As soon as we open our eyes in the morning, we should also open our spiritual eyes and keep them open all day long. You know how it is with those who have been on sentry duty for a long watch; they become weary on their watch and have to struggle hard against sleep, which often seeks to overcome them. Surely, death could be the result if they failed to stir themselves! In the same way, we should continuously rouse ourselves, keeping always in mind that this is no time to sleep, for the devil is stalking us, intent on destroying our souls. We should keep saying to ourselves, "Watch out! The devil is preying on us and stalking us in order to destroy us. Let us be on our guard and keep our eyes open so that we may be saved!" This is how we should motivate ourselves to watch and pray.

2. Watch what is approaching. If we exercise this vigilance, we will be able to clearly discern and detect occasions for good and bad from afar off. This will help us avoid and ward off bad influences and invite and encourage good ones. We will be like watchmen on the wall who are there for that purpose (Ezekiel 33). We know we are safest and best protected against evil when we keep it as far from us as possible and ward it off to keep ourselves from being touched by the evil one. As Scripture says, "We know that whosoever is born of God sinneth not; but he that is begotten of God keepeth himself, and that wicked one toucheth him not" (1 John 5:18). We need to be particularly vigilant from the onset to detect the evil promptings of the flesh and to nip these in the bud before they kill our souls (Isa. 59:2–4; James 1:14). On the other hand, we must care-

fully listen to the softest tapping of the Spirit and welcome his most tender activities and promptings for us to do good. We must be mindful to nurture and maintain these in every respect so that they are not wasted, which of course is what the devil would like (Luke 8:14; Rev. 12:4).

3. Be much in prayer. When he is on sentry duty, the Christian's heart should constantly be lifted to God in prayer. By these prayers—arrows shot directly from earth to heaven—he should make his requests known to God, his heavenly Father, so that he will not be dismayed about anything. We should lift our hearts to God in every situation, about everything we become aware of during our Christian watch, such as when we are moved to joy or sadness, when we detect right as well as wrong activities in ourselves, when something good or bad happens to us, or when we notice a special judgment or blessing of God. We should pray when we start an important task, while we work at it, and when it is finished. These are all situations in which we should watch and pray (Eph. 6:18), lifting our hearts to God and making our desires known to him. We must continually pray that he will lead us into all truth by his Spirit. We should also pray that he will bless us with all the good and beneficial things we need and to strengthen us so that we may use them wisely. And we should ask him to give us the wisdom and discernment to enjoy the spiritual blessings that come to us in them.

We should watch and pray so that we will be edified and, by the right use of the means, reach our true purpose in life and further godliness.

The Christian's Warfare against Every Hindrance

Just as having good rules for living and living according to them so that he may not neglect his watch but perform it well is necessary for a Christian, it is also necessary for him to be a devout fighter. A Christian who discovers that his enemies are trying to hinder him in a certain duty or to entice him to some sin, despite his vigilance, must put up strong resistance.

The necessity of this becomes very clear when we consider the existence of an undivided kingdom of darkness and its objective to hinder us in our godly walk. Clearly, it is nothing other than pure foolishness for a poor, ignorant man to presume that he will go to heaven and work out godliness well if he is making little effort to fight courageously against the devil, the world, and his own flesh. It was not for nothing that Christ the Lord spoke about the kingdom of heaven suffering violence and being taken by force (Matt. 11:12). The piety of those who serve the Lord their God only to the extent that they can serve him with ease, without loss of popularity, without danger, and without a struggle to overcome is worth nothing. Such people will fall away. True godliness is seen in the faithfulness of the godly who serve the Lord their God through trouble and strife, honor and dishonor, and in everything that opposes them. All those who earnestly desire to pursue godliness should begin by counting its cost (Luke 14:28). That is to say, the godly will have to fight long and fiercely to endure and persist in the practice of godliness. They will have to fight as long as they are here on earth, where the devil, the world, and the flesh constantly oppose them.

How this battle should be fought should already be plain from what we said earlier about the nature of the kingdoms of darkness and of grace. However, for the sake of the uninformed, we will explain the nature of the spiritual battle in more detail and deal with the following three things. First, we will show what we should especially concentrate on in our spiritual battle so that we may obtain the victory. Second, we will consider specific things our spiritual enemy uses to entice us. And third, we will look at how to know whether we have done well or failed in our spiritual battle. This is a difficult thing for inexperienced believers and people with tender consciences, for they are often doubtful; indeed, they often come to completely wrong conclusions in this matter. We will move on to discuss these things now, starting with the first one in this section.

In Ephesians 6:10–18, the apostle Paul teaches us specific things we should do in fighting our spiritual battle. We may summarize these in three points: We must be courageous and strong in heart, we must be equipped with good armor, and we must be much in prayer.

Have Courage and a Strong Heart

Regarding the first point, which is to have courage and a strong heart in spiritual battle, the apostle Paul says, "Finally, my brethren, be strong in the Lord, and in the power of his might" (Eph. 6:10). The apostle shows us where to look for our power; certainly not in ourselves but in the Lord (as taught in book 1). He also clearly teaches us in other passages that we must fight like heroes ("quit you like men") and to behave like men in battle (1 Cor. 16:13).

We are told to apply the same principles in spiritual battles as Israel applied in earthly battles when she set about conquering the land of Canaan. The people of Israel who were to occupy the land of Canaan had to fight hard against their enemies. So their officers told them in the name of the Lord, "What man is there that is fearful and fainthearted? let him go and return unto his house" (Deut. 20:8; cf. 1 John 2:14; Rev. 21:7). Having a courageous and fearless heart in fighting is most important in the Lord's battle because it is by means of steadfastness in faith that we oppose the devil (1 Peter 5:9) and overcome the world (1 John 5:4).

Christians should be undismayed and courageous in faith in their spiritual battles. They have very good reasons to be heroic in this battle because of the righteousness of their cause, the enemy whom they fight, and the commander in chief under whom they fight. We will look at this in more detail now, starting with the righteousness of our cause.

1. The righteousness of our cause. All true Christians have good reason to be courageous, for they fight the Lord's battles against the great tyrant and usurper, the devil. Like a pirate or a robber, Satan has no right to anything but tries to get his hooks into everything to rob people of what they have. The Lord himself declared war on Satan immediately after Adam's fall into sin and before he evicted our first parents from paradise (Gen. 3:15). We also know, as Abijah told Israel, that the Lord God of Israel gave the kingdom of Israel to David forever (2 Chron. 13:5). By a covenant of salt, he gave the kingdom to David and his sons and therefore also to Christ his Son. The devil and his cohorts, including many worthless men such as the children of Belial or Absalom, have risen up to disrupt the kingdom (2 Sam. 15:10–12). But the righteousness of our cause should encourage us to heed the exhortation of Joab to be strong for our people and for the cities of God (2 Sam. 10:12), for will God not stand behind his own work and bless those who fight for him?

2. The position of our enemies. They may behave fiercely and cruelly and put on a great show, but if they are what we claim them to be, which is enemies of true Christians, then we know that their power is already broken and their head crushed (Rev. 12:10). All their threats and toil are like the desperate struggle of a bull about to be castrated or like a wolf about to have its throat cut. It is true of our enemies what the Ethiopians said of the Assyrians: They are "a nation scattered and peeled . . . meted out and trodden down" (Isa. 18:2). Their sting has been taken away, their horn pulled out, and their power broken. They have been robbed of their superiority and openly triumphed over (Col. 2:15). Should this not inspire great courage in us? May we not be assured by faith of our victory against enemies who are already crushed?

This applies only to true Christians, however, who live here on earth but whose conversation is with heaven (Phil. 3:19; Rev. 12:11). The great enemy still rules in full force over those who are carnal and earthly minded. A curse is declared on those outside of Christ because of the irresistible advance and success of the enemy. But those who belong to Christ are comforted with the words, "In the world ye shall have tribulation: but be of good cheer; I have overcome the world" (John 16:33).

3. Our commander in chief. Our supreme commander is the Lord Jesus Christ, a wise and strong hero who is able to give counsel and perform it (Prov. 8:14), for he is the wisdom and the power of God (1 Cor. 1:24). He knows every device of the enemy and all his power, but he has already triumphed over all (Col. 2:15). Indeed, the Lord Jesus Christ, who is our commander in chief, our general, captain, and combat leader, is also the author and finisher of our faith (Heb. 12:2).

Knowing that the Lord was their commander gave great courage to Abijah and his people. They were able to say, "But as for us, the LORD is our God, and we have not forsaken him" (2 Chron. 13:10). They also declared, "And, behold, God himself is with us for our captain, and his priests with sounding trumpets to cry alarm against you" (2 Chron. 13:12). Likewise, Christians should be greatly encouraged to know that the Lord has crushed the head of their enemies (Psalm 110). He will go ahead of them in this battle, and he will also be their rear guard to protect them against attack (Isa. 52:12).

Everyone who knows anything about warfare knows well that the greatest power of the troops lies in the ability and courage of their captain and commander in chief. Our commander in chief is the one who sat on the white horse and went forth conquering and to conquer (Rev. 6:2). Should we, therefore, not have courage to fight against our enemies under the direction of such a victorious commander and chief? Every Christian knows well that all enemies are powerless against Christ the Lord (Matt. 21:24). Surely he will lead the hands of those who are on his side to war and their fingers to fight (Ps. 144:1).

Put on the Armor of God

As the apostle Paul tells us in Ephesians 6:11, we must be equipped with strong armor in our spiritual war. He says, "Put on the whole armour of God, that ye may be able to stand against the wiles of the devil." We could say much about the many weapons we have, as the apostle Paul does, but we will limit ourselves here to consider the most important weapon: the Word of God. The Word is like a rich arsenal of God or an ammunition storage facility containing all the necessary equipment an army needs for battle. The Word of God was the weapon Christ used to attack the devil and overcome him (Matt. 4:4f.). David also hid the Word in his heart that he might not sin (Ps. 119:11), which is to say that he might not be overcome by his spiritual enemies. We can say of this weapon as David did of Goliath's sword, "There is none like that; give it me" (1 Sam. 21:9). The Word of the Lord has three aspects or functions that are needed in our spiritual battle. These are as follows:

1. It completely arms a believer. Nothing remains uncovered and nothing is unprotected by this Word. It covers the mind, the memory, the will, the affections, and the desires with a good defense. It also covers the eyes, ears, mouth, heart, hands, feet, knees—indeed, everything. It completely provides every part of the believer with powerful weapons so that the man of God may be perfectly and thoroughly furnished unto all good works (2 Tim. 3:17). Anyone

who sincerely takes the Word of God into his heart will be able to draw and present every kind of spiritual weapon from this Word to resist his spiritual enemy and gain the victory.

2. It uncovers the schemes of the enemy. The Word reveals all the devices of the enemy—every attack, trick, obstruction, method, secret, thought, and plan that he uses with the intent to harm us. It is a phenomenal weapon. It is indeed a tool that dreamers fantasize about, such as the magical shields that enabled heroes to see the plans of their enemies. The mysteries of the kingdom of God, which are diametrical opposites of the devil's secrets, are revealed in the Word of God. It is like a bright light that clearly illuminates the enemy's secret strategies. Like Elisha, who knew beforehand the strategies the king of Syria would undertake against the people of Israel (2 Kings 6:8f.), we also will be able to discover and know every strategy of our spiritual enemy if we listen carefully to the Word of the Lord. Like David, we will become wiser than our enemies (Ps. 119:98).

Everyone knows how important and crucial it is to discover an enemy's plan in warfare. Kings and rulers pay much money to spies and informers to supply them with intelligence about the plans of their enemies.

3. It leads us to victory. Apart from it being a most wonderful, indeed, a wholly godly weapon, the Word of God teaches Christians how to use it and all other weapons to stand in the evil day and emerge victorious over all their enemies. The Word gives Christians good counsel and teaches them how to conduct themselves in every situation. God's Word helps them in all things, no matter how they are attacked, whether they are young or old, whether they have a high position or take orders from others, or whether they are in prosperity or adversity. Whatever situation they are in, whether they are working or eating a meal or are engaged in serving God, his Word will be their aid. As Solomon says, "My son, keep thy father's commandment, and forsake not the law of thy mother: bind them continually upon thine heart, and tie them about thy neck. When thou goest, it shall lead thee; when thou sleepest, it shall keep thee; and when thou awakest, it shall talk with thee" (Prov. 6:20–22).

The Word of God also reveals God's promises to us, encourages us, and shows us how we may obtain God's help and assistance to gain victory. Those who persevere in the spiritual battle and abide in God's Word will in the end be like the young men described by John: "Ye are strong, and the word of God abideth in you, and ye have overcome the wicked one" (1 John 2:14). The foremost cause of Adam's fall was that he neglected to hold fast to the Word of God (Genesis 3). If he had held firmly to God's Word, he might have been able to stand in his innocence through that hour of trial.

We have adequately dealt with the second point. Let us move on to the last.

The Importance of Prayer

It is necessary that the Christian quicken the spirit of prayer and cry out to God in his spiritual battle. The apostle Paul clearly shows this in Ephesians 6:18. It is actually quite natural for man to call out to God in prayer when he is in great danger (Ps. 107:28; Jonah 1:5). We read that King Jehoshaphat cried out to the Lord when he was anxious and in great distress because of his enemies, and the Lord helped him (2 Chron. 18:31). On another occasion, when his enemies seemed too numerous, too great, and too strong for him, King Jehoshaphat cried out to the Lord of heaven for help, saying, "O our God, wilt thou not judge them? for we have no might against this great company that cometh against us; neither know we what to do: but our eyes are upon thee" (2 Chron. 20:12). We also read that our Lord Jesus Christ earnestly prayed when he was in the midst of a fierce struggle (Luke 22:44). He offered up prayers and supplications with strong crying and tears (Heb. 5:7).

When we are in spiritual battle, prayer is an express messenger that swiftly ascends to heaven to present our need to God and bring down the help we need, for the Lord promised, "And call upon me in the day of trouble: I will deliver thee, and thou shalt glorify me" (Ps. 50:15). The psalmist who experienced this help tells us, "In the day when I cried thou answeredst me, and strengthenedst me with strength in my soul" (Ps. 138:3). Thus, the apostle Paul says to the Romans, "Ye strive together with me in your prayers to God for me" (Rom. 15:30).

Note this well: The Lord our wise God gave all creatures, to which he gave life and who require nourishment, an instinctive force to draw to themselves those things that would strengthen them. Man thus has a certain impulse in his stomach that draws him to food to strengthen him. In the same way, the Lord God has provided the soul with such an impulse toward the prayer of faith, by which we may draw the power of the almighty God into our hearts when we need strength in our spiritual battle. By this we will gain the victory (1 Peter 5:9). Our first parents, Adam and Eve, neglected this weapon in their spiritual battle and were ambushed and defeated in Paradise (Genesis 3). Paul, however, applied prayer when he was buffeted by Satan and so won the victory (2 Cor. 12:8–9).

We should thus be fervent and persevere in prayer in our spiritual battle. We always ought to remember to lift our hearts to God and cry out of need by means of quick prayers darted up to God. To receive suitable help from God and to be truly strengthened by him, we should tell God these three things:

1. How strong our enemies are. We should tell God how numerous, fierce, bitter, sneaky, and evil our enemies are. When we are being attacked by them, we should pray to God about the intention of our evil enemies to defeat us and to make us break and violate God's holy commandments and laws. Indeed, these enemies rise like Goliath to scoff at the living God (1 Sam. 17:26). Thus, we should fervently pray to God, beseeching him not to allow these enemies to succeed in performing with their evil hands what they have planned against us in their crafty hearts. We should ask God to fight with us in this battle and affirm his cause and be an enemy unto our enemies and a foe unto our foes (Exod. 23:22).

2. How weak we are. We should confess to God our powerlessness, insignificance, carelessness, slothfulness, and great weakness in confronting our enemies. We should acknowledge our unimportance or nothingness or smallness in order to magnify our great God. Like Asa (2 Chron. 14:11), we must confess and acknowledge that there is no strength in us against the great number of spiritual enemies who plot against us. We are so weak that we do not know what to do. Indeed, we can only look to God, from whence our help comes. We should throw ourselves at the feet of our God

and gladly acknowledge before the whole world that there is no strength in us. Like David, we must acknowledge that our help and power come from the Lord our God alone (1 Sam. 17:45–47).

3. How we may expect help through Christ the Lord. We may expect God's help and assistance in our spiritual battle on the basis of the merits of Christ alone, because of his bitter suffering and death and the glorious victory he has won over his enemies. Let us bring the case to the Lord our God that the cause we are fighting in this battle is also Christ's cause. Have we not become members of Christ the Lord by God's grace? Should we then not fight his battle "and fill up that which is behind of the afflictions of Christ" in our flesh (Col. 1:24)? By faith, we should emphasize this in our prayers so that the Lord our God will not refuse to answer us. Indeed, we know that the Lord our good God is willing to listen to all who ask for something in the name of Christ (John 16:26).

Let us cry out like Daniel in our fiercest battles, saying, "Now therefore, O our God, hear the prayer of thy servant, and his supplications, and cause thy face to shine upon thy sanctuary that is desolate, for the Lord's sake" (Dan. 9:17). If we pray like this, our good God will surely send us relief. He would rather send an angel from heaven to comfort us than leave us in trouble. So our prayer, sent up to heaven, will be like a scourge or whip to our spiritual enemies. It will make them flee in terror, and we will win the victory to our eternal comfort. However, we must pay close attention to the particular transgressions with which our enemy tries to tempt us in our spiritual battle. We will discuss this further in what follows.

Sins That Our Enemies Tempt Us to Commit

Our spiritual enemies are so completely evil that nothing is too evil, gruesome, or sinful for them to invent with which to tempt us. The detestable sins into which our enemies try to seduce us consist mainly of three kinds: pride or arrogance in our attitude toward God's grace, which leads man to commit all kinds of grievous sins against good Christian morals or mores; every kind of blasphemy or sacrilegious thought; and the evil of despair or despondency. We will consider each of these in more detail.

Pride and Presumptuous Arrogance

These detestable sins lead us into every kind of transgression that opposes good Christian morals. For example, they include sensuality with its fruits of flirting, lechery, frivolity, unchaste conversation, silly talk, overindulgence in food and drink, fornication, indecency, prostitution, and anything related to such immorality. They also include greed, love of money, and avarice with its fruits of deceit, false measures, shoddy merchandise, lies, usury, theft, robbery, throwing dice, card playing, and gambling. It includes everything of a dishonest nature: seeking the homage of men, wrong ambition, wrong aspirations, and their consequences, such as self-conceit, pride, vanity, false servility, revenge, envy, jealousy, excess in apparel, notoriety, idle fame, quarreling, fighting, spitefulness, murder, and other ghastly things.

You see, our spiritual enemy seeks to tempt us into these and thousands of other sins of that nature whenever he notices that we have a weakness for or an inclination toward these sins. Our enemies also try to fool us into thinking that it is no big deal to occasionally violate God's law. Be on your guard against such things. To keep from giving in to even one of these temptations from Satan and his allies or falling into any of these sins, we should take care—no matter how strong the provocation may be—not to retaliate with flesh and blood, even though we may be provoked to do so. If we do, it will betray, mislead, and destroy us. And so we should fight and resist in accordance with what the Lord reveals in his Word. We see here that apart from the great importance of prayer, which we have already discussed in a general way, it is especially crucial to involve ourselves in a painstaking study and holy contemplation of what we will discuss in the next three books to help strengthen us against pride. In this, we must be sure to comply with the following three teachings and warnings.

1. Do not consult with the enemy. We should never consult with our spiritual enemies, either to debate the sin we are being tempted to commit or to listen to anything that suggests that it would not be so bad to commit this sin just once. Clearly, we ought to be on our guard against this, just as an honorable young woman refuses to think of letting herself be dishonored. However, a young girl who

rejects a debauched man somewhat halfheartedly encourages him to pursue her even more.

There is not a single good reason for man to dare to sin. The greatest obligation we have is to refrain from sin altogether, were it possible, and to die rather than sin. In truth, sin brings forth death (James 1:15). Eve, the mother of us all, was deceived when she considered the matter that the serpent presented (Genesis 3). For that reason, as soon as we notice that we are being enticed into some sin, we should flatly refuse even to deliberate it and firmly resolve that whatever happens, we will refuse to sin, even if we would be burned for refusing it.

This decision is like a shield against temptation and greatly protects the soul. Daniel used this shield when he "purposed in his heart that he would not defile himself with the portion of the king's meat, nor with the wine which he drank" (Dan. 1:8). Thus, he was delivered. The apostle Peter repeats the same teaching when he says, "Forasmuch then as Christ hath suffered for us in the flesh, arm yourselves likewise with the same mind: for he that hath suffered in the flesh hath ceased from sin" (1 Peter 4:1).

2. Flee from temptation. We must refuse to open our eyes or heart to behold the loveliness, beauty, or pleasantry of lures such as profit, pleasure, or worldly esteem, which sin pretends to promise if we will yield to these temptations. Let us be much on our guard and turn our eyes away from these things. Unless we do, we will be taking burning coals into our bosom and playing with fire (Prov. 6:28).

Our ancestor Eve was led further down the road to ruin when she had the impudence to behold the beauty of the fruit (Gen. 3:6) during her conversation with the serpent about eating the forbidden fruit. This was not the case with Joseph, who did the opposite and so was saved from sinning (Gen. 39:12). Thus, we should not only make a positive effort to flee from the delightful appearance of sin but also, like Joseph, diligently avoid every occasion that may tempt us to commit the sin that entices us. How many foolish young men could have been freed long ago from the object of their foolish infatuation, now a burden to be borne, if they had avoided looking into the face of their temptress at her home, her door, or her window! Solomon counsels us to keep ourselves far from her and not come near the door of her house (Prov. 5:8).

3. Arm yourself with Scripture. Make a habit of having the right Scripture ready to dissuade you from those sins that have the power to entice you. For example, if you are tempted to overindulge in eating and drinking at a festival or a wedding, stop thinking that a wedding is a special day or that your son or daughter only gets married once. Remember Luke 21:34, which says, "Take heed to yourselves, lest at any time your hearts be overcharged with surfeiting, and drunkenness, and cares of this life, and so that day come upon you unawares."

Take care not to let your heart be carried away at a festival or a wedding, not even when your son or daughter gets married and when the sweetness, loveliness, and pleasantry of the occasion strongly tempts you to sin. Think about the bitter taste that sin leaves and of what God's Word reminds us: "What fruit had ye then in those things whereof ye are now ashamed? for the end of those things is death" (Rom. 6:21). Remind yourself that sin may be very sweet to the flesh, but the punishment of sin is very bitter. When you feel strongly tempted, consider that Abraham, the father of believers, chose not to spare his only beloved son in order to serve his God. Seek to walk in his footsteps. Ask yourself, if Abraham would not spare his own son, the son of God's promise, the son who had already given him so much and from whom he could still expect so much that was good, then should I excuse my awful sins when sin promises nothing and threatens only hell and damnation? Did sin ever really profit me, and can I ever expect it not to harm me? Shall I give in to sin instead of holding fast to my God and trying to seek and please him? No!

Remember also what the Word of the Lord says about your end and how you will have to appear before his judgment seat (Heb. 9:27). Does this not strengthen you to fight courageously and gain the victory? Clearly, yes, for when the battle is fiercely fought, remember that you can still be upheld by reflecting on all the incentives you are given for godliness in the Word of the Lord. We will show you these in the next three books, and they may be a great help to you.

Blasphemous and Sacrilegious Thoughts

We move on now to consider the second type of sins that our spiritual enemy uses to entice us in our spiritual battle, which is to accept blasphemous and sacrilegious or, at least, irreverent thoughts. This battle is particularly painful and frightening to the godly in heart, for even the best and the most godly among us are not free from such temptation.

This impertinent spirit, the devil, who had the audacity to tempt Christ the Lord to worship him (Matt. 4:9), will not hesitate to rouse the most detestable and blasphemous thoughts in the minds of godly people. He has the nerve to interfere with the hearts of the godly to test them and see if he can make them doubt the existence of God, the Holy Trinity, the divinity of Christ, the truth of God's Word, the reliability of the gospel, and even God's providence or fairness. Truly, he often seeks to probe all their vices at the same time so that they feel this in their flesh like stings from a hellish monster. He then stirs up such terrible, shameful, filthy, and hellish thoughts and ideas in them regarding God's majesty and the holy things of God that these godly folks are appalled, discouraged, and apt to lose heart when they become aware of them.

The apostle Paul must have experienced something similar when Satan's angel buffeted him and a thorn that severely tormented him appeared in his flesh (2 Cor. 12:7). We cannot imagine how distressed God's children become when they experience these things in their hearts. They feel like they are encountering crafty Satan himself, who boldly confronts them. Every blasphemous thought that rises in their hearts hurts them and pierces them like a hellish fiery arrow through the most tender and noble part of them that they have: their precious and God-loving soul.

We have often seen sensitive young Christians become so extremely distressed in these circumstances that they have almost broken down and succumbed, even though they were normally quite sensible. Clearly, these blasphemous thoughts are like hellish sparks burning in the flesh of the tenderhearted and new believers who do not yet understand God's ways with his children. They dry up their youth and life sap, just like the sun dries up puddles of rain on a hot summer day. These wicked thoughts penetrate, erode, and burn as it were the marrow in their bones so that they become faint-hearted and increasingly weak, languishing until they have to be helped to stand against this and comforted until the day of their restoration.

We will briefly point out three remedies for this affliction. If we apply these remedies well, we will gain the victory in our spiritual battle and find something good in it. However, we will not attempt to analyze in depth here where these blasphemous thoughts come from—whether they come from our own heart and are stirred up by the devil or whether they are put into us by the devil and then stimulated further. Still, it may relieve the distressed in spirit to know that the blasphemous thoughts that torment them may be put in them by Satan and so may be Satan's sins rather than their own. Regardless of where they originate from—whether from Satan or from the old fleshly nature remaining in us—those who carefully follow and apply these three instructions against blasphemous and sacrilegious thoughts will be not only sufficiently strengthened against them but also comforted.

1. Arm yourself with Scripture. A Christian should equip himself as much as possible with appropriate Scripture passages about the nature of the things of God. He should use these verses to fight the blasphemous and profane thoughts that rise from his heart against God's majesty, the Holy Trinity, the certainty of Holy Scripture, the justice of God's providence and decrees, and so on. I repeat, the Christian should arm himself with appropriate verses, which he will find by reading the Scriptures or by hearing and learning them from others by means of catechizing. To battle against filthy, dishonorable, and shameful thoughts about God or the things of God, believers should have ready an armory of appropriate texts from the Holy Scriptures.

For example, Habakkuk 1:13 tells us that our God has such pure eyes that he cannot look upon evil. The Christian should equip himself with such verses and mix them with faith. Then he should hold fast to them and apply them whenever blasphemous thoughts rise in his heart. That was the practice of our Lord Jesus Christ. Christ the Lord attacked Satan with what was written in Scripture, Matthew 4:6 tells us. The Christian should do likewise. Indeed, he should seek to press God's truth on his heart in his fight against such thoughts and hold on to it, taking care not to respond to these blasphemous thoughts or to dwell on how filthy, scandalous, and fearful they are, for these thoughts are the devil's merchandise, and they are very infectious. The more we stir them and the more we are occupied with them, the more they defile us. It is, therefore, wise that a Christian fortifies his heart against and resists blasphemous thoughts as soon as they enter his mind. With a resolute heart and mind, he must wage war on them as something evil, hellish, and demonic. He should firmly keep in mind that one text from Holy Scripture that refutes them or helps the light of his conscience see things better is more effective than a thousand fiery arrows shot by a lying, hellish spirit or that rise from his loathsome depravity.

2. Pray to God for help. When certain blasphemous and sacrilegious thoughts arise, the Christian should immediately lay these before the Lord his God in prayer with holy self-accusations as King Hezekiah did when he spread the letter of Sennacherib before the Lord and prayed against it, beseeching the Lord to deliver him (2 Kings 19:14–19). That was also Paul's practice; he went to God in prayer at least three times when he felt a messenger of Satan stirring up his depravity (2 Cor. 12:7).

Note this well. If a shameless rogue brazenly forces an honorable lady to listen to his disgraceful talk in order to seduce her into being unfaithful to her husband, could she not be easily delivered from him if she immediately tells her husband what this brute intends and wants from her? Just as it is not right for an honorable lady to consider such a filthy overture because her heart opposes, detests, and abhors it, so believers should do the same thing. They are to lay blasphemous thoughts, whether they originate from the devil or from their old nature—which we might label "the devil's oldest son"—before the Lord their God and charge their tormentors before him, saying like King Hezekiah, "LORD, bow down thine ear, and hear: open, LORD, thine eyes, and see: and hear the words of Sennacherib, which hath sent him to reproach the living God" (2 Kings 19:16).

Let them loathe these thoughts to the very abyss of hell, from where they came, and beseech God for grace, on the basis of the pure and spotless merits of our Lord Jesus, for any depravity they may have mixed with it. Let them be satisfied and assured that the grace they have already received is no small thing, which is evident by their sorrow and distress for even the most hidden, corrupt thought. Being saddened and distressed about those things that would never disturb the world and by which we do not have to fear worldly harm or shame actually prove that the fear of God lives in our hearts.

3. Find the source of such blasphemy. Let the Christian who is greatly attacked by blasphemous thoughts also try to halt them by finding out, as much as he can, the root or origin of them. There are many and various sources but mainly these three:

Irreverence and carelessness in serving the Lord our great God. Our God is a consuming fire (Heb. 12:29) who requires us to serve him with reverence and fear. We may have disrespected this and become fearless and insolent toward him. We may treat his holy service as if God were just an ordinary person who does not need to be revered. Perhaps we failed to give much attention to his concerns. If that is the case with us, then be convinced of this: It would be just for God to give us over to our own depravity and to allow Satan to assault us with his schemes. It would be just and right for him to allow us to be attacked by the fiery arrows of sacrilegious thoughts that deprecate the great majesty of our God.

Surely, if we fail to adore our great God because of our inattention, love of ease, carelessness, and irreverence, and, as far as our attitude is concerned, demote and nearly stop worshiping God or treat God as if he were only an idol, is it any wonder that we should be weary with blasphemous thoughts? Is it only right that we who have provoked God and grieved the Spirit by our inattention and indifference should be tormented, wearied, and afflicted in our spirits by Satan's many fierce and fiery arrows? Should we not be attacked in the very things that we purposely exposed ourselves to when we began to doubt whether God really was as glorious and righteous as his Word reveals him to be? Could we doubt his revealed greatness and serve him badly for such a long time as if he were unimportant?

Note this well. We must be on our guard against this cause of blasphemous thoughts. If a Christian wants to be delivered from these assaults and strengthened against these attacks, he should make sure that he serves the Lord his great God and Savior with the greatest reverence. His dedication to the almighty God and adoration of his highest and eternal majesty should be the best he can offer. This will strengthen him greatly against every blasphemous thought that seeks to deprecate our great God.

Depending on worldly things rather than God. We are also attacked by blasphemous thoughts when we care little for the things of the Lord our God but instead become very attached to outward means, relying on them and binding God to them by the feelings of our hearts. This often results in our becoming impudent, foolhardy, and arrogant. We promise ourselves all kinds of blessings, happiness, and prosperity if only we had an abundance of outward resources. We assume that by possessing material things in abundance we will prosper and be happy. Yet all that time we are clearly not right before God or at least no better than what we were when we were not as prosperous and were being kept poor.

Similarly, we may become very fearful and greatly despondent when material things escape us. Yet in reality we are really in as good a relationship with God in these times as in the times when we were outwardly more prosperous. You see, this is how many people react, even true Christians at times. They bind the Lord God to material things, as if he cannot help us when these are lacking but helps only when we have plenty. Is this not making the Lord God Almighty only another pagan idol who neither can help nor harm us (Jer. 10:5; Lam. 3:37)? Surely you must agree that this is what such an attitude promotes.

This is also, under God's righteous providence, a great occasion for blasphemous thoughts against the almighty God. Christians may be sorely attacked by blasphemous thoughts against God's majesty, particularly when they, out of worldliness, have so diminished and limited God in their thoughts and bound him to material things that they feel cheated by him. When they glorify him for his divine providence only as far as they can recognize his hand in providing them with material things, they are easily waylaid by slanderous thoughts against God's majesty, as if he were not an almighty or a righteous God.

The Christian who wants to be delivered for good from blasphemous thoughts or wants to be thoroughly armed against them when they arise should be careful that he does not treat the almighty God like an idol through this kind of behavior. In the fear of the Lord, he should make it his habit to depend not on the means but on the Lord God himself. He should trust God and cling to him in every respect as the almighty God who is not bound to any means either to help or to harm him. It will greatly strengthen him if his thoughts of and meditations on the Lord his God are most reverent and if he immediately resists, loathes, detests, and thereby overcomes any blasphemous thought as soon as he is aware of it or even sees one coming.

Surrendering to errant thoughts. A Christian may become so wrong-minded that he considers himself above being harmed by unchaste, revengeful, egotistic ideas and thoughts. He surrenders to them or enjoys them, even if he does not intend to put them into action. But crafty Satan senses an opening and increasingly feeds those thoughts in order to move the person from thought to action. Even thinking bad thoughts is like giving permission to Satan, who, having received permission, will then take full advantage of it and assault people who have not controlled their vain thoughts. Satan replaces those thoughts with such awful blasphemous urges that these people, who still possess some godly fear, will be exceedingly frightened.

The Holy Spirit allows this for a reason, for it is righteous that the Lord God permits these great terrors into our thoughts when we fail to take our thoughts seriously. We must realize that our thoughts can exact a toll from us and that the Lord God loves truth in the inmost parts of our hearts (Ps. 51:6) to sanctify our thoughts. We learn that God can also frighten and distress us in our hearts. Therefore, it is very essential to sanctify our thoughts before God.

These thoughts are most perilous when a Christian is arrogant and exalts himself and when he despises and belittles others around him. Oh, when a Christian starts trusting in his gifts and imagines that he is better and more important than others, then it is time for a thorn in his flesh and for a messenger of Satan to buffet him! Yes, because of such haughty thoughts, he will be tormented and exercised by troublesome, blasphemous anxieties or with painful bewilderment. We have seen how God dealt with the apostle Paul when he was about to exalt himself through the abundance of revelation (2 Cor. 12:6–9). Whoever wants to be delivered from or strengthened against blasphemous or other terrible thoughts should take care not to succumb to evil thoughts and certainly not to foster haughty and lofty thoughts of himself and his gifts.

We have seen how these aids strengthen the Christian in his spiritual battle to enable him to resist blasphemous or terrible thoughts that may rise up and torment him. We will now consider the third kind of evil with which our enemy afflicts us.

Desperation and Despair

This is the third kind of base sin to which our spiritual enemies try to seduce us in our spiritual battle. A Christian may give up all hope of salvation because of his conviction of sinfulness and his understanding of God's severity against sin as well as his inability to hold fast to Christ the Lord by faith. He grows despondent and begins to despair, as if the door of grace had already been closed to him and the gates of hell were opened wide, with Satan's jaws gaping before him, ready to devour him.

When this temptation and despair fiercely assault the Christian, it is difficult to say how greatly they distress and dishearten him. Truly, from experience we know that dear children of God—often God's dearest children—find themselves in such anguish that they feel as if they were already in hell. They see so clearly the awfulness of their sins and the severity of God against sin. They also feel their inability to help themselves. In their soul, they vividly sense the terrible, unutterable, and unbearable hellish pains and their eternal nature without end. This deeply distresses them and so terrifies their heart that we know of several who had every material possession they could wish for and good physical health who nonetheless languished and broke down under these assaults, like people suffering from tuberculosis.

As Solomon says in Proverbs 18:14, "The spirit of a man will sustain his infirmity; but a wounded spirit who can bear?" All the power of our life lies in our soul. When the soul is afflicted with such a venomous sting as the hellish, tormenting thorn of Satan, we can scarcely imagine how terribly distressed and anxious a person can become.

The devil, that merciless and dishonorable spirit, takes advantage of this poor Christian's extraordinary distress. When the believer is most distressed and anxious, the devil will often speak loudly and impressively to his mind, trying to convince the person by saying, "You are totally lost. You are mine. It will not be long now before I come and take you and drag you into the abyss of hell!" This terrifies the person so much that unless he has the hidden, favorable, restraining power of God within him (though he may not be aware of it or even search for it), he may want to hasten his own death by suicide, or throw himself into the hell and perdition that so terrifies him and which he so fears will be his destiny soon. These anxieties and doubts occur in even the best Christians because of those awful thoughts about a certain sin, as we mentioned.

This condition is aggravated if a person has a natural inclination toward melancholy and depression. If the latter is the case, then it is imperative that we offer the person the assistance of a physician so he may be restored both spiritually and physically. Nonetheless, we will show you some spiritual aids by which true Christians (whom we are addressing here) may be strengthened and helped to gain victory in this great battle. However, when we speak about this matter, we will refrain from any interpretation because that would require another volume to cover this material, which is so exhaustive and weighty. We will briefly consider the most important things concerning these matters, three in particular:

1. The first aid: Realize that this affliction is God's way with his children. The Christian who is distressed should know that God often deals with his children in this way. No temptation will befall a believer but that which is common to man (1 Cor. 10:13). Other true Christians have also experienced these temptations and have been delivered from them. The afflicted person should remember this, reflect on it, and take it to heart so that he will be assured that there is hope for him, seeing how others who were in the same position were delivered and saved from this condition. Truly, many Christians get completely discouraged, lose all hope of salvation, and convince themselves that they are lost at such times because they do not acquaint themselves with God's ways. They fail to realize that sometimes God's way of dealing with his dearest children is to take them by their heels, as it were, and hold them above the opening of hell as if he were about to throw them in. Yet the Lord uses this method for no other purpose than to scare his children away from those practices, ways, and habits that lead them to hell so that he might lead them back to heaven. To confirm this truth

of God and to further explain God's ways with his children, we will take careful notice of the following three things:

Every sin repented of will be forgiven. There is no sin for which man has repented and struggles against and from which he desires to be delivered that is unforgivable. This becomes clear when we consider the following: Christ the Lord, the Savior of the world, emphatically declares that all kinds of sin and blasphemy will be forgiven of men except the sin of blaspheming against the Holy Ghost, which will not be forgiven (Matt. 12:31). Theologians understand (to let other proofs rest for the moment) this blasphemy against the Holy Ghost to mean that the person who commits this sin has become so hardened and callused that he is not able to repent of sin and no longer becomes saddened over it. Indeed, he wants to keep on sinning and does so without the least contrition or hesitation. Whoever is in this condition cannot be brought to repentance and will therefore be forever lost (Heb. 6:4–6).

But if man is so disposed that he hopes and desires to be delivered from his sin and longs to do better if he were able, then he may still repent and be saved. Anyone who doubts his salvation and lies down in despair, so to speak, should remember this. So should those who yearn to be in a better state so that they may fear and love their God, trust in Christ, and be saved. These people may yet be saved and can trust that it might still happen. They should remember that not one word of God is against them, for we know that with God all things are possible and that he is even able to raise up stones to become children of Abraham (Matt. 3:9).

This affliction is brief compared to God's mercy. We need to realize that God deals with his children in such a way that he may seem to forsake them but that is only momentary in comparison with the great weight of eternal glory, for he will truly embrace them with mercy. As the Lord himself says through the prophet Isaiah, "For a small moment have I forsaken thee; but with great mercies will I gather thee. In a little wrath I hid my face from thee for a moment; but with everlasting kindness will I have mercy on thee, saith the LORD thy Redeemer" (Isa. 54:7–8). He speaks earlier through the same prophet, saying, "But Zion said, The LORD hath forsaken me, and my LORD hath forgotten me. Can a woman forget her sucking child, that she should not have compassion on the son of her womb? yea, they may forget, yet will I not forget thee. Behold, I have graven thee upon the palms of my hands; thy walls are continually before me" (Isa. 49:14–16).

Clearly, this shows that when God's children think the Lord has forsaken them, he still thinks of them. He has written their names in the palms of his hands. The Lord sometimes treats his children in the same way that Joseph treated his brothers, whom he knew well even when they did not recognize him. He acted harshly and severely toward them as if he were very much against them, but that was not his real attitude toward them. He meant only to do them good, as we see in Genesis 42–45.

This distress will sanctify them in the end. There are many examples of godly people and dear children of God who were distressed by almost hopeless situations at one time or another, but the Lord still accepted them by grace and sanctified them (Psalms 77; 88; Isaiah 63; 64; Jeremiah 14; 49). We read that such people of God, his dear children, were for a time in such anguish that they lost all hope of ever again finding the grace of God. But this was just what they assumed in their weakness, because their end was very different. In times of deepest distress, the Lord treated them like a mother sometimes treats her child. She may hide for a moment behind a door, but she keeps an eye on her child through the keyhole. She does this so that her child may learn to further appreciate the presence and affection of his mother.

Look at how it was with Christ, who cried out, "My God, my God, why hast thou forsaken me?" (Matt. 27:46). Did it not seem that Christ in his humanity was forsaken of God? Yet all that time he was the only beloved Son of God in whom God was well pleased! So a believer can be in God's favor yet find himself in the greatest possible anguish of conscience.

Still, God has not left us without witnesses, not even in our time and in our church community, for we know that there are many dear children of God in our church who can testify, and others who can confirm it, that at times they have been most fearful and in great doubt. But God delivered them from despair in his own right time. Today, they are encouraged and comforted by God's grace and live joyful, peaceful, and quiet lives in the fear of the Lord. They are also looking forward with great longing and desire to the glorious appearing of their Savior, the Lord Jesus Christ. Let everyone in this sorrowful state take note of these examples and have courage. They will progress to the present blessedness of these people who were delivered from despair if they will only (and this is the second thing they should do) reveal their state and condition to a few experienced Christians or pastors.

2. The second aid: Confide in mature Christians. We will consider another spiritual aid for the strengthening of the Christian who is in distress. It is important that the Christian who is assaulted and tempted in the way previously described make his pitiful and sorrowful state known to some wise, experienced, and godly persons, especially to preachers (James 5:16) who have the tongue of the learned and know how to speak a word in season (Isa. 50:4). They may thus receive counsel and direction in their distress. We must pay close attention to this and never neglect it.

In his craftiness, Satan tries to keep God's beloved children from revealing their distressed state to others. He admonishes them to be silent and deceives them into thinking that people will become suspicious if they hear about their desperate state. He tells them people might think they have a great crime or evil on their conscience and regard them as detestable folk indeed! In this way, Satan tries to make them so ashamed that they keep silent. He keeps pressing them on this until they become thoroughly confused and cannot remain silent any longer. Then they pour their heart out to everyone, usually at the wrong time, as experience has shown us. If they had kept their wits about them and shared this trouble promptly with trusted Christian friends, they might have been comforted without having let everyone else know about their trouble.

Observe, there are three specific benefits for people who expose their pitiful state promptly to wise and experienced people:

An immediate sense of relief. When you make your difficulties known to a faithful friend, you will feel a sense of relief that lifts your weary, crushed, and bruised heart. Note this well, for experience shows us that just talking about our difficulties and anxieties brings some relief. Before doing this, you felt as if you were about to suffocate from the pressing anxieties that attacked you, but you are refreshed just by talking about them.

Elihu says that the spirit constrained him when he was full of words until his belly was like an unopened bottle of wine and he was gasping for air (Job 32:18–20). Just as Elihu found relief by speaking, so godly people often get relief by opening their hearts. No one who seeks deliverance should neglect this.

Comfort and encouragement. After you have revealed your difficulties and anxieties to a godly and faithful friend, this person will offer you comfort, strength, and all the advice he is able to give. Everything he has learned from God's Word and from experience he will gladly offer for your comfort and strength. He will use all the powers of his mind to give you the best counsel and to warn you against the sly ploys and craftiness of Satan. He will talk to you of God's ways with his children and God's eternal mercy and grace. He can disclose the troubles he himself has experienced (James 5:16), which may be just like yours, or give you examples of other honorable and honest people whom he knows have been assaulted in the same way you have but have come through it well.

You will then see and understand that no temptation can overtake you that is not common to man. You can expect a good outcome (1 Cor. 10:13) and may yet say along with David, "The entrance of thy words giveth light; it giveth understanding unto the simple" (Ps. 119:130). Your godly friend will gladly and wisely endure your despondency and your repeated self-accusations. And although he has heard you repeatedly explain your condition, he will not become weary in comforting you again and again—the next day or even the following week—because he is full of compassion for your sorrowful state, which he understands to be one of the most difficult on earth. He knows how to encourage you in your situation and will speak wisdom to you (Jude 24–25). It is easy to understand what great help and strength this brings to someone with a crushed heart. Thus, anyone who seeks comfort for his soul should not wait too long before making his state known to a godly, experienced person.

The faithful prayers of others for you. In confiding your concerns to godly and faithful friends, you will enjoy the privilege of having them pray for you and your concerns, which you find difficult to lay before God in this distraught state. These friends will steadfastly lift up your problems to the Lord your God and beseech him to grant you grace and deliverance (Rom. 15:31).

In a similar way, the paralyzed man in the Bible who was unable to walk to Christ was carried by his friends on a stretcher to the house where Christ was preaching and was laid down before his feet (Mark 2:2–4). We also read in the Scriptures that it was common for the saints to pray for one another but most of all when they knew and heard more about one another's problems and difficulties. Even nature teaches us that when we see someone in great difficulty and cannot help him, we call for assistance. If there is no human assistance available, we call more fervently upon the Lord to take the miserable condition of that man to heart and deliver him. It is difficult to say how precious and how encouraging it is to know that many of God's dearest children are constantly petitioning their heavenly Father for us.

3. The third aid: Keep struggling. The Christian who is under assault should help himself as much as he can in the situation. It is part of man's nature to do his utmost in an emergency to be saved. This principle may appear superfluous, but those who have experienced severe assaults know very well how essential this rule is, for in such a case, a man is like a woman in labor who has no strength left to bring her child into the world. We must encourage the woman to give birth, urging her to help herself or the infant may be lost.

But crafty Satan also involves himself here. We know he is a most devious spirit who steers a situation in such a way that poor man unwittingly takes his side and assists him, distressing his already anguished heart even more with every sad and melancholic thought. No matter what we say and whatever we do to comfort such a person, he immediately disregards our efforts and becomes weighed down even more. The crafty deceiver abuses his mind, turning everything he knows from Scripture and his own life pitifully against him. A poor man in this condition has no stronger opposition than his own mind, heart, and reason.

When we fail to warn a poor man in this spiritual battle, he may go on without the slightest suspicion that Satan could be feeding his mind with serious thoughts and speculations against himself. He may recall everything from the past that burdens him, then apply every severe text in Scripture against himself. He tells himself that he is fighting for God's truth, but in reality his conduct leads him to side thoughtlessly with the crafty deceiver who turns things upside down (Ezek. 13:22). Satan applies every word of comfort to those who live lasciviously. These words are of no use to them, for they do not apply to them. All the while, he uses terrible threats to crush those who are downhearted and despondent because of their sins. They could better listen to Christ's comforting words: "Blessed are they that mourn: for they shall be comforted" (Matt. 5:4).

Anyone with a sad and anguished heart should pay particular attention to this trick of Satan. He should diligently guard himself against Satan's work against his soul to fill him with fearful memories and melancholic, sad thoughts. Instead, he should try to help and encourage himself. To achieve this, he should keep three things in mind:

He should accurately examine himself. A man should accurately and thoroughly examine the state of his conscience according to the law of God. He must do this to be humbled for his sins, not only generally but also for those sins in which he has rested and slumbered for a long time without any concern. We must pay serious attention to this, for our wounded and bruised consciences are like infection in an old dirty wound that cannot be healed unless the pus is squeezed out and the wound cleaned. We can get rid of the infection in our souls only by holy examination, confession, and humble repentance of our sins (cf. Ps. 32:5; 2 Cor. 7:10–11). Indeed, let us conduct our lives as recommended in book 1.

Note this well. Some people may be distressed over their sins, but they keep fiddling with them because their own minds and hearts, when they are disturbed and upset enough, sort of throw up dirty froth and filth. Hence, they constantly and forcefully remember all their old sins. What is more, they see some sins so clearly that it is like they were committing them all over again.

We should not reprimand people like this too much at this point but let them search their hearts and consciences according to God's law. Otherwise, it would be like taking blood from someone with a bad nosebleed who should be treated with scientific skill to stop him from bleeding to death. We should apply this to troubled souls so they might be led into doing things right and come to a godly sorrow and yearning for God on account of their lamentable state rather than just wallowing around in a confused and aimless condition. Though this approach may seem to disturb and distress them even more, they are experiencing the same thing as sick people who have to take a much needed and strong medicine that may initially seem to make them worse before they are cured.

Experience teaches us that those who neglect this and are too quickly comforted with consoling words may appear to have been restored. But, sadly, they are like a wound that has been closed too quickly before healing. The wound will become even more infected and later on will burst open again.

Another result of such treatment is that these people may get beyond feeling. Then they will greedily succumb to sin without feeling sorrowful or disgusted with themselves (Eph. 4:18). We have often noticed how this great haste for deliverance from a troubled conscience has harmed souls because they have not been thoroughly cleansed and patience has not been allowed to do her perfect work (James 1:4). Let everyone who has a troubled conscience examine his condition more seriously in accord with God's law. Take care not only to examine and test yourselves and your earlier conduct but also to try to see what you should do from now on.

Clearly, how we lived in the past does not really affect our enjoyment of comfort and assurance, but it matters very much how we conduct ourselves in the future. The great sinfulness of our past is in the past, so we can be comforted if we earnestly reform our lives from now on and have a sincere and upright heart before the Lord God, who knows us inside out. We may no longer succumb to sin but resist it and practice those holy exercises described in book 1. We might then embrace consolation, for it is written, "Let him that is athirst come. And whosoever will, let him take the water of life freely" (Rev. 22:17). However, if we believe we have lived virtuously in the past and have no intention of repenting of our sin and practicing godliness, then there will be no comfort for us in God's Word. The murderer Manasseh, Levi the tax collector, Saul the persecutor, and the harlots and publicans of Jerusalem could all expect salvation because they wanted to change their lives. By contrast, haughty and sanctimonious hypocrites were without any hope of salvation as long as they failed to change their minds and repent (Matt. 21:31).

If, after having carefully searched his conscience, the Christian discovers that in his heart and mind, he by God's grace intends to walk from now on in God's ways, even though he is deeply melancholy and arms himself against every kind of sin, he may, yes, he must take courage and conclude that the root of the matter is still found in him (Job 19:28). Truly, somewhere, the hidden power of God is still at work in him to affect him this way, for flesh and blood do not teach him this. What is more, the Lord still has thoughts of peace and blessing toward him.

He should open his heart to God's promises. The Christian must try with all his might and by every means to open his heart and lift it up to God to find out, think over, and appropriate all those comforting texts that the Lord God has so richly written down for us in his Word. Those texts are for all who mourn in Zion and for all who sincerely desire to change their lives and seek the Lord in all earnestness, holding fast to him.

Note this well, for much confusion comes to people who do not pay enough attention to God's Word. We have often seen how many good Christian souls were greatly confused by Satan's wiles and their own heedlessness and so passed a long time in an anxious state simply because they did not pay enough attention to the Word of the Lord. We also see all around us people who are reckless, careless, and without zeal for God. With a conceited imagination, they promise themselves everything good—even heaven itself—and boast without any hesitation of their complete assurance of salvation. They are so sure of God's favor toward them that if only two people are saved in a particular place, they think they would certainly be one of them. The reason for this deception is that they have failed to pay sufficient attention to God's Word. They have let the deceiver stuff some comfortable texts of Scripture into their hands that really do not refer to them. They are not eligible for such promised blessings, much less are entitled to share in them. Yet they go on living without paying attention to thousands of other terrifying texts that are more applicable to them and are each more designed for them.

On the other hand, we see many defeated, crushed, and brokenhearted souls who keep on living without any comfort; although they are sincerely sorry for their sins and hunger and thirst after righteousness, they think they are entitled to nothing but hell and damnation. They have been deceived by the liar Satan, who took some frightening texts of Scripture, which never really applied or referred to them, and misled them into thinking that they did. He so convinced them that these were meant for them and applied them to their mind and conscience that they were deceived and became despondent, when those texts never referred to them at all. Meanwhile, Satan hid from their eyes all those pleasant and precious words of comfort as well as positive and definite promises and pledges that the Lord has made to all those who mourn in Zion, that is, to everyone who labors and is heavy laden on account of his sins (Matt. 11:28) and mourns over them, hungering and thirsting after righteousness (Matt. 5:4, 6).

All those anguished souls who honestly and earnestly desire to fight against their sins and walk in the way of the Lord should open their hearts and eyes to pay attention, not only to the threats of the Lord against hardened sinners but also to every comforting and joyful promise offered to those who genuinely desire to fear the name of the Lord (Neh. 1:11; Rev. 22:7). They should make sure they do not sadden their hearts more than the Lord makes them sad (Ezek. 13:22). They must also be careful not to let their hearts, consciences, and minds become heavy or downcast because of unexpected ideas that come into their minds or by wrong ideas that are put there by Satan. They should let themselves be saddened, burdened, quickened, or comforted only by the clear Word of God, well taught and correctly applied, for they will be judged by what the Word of God says (John 12:48), not by the suggestions of their own hearts or minds or of Satan's. Keep this in mind, and it will benefit you greatly in many ways. Indeed, it will deliver and save you from many troublesome and disturbing perplexities.

We have three things to offer from the Word of the Lord to comfort all those with downcast and sorrowful hearts who desire to live righteously and who can testify before God, who knows them inside and out, that they wholeheartedly want to change their lives. They are as follows:

The work of our Redeemer and Savior, Jesus Christ, is sufficient to cover all our sins. God gave his Son to help and comfort us in all the troubles of our souls (Col. 2:10; Heb. 7:25). Truly, Christ is our Redeemer and Savior, given to us by God's great and wonderful grace. Although we are sinful through and through, he is perfectly holy, even holiness itself (1 Cor. 1:30). Through that holiness, we are sanctified and reconciled to God (Col. 1:21). Christ, indeed, has done all things well (Mark 7:37). As we have offended and angered the Lord God to the uttermost by our sins and transgressions, Christ has pleased and satisfied the Lord God to the uttermost by his virtues and goodness. As we have earned death, hell, and damnation with our disobedient and evil lives, Christ has obtained life, heaven, and eternal salvation for all who seek him by his obedience and his bitter suffering and dying (2 Tim. 1:8). All you who are sorrowful in heart should note this well.

God earnestly wants to save and bless lost people through this Redeemer. This earnestness of God is beautifully shown in the following ways. First, God extends the free offer of grace in Christ without distinction to all people who are brokenhearted and truly seek him (Isa. 55:1; Matt. 11:28; Rev. 22:17). The end of those who positively respond to his offer is wonderfully blessed, for no sooner does a person sincerely mourn and repent of his sins than salvation in Christ is immediately given to him. Second, this is such a serious matter that the Lord God himself begs and pleads with lost man to receive Christ in order to be reconciled to God (2 Cor. 5:19). And third, God is so earnest about this that he becomes very angry and terribly offended when someone refuses his invitation to receive forgiveness in Christ (Luke 14:21; Rom. 10:21).

We may, therefore, conclude that the Christian who confesses and mourns his sins is also required to believe that his sins have truly been forgiven through salvation in Christ. He must believe this if he earnestly desires to forsake and strive against his sins. From now on, just as you must not let yourself be led into a grievous sin but must resist it, so you must also resist the sin of despair with the same determination and persistence. And just as earnestly as you now seek to break from sin in order to forsake it and fulfill all your Christian duties, so you must just as earnestly and seriously—indeed, with all your mind and strength—urge your heart and mind to believe and appropriate all of God's promises of the forgiveness of sins given in Christ Jesus to all who mourn. God strongly commands this, and it is most pleasing to him.

Furthermore, the Lord God continues to reach out to poor sinners who live in utter despondency. God does not abandon such defeated ones and allow them to come to complete ruin. While they are still alive they are surrounded by godly people and instructive writings to counsel them and show them the way to salvation. Oh, if we rightly understood these blessings, we would see how many proofs they contain that the Lord God still has thoughts of peace toward us. To encourage our hearts, we would be able to say with Manoah's wife, "If the LORD were pleased to kill us, he would not have . . . shewed us all these things, nor would as at this time have told us such things as these" (Judg. 13:23). The Lord certainly does not want to fulfill the expectations of miserable man himself regarding his eternal death (Ps. 9:18).

We should earnestly reflect on this matter so that we might believe again with all our strength and be assured that, because of Jesus Christ, we will again find grace and mercy with the Lord our God, for he is good and is full of mercy and compassion toward all those who seek him.

The Christian then should wait patiently for the Lord to deliver him. If a man applies and practices all this and is humbled and believes the Lord has forgiven his sins, then he should wait patiently for the Lord to deliver him. He should not be impatient about being delivered. Rather, he should remember how the Lord called him a long time ago and many times invited him to come to him. But he was unrepentant and did not listen to him or follow him right away. He should therefore not consider it strange when God lets him pray to him, call out to him, seek him, and follow after him for some time before he finds any comfort—indeed, even when God seems to have turned a deaf ear to his pleas. He should realize that this is the Lord's way of testing him and teaching him to discover whether he is serious about his salvation and has a sincere desire to cling to him and serve him forever. When he has given God solid evidence of his sincerity, God will give him the crown of comfort and glory (James 1:12). He should also remember the verses in Scripture and the examples we have mentioned that show how the Lord God sometimes hides his face for awhile, even from those toward whom he has special thoughts of peace and whom he wants to embrace with eternal compassion.

Bear this in mind and strengthen your heart with it so that you may be able to hold fast in the evil day, having done all that you could (Eph. 6:13). When you are distressed and anxious, you should imagine that you are living through the travails of rebirth (Hosea 13:13) and that if you persevere in this you will be delivered in the end, according to the Lord's promise, as we mentioned before. You will then forget your anguish (John 16:21). You see, when you consider that you have been conceived and reborn in Christ the Lord, whereas prior to that you were conceived and born into the sin that leads to death (James 1:15), you will not remember your anxieties anymore. Everlasting joy will be on your head; you will obtain "gladness and joy; and sorrow and mourning shall flee away" (Isa. 51:11).

How to Know If We Have Fought Well in Our Spiritual Battle

We have much to say about this, but we will try to keep it brief. In the previous section, we noted three sins in particular that our spiritual enemies try to entice us to commit. These are presumption or pride, blasphemous thoughts, and despondency or despair. We will look once more at all three.

Pride or Presumption

The purpose of these sins is to make us fall into one or more grievous sins that conflict with good morals. We should realize this when the enticement leads to a sin of action that we commit with the body, such as lying, usury, drunkenness, fornication, vanity, excess in dress, slander, cursing, quarreling, haughtiness, or preening self-importance. Obviously, we are quite capable of knowing whether we have committed those sins or not. Thus, we will easily know if the devil has succeeded in gaining victory over us in this temptation. Yet it is not as easy to determine if we have been overcome by presumption and conceit if the loathsome sins that it leads to are not as tangible and nestle deep in our hearts and include such things as greed, lust, or ambition. These sins are rooted in our hearts and so must either reign or be subdued there. Many people think that greed, lust, or ambition do not rule over them when they really do. We can find out whether we have these sins by examining ourselves as follows and asking the following questions:

1. How do our hearts, desires, and wills confront these sins? Do we have a tendency, desire, or inclination to commit the sins of greed, lust, ambition, usury, illicit pleasures, vain aspirations, or

desire for prominence? Do we find some pleasure in these inclinations, or do we defend ourselves against them?

If we like and approve of our hearts' inclinations and want to keep them that way, and if we find that we also like these inclinations in others (Ps. 50:18; Rom. 1:32), then the evil one has certainly gained the victory over us and mastered us, for our own wills consent to these sins. On the other hand, we may have noticed this tendency and inclination but have not taken pleasure in it. We are concerned that we have these faults and want to be free of them. If we want to be different and act differently, then that is a good sign. We feel an inclination toward such sins but do not want to give in to this urge. Clearly, if we truly desire not to succumb to this force and say in our hearts, "We will not ride upon horses" (Hosea 14:3) and "I will no longer do that evil," then this is proof that there is something in us that opposes this evil tendency. It is certainly a good sign to find this opposition, especially if it is accompanied by other signs that we will examine a little closer in the next point, and if this resistance is firm and genuine. Incidentally, servants of sin may also have a weak and feeble aversion to sinning, but they still give way to foolish sins in all kinds of situations.

2. What is the inner activity of our hearts? What else would we do in these circumstances? If we find that we are inclined to greed, lust, or ambition, do we just carry on without avoiding the situation that leads to that sin, without applying the means to withstand it? Do we continue to walk heedlessly and without discipline and without paying attention to what is happening inside our hearts? Surely, if this is our disposition, then we already have been conquered by these sins. These sins have us in their power, for there is no real resistance in us to them. Although some people want to be liberated from certain masters, they will remain their servants as long as they do not apply any means to obtain their liberty from them.

We prove that we are not mastered by avarice, lust, or ambition if we resist them wholeheartedly as soon as we feel an urge toward them and are concerned and troubled about this and carefully avoid situations in which the evil inclination toward them burns fiercer in us. As Jude 23 says, we must hate the garment that is spotted by the flesh. We must close our eyes to the enticements of the world and this life (Job 31:1) and avoid the company who commits such evil and places where such evil is most committed.

We resist this inclination when we use the means that can strengthen us (Ps. 119:11) and when we open our eyes to see the vanity and futility of all worldly things as well as the beauty and glory of heavenly things as we are much in prayer about this. Furthermore, we resist when we plead for God's help, pray about our depravity, beseech God to help us resist these evil temptations, and diligently use God's Word and the means we have mentioned in order to resist these sins. If we continue to act like this, it is a sign we have not been conquered by this inclination to sin and are judiciously resisting the devil. As James 4:7 says, if we resist the devil, he will flee from us. We will thus be victorious over him and bruise him under our feet.

3. What do these temptations lead to? When we have been tempted to give way to greed, lust, or ambition, do these temptations result in our lying, deceiving, or breaking the Sabbath to satisfy our greediness? Do we satisfy our lust for pleasure by drinking and reveling? Do we flatter, bow, and scrape to feed our ambition? If the answer to these questions is yes, then no matter how we argue, clearly sin has overcome us and enslaved us, for we are obeying sin and our inclination toward it (Rom. 6:12).

This is not the case if we resist this inclination and do not succumb to these sins of greed, lust, and ambition. Although we feel a strong tendency and urge to commit these sins, we refuse to lie, deceive, or break the Sabbath. We do not commit usury and chase after worldly profit to satisfy our greed, and we do not succumb to drinking and reveling—to jesting, singing, and dancing, and so on— to cater to our appetites and to give free rein to our lusts. Moreover, we recoil from flattering people and refuse to bow and scrape to them. We are not hypocritical toward those from whom we expect some profit or advancement, and we do not put down people or speak evil of those who stand in the way of our ambitions. Rather, we keep ourselves from all sins and sinful attitudes, no matter how much they beckon us. We deny ourselves dishonest gain and fleshly lusts out of submission to God and reverence for him and because we love and desire to obey his holy commandments. If we do all this, it is a sure sign, a clear proof (even though depravity is still strong in us), that sin does not have the upper hand in us because we do not obey sin and its lusts (Rom. 6:12). Sin is then like a fierce, devouring wolf or bear that would like to devour us but is fastened to a chain and unable to reach us.

Observe, the Christian may determine from these three signs whether he has been overcome by his spiritual temptations to commit these sins of pride and arrogance. We may illustrate this by showing you the picture of a young man in love with a girl who is not a good match for him and would not make him a happy husband. Although the young man clearly sees that marrying her would not be a success, he still cherishes his love for this girl and approves of it to such an extent that he refuses to avoid opportunities that continue to ensnare his heart. If he fails to use every means to withdraw his love from her but takes every opportunity to gain her love, if he constantly seeks her company and talks to her, if he thinks about her all the time and asks her to marry him; and if he sends her presents and gives her the best of whatever he has, who would not conclude that he is overcome by love?

However, if this young man really wants to be released from his foolish infatuation for this girl and would give much to be freed from her and avoids every opportunity that could ensnare his heart, avoids her company, and stays away from the door of her house, if he uses every means to end the relationship and to be liberated from this love and stops giving her proofs of his love but keeps a distance—even though he feels a strong and powerful love for her, cannot immediately let her go, and is not able to stop loving her dearly—because he realizes that marrying her would lead to unhappiness and misery, then we know for certain that this young man is not overcome by a foolish love. Even though he still has strong affection for the girl, he offers evidence that he wants to be delivered from his foolish infatuation and would give everything to be rid of it. He avoids situations that would further ensnare his heart by avoiding her company and the door to her house. And instead of courting this woman and sending her presents, he now shuns her. This shows he has conquered and withstood his passion. We can trust that all will end well for him.

Well now, this is an illustration of how it works with temptations to sin. From the proofs mentioned above, we are able to determine how we must confront temptations to pride and arrogance.

Blasphemous Thoughts

We will now examine blasphemous or other dreadful thoughts and consider how we may determine whether we have succumbed to these temptations. The following three questions will help us decide.

1. How do we deal with such thoughts? If we do not resist these thoughts as soon as they arise within us or we become aware of them but coddle them and let them divert our minds, willfully speculating on them, then we somewhat welcome them and give way to the devil. We let the devil come too close, where he gets the best of us, for we have accepted the devil's wares, and they will inevitably defile us.

On the other hand, our hearts may immediately reject these profane thoughts as soon as they appear and as soon as we get a whiff of them, and we may abhor them just as the Lord Jesus Christ did (Matt. 4:4). Should these thoughts persist in rising again and again and be a complete torment and anguish of soul to us, indeed, if we discover they are a heavy burden and an unbearable weight from which we constantly desire and seek to be delivered, then these blasphemous and detestable thoughts are what they were to Paul (2 Cor. 12:7). They are like buffeting fists of Satan, from which we pray to be delivered as if we were in the claws of a lion or a bear. This is proof that these sins are not of our doing; we have no part in them, and the devil has not gained the upper hand in us.

2. How strong is our resistance to such thoughts? Surely, the evil one has an advantage if we take off our Christian armor, which we should always wear (Eph. 6:14). If we ignore and slight God-given means such as reading and hearing God's Word and praying and if we delay the duties of our daily occupation (many weak Christians are strongly tempted when Satan attacks them, telling them to set aside their religious duties and the duties of their professions), then the evil one has truly deceived and confused us, and we have been hit by his fiery arrows. However, if we keep our whole armor on and use the scriptural means previously mentioned or any others to valiantly resist these thoughts, if we try to strengthen ourselves with God's Word, if we pray much and call upon God for help, as Paul

232 The Path of True Godliness

did in 2 Corinthians 12:9, then it may still be well with us. We will gain the victory if we persevere and withstand the devil, for the Lord God has made it abundantly clear that if we resist the devil, he will flee from us (James 4:7).

3. How are we daily conducting ourselves in word and deed? When we are assaulted by blasphemous or sacrilegious thoughts that greatly increase and form seeds of blasphemous words and works in us, then the devil has gained too much ground. Truly, he has won the victory and has caught us alive in his snare (2 Tim. 2:26).

On the other hand, it is a good and sure proof that the devil is not able to stand up against us and oppose us, indeed, that we have won the victory over him when we constantly fight against these evil thoughts even when our heads and minds are still full of them and they often arise in our hearts. Moreover, when we sprinkle the words of our mouths with salt and do not spew out blasphemous words and when we guard ourselves against offensive and ungodly works and enterprises that slander the name of God, then we behave in an edifying and Christian way in word and deed (2 Thess. 2:17). We become more diligent with a holy concern and vigilance about what we say and do because of these blasphemous thoughts inside us so that we honor God and magnify his name as much as we are able to.

The following illustration of a young woman who is tempted to indecency by a rogue may help us understand this better. She cannot help it that this ungodly person unexpectedly whispers grossly indecent words into her ear. However, these words immediately create a picture of the actions in her mind. We see that the heart of the maiden immediately rejects these suggestions and is disgusted by them. She continues to resist them even when these words are repeated. She runs as fast as she can to her friends to complain about her predicament. She is so troubled that she immediately decides never to wear anything that may offer suggestions of impropriety on her part. In all of these actions, we can plainly see that she in no way cooperates with the evil suggestions of the immoral man.

On the other hand, she may take pleasure in this man's suggestions, allowing them to enter her mind and offering no resistance to them. She may even show signs of accepting his suggestions; although she outwardly remains moral, inwardly she entertains thoughts of promiscuity and unchasteness as a result of being tempted by his suggestions. That is a sure sign that she may soon capitulate and fall outwardly into sin. Likewise, the Christian who has no pleasure in a temptation but resists it and endeavors to practice the opposite still has not been overcome.

Despair and Despondency

In regard to the sin of despair and despondency, we will be able to determine whether we have been overcome in such by the signs we presented earlier. But for good measure, we will offer more applicable advice about this temptation, specifically three questions we should ask ourselves.

1. What is our hope regarding eternal salvation? Do we have so little hope of eternal salvation and joy that it would seem beneficial if a sorcerer or witch could have our souls pledged to perdition on the condition that we could have everything we wanted during our life here on earth? Is our hope of eternity so small that we would trade it for the temporal pleasure of sin? Could we say with the ungodly, "Let us eat and drink; for tomorrow we shall die" (Isa. 22:13)? If so, then surely we are in a pitiful and desperate state. Indeed, if we do not attend to this immediately and take great care, our portion will be eternal separation from the presence of the Lord.

Now, this is not the case if we do not give up all hope of being saved and being sanctified, not for all the wealth in the world, even if our hearts are full of confusing, sorrowful, melancholic considerations and thoughts. Do we still occasionally have vivid thoughts that show clearly how wonderful it must be to be saved? Do we still desire and seek eternal life with the hope that the Lord may still save us and that the future may yet bring a change for the better? If so, this is a good sign that our state is not totally hopeless.

2. What is our hope regarding Christ the Lord? Our situation is lamentable indeed if we feel in some measure the sorrow and awfulness of our sins and our condemned state but fail to most highly esteem Christ the Lord. If Jesus is not precious to us, we fail to value

him and refuse to seek him and pay attention to him. Instead, we drift along, seeking to expel our melancholy thoughts with cheerful company or something else. Like Judas (Matthew 27), we choose the noose rather than seek Christ. We should immediately seek better counsel, or it will not be well with us. Indeed, we should make use of the means shown in the previous section, or it will go very badly for us.

On the other hand, it is a good sign if we know our pitiful, miserable, sinful, damnable, condemned, and accursed state, and we look to the all-sufficiency of Jesus Christ. If we esteem him highly, seeing him as precious and honorable, then we know we would rather partake of Christ's merits than rule over the whole world. If we could have our hearts' desire, we would choose Christ the Lord above all that is esteemed precious, valuable, and most desirable in the world. You see, when Christ the Lord is precious in our eyes, then we have not been completely overcome by despair and unbelief. However desperate our situation may seem to us, we still have the root of the matter within us (Job 19:28). Clearly, we are believers who regard the stone that the builders rejected as precious in our eyes (1 Peter 2:7).

3. What is our hope regarding the use of the means? It is a bad sign if we find ourselves in this sinful, damned, and condemned state and are so assaulted in our minds and consciences to despair and hopelessness that we throw off all defensive weapons. It is a bad sign if hopelessness and neglect have made us indifferent to all the means that God has offered and presented to men for their salvation. It is a bad sign if we no longer pay attention to the Word of God, no longer pray or go to church, no longer meet with the godly, and no longer complain to them about our dilemma or ask for their help and counsel. Surely, it is a bad sign when they come to us to encourage us to resume our holy duties, and we answer them as the Israelites answered the prophet, saying, "If our transgressions and our sins be upon us, and we pine away in them, how should we then live?" (Ezek. 33:10). Clearly, it is not a good sign if we no longer take counsel from the men of God. Oh, what a bad sign it is when Satan has come so close to us that we are about to be defeated by despair and desperation.

However, even though our hearts and consciences are full of despair and hopeless questions, thoughts, and anxieties, it is a good sign that we have not yet been defeated by these temptations if we still subject ourselves to the Word of God. Even if our hearts and minds are full of comfortless and hopeless considerations, thoughts, and concerns, and we have no hunger for God's Word, the Lord's Supper, or meeting and having fellowship with believers, it is a hopeful sign if we still submit to the Word of God. It is a good sign—even though we have no desire for prayer or any other holy and spiritual exercise, no relish for anything that is of Christ or of God—that despite all this we still participate in the Word of God, attend the Lord's Supper, meet with other believers, have fellowship with the godly, give ourselves to prayer and all kinds of holy exercises and to everything that is of God and of Christ.

I repeat, doing all this is an excellent and beautiful sign that we still have not succumbed to Satan's assault, yes, that there is still a mighty strong and godly power from on high within us that resists our flesh and the devil, despite our weaknesses, enabling us to deny ourselves and consecrate ourselves to God. It may not be a holy, living, pleasing sacrifice in our eyes, but it is still a sacrifice that we can present and offer to God. This shows us very plainly that greater is he that is in us than he who is in the world (1 John 4:4). We should be encouraged by this. As long as we hold on to our armor in this way, as long as we still use and apply the means to resist, as long as we keep confronting our enemies and put up a defense, we show signs that we are not defeated, no matter how desperate and hopeless our situation may seem in our eyes.

This last point can be clearly illustrated by the following. When a soldier in battle throws away his weapons, falls on his knees, folds his hands, and prays for mercy, this is indisputable evidence that he has been defeated. However, as long as the soldier stands firm and puts up a good defense, holding on to his weapons and making an effort to stab, fight, and struggle, he has not been defeated. He may be covered in blood from many great and horrible wounds, he may have been knocked down and trodden underfoot by his opponent, but he has not yet been defeated. A change in his situation is still possible. Often, such a soldier, by encouraging himself and making a great effort, gives his enemy a final deathblow and so becomes the conqueror.

It is the same with us in the spiritual battle. We have not been defeated until we no longer resist. As long as we hold on to our spiritual weapons, using the means to deliverance and resisting our enemy, then we are not defeated. Truly, we then confidently hope that our spiritual enemy will have to flee and that we will obtain victory over him (Eph. 6:14; James 4:7).

We have now considered the proofs and signs whereby we may determine whether we are still in the process of conquering or have already been conquered by our sins.

Let me answer a final question: What if a poor Christian has already been crushed and defeated? He really is in a wretched state. But there is still hope, as Shechaniah testifies in Ezra 10:3, for restoration and reconciliation can still be found in Jesus Christ our Lord (1 John 2:1), whose blood cleanses us from all sin (1 John 1:7). As long as we do not remain in the sin in which we are entangled but get up and amend our lives, we may still find reconciliation (Ezek. 33:10–11; Isa. 1:16–18). The Christian, therefore, should diligently apply the three duties discussed in book 1 so that he may still be helped.

BOOK
7

Motives to Practice Godliness Derived from God's Attributes

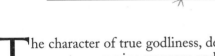

The character of true godliness, described in book 1, should prompt an amazing response and love in the hearts of men. But even if he could see the true beauty of godliness with the physical eye, man is so ungodly by nature that he has neither the desire nor the will to practice true godliness. Even God's true children are often lukewarm and slow in practicing godliness. Because of the interference of worldly things and the spiritual enemy's tricks, they are so distracted that they become quite careless in their practice of godliness. They then omit or fail to maintain the study and contemplation of Scripture, which motivate them to godliness. We will consider some of these motives toward godliness and show that the most important ones are derived from the attributes of the Lord our God, whom we should serve in holiness. Others are derived from our own disposition, and still others from the nature of other related things that should motivate us to practice godliness.

Motives for Godliness: The Attributes of God

We will start this book with the attributes of the Lord our Tri-une God, who is Father, Son, and Holy Spirit. Concerning the person of the Father, or the Lord God, we should generally observe God's wisdom, power, and goodness. We will begin by discussing God's wisdom as a motive for true godliness.

God's Wisdom

Well now, Christian, whoever you may be, when you find yourself slow to practice true godliness and failing to order your life in accordance with the Lord's will, you must give serious thought to the nature of your God, for the Lord God, whom you seek, calls you to walk in godliness. Is the Lord God, whom we encourage you to serve by regulating your life according to his Word, not the wisest one, the adviser who can give you the best counsel (Prov. 8:14)? Did he not give his people his beloved Word, in which his great wisdom is revealed as well as the path that you must follow (1 Cor. 2:7; Gal. 6:16)? Shall we Christians continue as if God the Lord does not care more for us than for pagans (Ps. 147:19–20)? Should we, to whom godly wisdom has been revealed so that we should live in holiness, continue to conduct our affairs without restraint? Should we not rather choose to live in accordance with the beneficial standards prescribed in God's Word? Do we acknowledge God's book, the Holy Bible, which contains the best rules ever given for living, so that we may live accordingly? Would we then still follow other rules, such as those of the world, of our own minds, or of the lusts of the flesh?

1. The danger of following our own wisdom. Surely, we know that all the slyness of the devil's schemes and of his hellish, demonic advisers is actively working against us in order to deceive, mislead, and bring about our eternal ruin (Gen. 3:1–5; Rev. 12:9). Why then should we follow our own wisdom when we know it leads us in the wrong direction? Have we failed to see that we will be lost if we do not heed God's wisdom as revealed in his Word and neglect to follow it?

2. The foolishness of following the wisdom of others. If students of men such as Pythagoras or Epictetus obey the words and lec-

tures of their masters, who were only frail men, and faithfully accept them and diligently observe them, why should Christians pay no attention to the doctrine of Christ and the wisdom of our almighty God as revealed to us in Holy Scriptures? What could be more foolish than ignoring God's wisdom?

3. The folly of ignoring God's wisdom. The Lord God, in his righteous judgment, will give those who do not wholeheartedly and, out of love, accept his wisdom and truth over to strong delusions so they will believe the lies and be damned, for does God not reveal his wisdom and truth with tremendous grace in his Word in order to help men work toward true godliness? Clearly, a great and severe condemnation awaits many so-called Christians who have regarded the wisdom, counsel, and will of God, faithfully made known in his Word to show them how to live godly lives, as a strange doctrine (2 Thess. 2:10–12). This will bring eternal damnation to many who pretend to be Christians but who have regarded God's wisdom and intent for the way of salvation as if they were only strange opinions (Hosea 8:12; John 15:22). Instead of following God's counsel and instruction, they have made their own opinions or that of the world their rule and guide in life. Let all who are courageous sincerely consider this, and whoever is wise, use that wisdom!

God's Omnipotence

Is not the Lord God, to whose service we invite you, the almighty God? Does he not hold your life and your death in his hand (Deut. 32:39)? Is he not able to raise you into heaven's glory or throw you into hell's abyss (Matt. 10:28)? Should you then not embrace the Lord, gladly extend your hand to him, and perform all your affairs according to his will and instruction, as true godliness teaches you, so that you might enjoy his blessings upon it? Let us consider the following:

1. God's final control. Is not the power of this almighty God so great that even if you were to suffer the greatest possible distress for his sake and cause, yes, even if you were to be thrown into hell for carrying out his will, the flames of hell would not set you on fire (Isa. 43:1–2)? This is clear from the example of the three godly men

who allowed themselves to be thrown into a fiery furnace rather than disobey God's will (Dan. 3:17).

2. God's final judgment. Furthermore, even if you had obtained an earthly paradise by serving the world, even then the omnipotent God could make this world a hell, for we have seen how paradise became a hell, as it were, for Adam and Eve after they made almighty God their opponent. God turned Eden against them so severely that they could no longer be happy or remain there, and they tried to hide themselves among the trees (Gen. 3:8).

3. God's final grace. Finally, everything depends on God; therefore, all your toiling and fretting will not help you obtain or win anything in the world unless God gives it to you (Ps. 127:1–3). How then can we not fear and revere the almighty, all powerful Lord, who is able to save and to destroy us (James 4:12)? Indeed, should we not serve him above all, as true godliness teaches us?

God's Loving-Kindness

Is not the Lord God, to whose service we invite you, also the most compassionate one? Surely, he is completely and solely good (Luke 18:19)! Therefore, should we not trust that his laws and ordinances, indeed, all his commandments that he gives as a rule of life, will serve for our own good (Ps. 19:11)? If you doubt this, pay attention to the following:

1. God's great sacrifice. Has the Lord God not given comprehensive proof of his heartfelt compassion and love to us in what he has done to save us from death (Rom. 8:32; Titus 3:4–5)? How could we imagine—as do the ungodly who reject God's commandments and follow their own understanding or the customs of the world—that he, who gave up his Son to save us eternally, would give us commandments that would destroy us?

2. God's loving directives. If you examine God's directives a little closer, you will see how even the sternest of God's commandments are intended for our own good. If he demands that we deny ourselves for a while, it is so that we might enjoy him forever (John 21:22). If

he asks us to humble ourselves, it is so that he may one day exalt us (James 4:6). If he commands us to give up our sinful pleasures and indulgences, it is so that we might receive eternal joy (Mark 10:30). If he commands us to pluck out or cut off an offensive eye or hand, it is so that we might not sink into the fires of hell with both eyes, both hands—indeed, with both soul and body (Mark 9:43).

That is exactly how it is with the sternest commandments of God, for they are all intended to serve our good. Is it then not reasonable to think that every other commandment of our God, without exception, is also for our good? Should we then not delight in practicing all of them, as true godliness teaches us? Do we not seek our well-being above everything else? Clearly, God's counsel, most of all, serves our well-being. We thus will never be better off or happier than when we follow the will of our omniscient, almighty, and good God. Why should we not do so immediately?

3. God's great compassion. Is it not also true that the Lord God, according to his eternal and inexpressible loving-kindness, was long-suffering toward us in the days of our rebellion and ignorance, when we daily taunted him and defied him with our sins and transgressions (Acts 17:30)? If it were not for God's compassion, we would have been totally consumed a long time ago (Lam. 3:22). The only reason we were not thrown into the abyss of hell (which our sins earned a thousand times over) but were spared to live in the land of the living was that God wanted us to lament over our sins and repent of them, seek him, and devoutly serve him. Is this not, in every respect, due to the loving-kindness of God?

Have we not had enough of following after the heathen's will, walking in lasciviousness, lusts, and passions? Have we not had enough of wallowing in our sins for so long, satisfying our carnal, pagan wills by living for our pleasures and satisfying our fleshly desires (1 Peter 4)? We should then gladly serve our good and long-suffering God, who, out of his steadfast love, daily invites us so kindly to repent (Rom. 2:4). Surely, we should no longer live according to the lusts of men but according to God's will (1 Peter 4:3), for if we do not let the loving-kindness of God win us over to true repentance and the practice of godliness, we will rightfully treasure up wrath for ourselves in the day of God's righteous judgment (Rom. 2:5).

Motives for Godliness: The Son of God

Beloved Christians, if you are still unmoved by the preceding discussions as to why you should practice godliness, then give further thought to the person of the Son of God, our Lord Jesus Christ: his incarnation, his example of godly living, and his friendly and kind invitation to practice godliness.

The Incarnation

Did not the Son of God, who is truly God and who should be forever praised, become a man so that you might become a child of God (Gal. 4:4)? Should you then continue on as a worldly person, living heedlessly as is the custom of the world instead of walking according to God's will? Consider the following three regarding this point:

1. Why did God's Son become flesh and blood? Did Christ not become a partaker of our human nature (Heb. 2:11) so that you might partake of his divine nature (2 Peter 1:4)? Should you then not make an effort to express this divine nature through Christian conduct? You will do this when you practice true godliness.

2. Did the Son of God become a servant? He did (Phil. 2:7) so that you might be freed from bondage by the Lord (John 8:36; 1 Cor. 7:22). Should you then not unshackle yourself gladly from the bondage of sin in order to serve the Lord from now on by practicing true godliness?

3. Was Christ obedient to his Father unto death? Yes, he was obedient even to the accursed death on the cross (Phil. 2:8) to deliver us from death and enable us to walk in newness of life (Rom. 6:4). Should we then not exert ourselves and strive to be obedient throughout our lives?

Since the Son of God became man and died a cursed death for us, should we then not live a blessed Christian life for him? What kind of Christians are we if we fail to live up to this? Did not Christ the Lord give himself up and bear our sins in his own body on the tree so that we, being dead to sin, might live unto righteousness?

Did he not do that to purify unto himself a peculiar people, zealous of good works (Titus 2:14)? Should we then not take care, as much as we are able, that the design and the purpose of his suffering do not fail? Should we not in all earnestness strive to die to sin and live unto righteousness (1 Peter 2:24; Titus 2:14)? Should we not do all that we can so that his intention and purpose are not in vain in our lives? Surely, this should inspire us to true godliness! We are truly miserable Christians if we do not do this for the Son of God, Christ our Lord, who has done so much and suffered so much for us.

The Example of Our Lord Jesus Christ

Is it not true that the Son of God has left us an example of a godly life so that we should follow in his steps (1 Peter 2:21), become his followers (1 Cor. 1:9), and do as he has done (John 13:15)? Has the only beloved Son of the mighty God not shown us how to live according to his example so that we might live blessedly with him in eternity? Should we Christians not be diligent in practicing true godliness? Surely, we should manifest the life of our Lord Jesus Christ in our mortal flesh (2 Cor. 4:10f.) according to the following:

1. His perfect example. Clearly, we have a perfect and infallible example of godliness in Christ's actions and walk in ordinary, daily activities and work. As long as we continue to follow the direction shown by the Lord and follow his actions and daily walk, we will not fall or turn from the right path. Any examples of other godly persons might mislead us. That is why the apostle Paul urges us not to be followers of him except in how he follows Christ (1 Cor. 11:1). The example of Christ is infallible. He has done all things well (Mark 7:37). All of us should therefore try to follow Christ the Lord and his precepts as much as possible, even to the letter, and so practice true godliness. Christ has set us an example in everything. We are to follow that!

2. His strengthening power. The perfect and infallible example of God's Son, our Lord Jesus Christ, has the special power to help and strengthen all those who follow it and are willing to work toward shaping their lives and actions by it. This power enables them to do this and to succeed in it. Other good examples show us what we ought to do, but they have no power to strengthen those who follow them and

to enable them to follow their examples. But the example of the Lord Jesus Christ has a marvelous, powerful quality that enables all who sincerely apply themselves to following it to succeed in some measure (2 Cor. 3:18). Should we then not gladly follow such a perfect and powerful example of Christian living in practicing true godliness?

3. His transforming person. The example of God's Son, our Lord Jesus Christ, has yet another distinct quality. All who faithfully seek to follow his example, as we have shown, not only have a perfect example to direct them and to strengthen them but also gradually become conformed to the life of Christ. As they are conformed, they will also partake in some measure of the life of Christ. This is what is meant when we are told that those who follow Christ will be made kings and priests of the almighty God, just as Christ is in the highest degree (2 Cor. 3:18; Rev. 1:5–6).

Consider if that were true of an earthly, mortal king. Those who conducted themselves like him and sought to follow his example would then share in the king's splendor and status. Would we not find all kinds of courtiers everywhere who would be following the examples of Alexander the Great and other world rulers like him to the smallest detail? This is not possible with earthly kings; however, it is the case with Christ the Lord, King of kings and Lord of glory. Everyone who follows Christ in his life and actions will be changed into his image from glory unto glory. Should we then not do our utmost to follow the Lord Jesus Christ in the practice of godliness?

The Kind Invitation of the Son of God

The Lord gently calls us to come to him and graciously invites us to bear his yoke so that we may find rest for our souls (Matt. 11:28–30). Does he not counsel us through his messengers and servants, with tears in their eyes and pleas in their mouth, to deny ourselves and follow him for our eternal comfort (Matt. 16:24)? Indeed, on the basis of his bitter suffering, bleeding wounds, and awful death, does he not beseech us to no longer grieve his Spirit by our worldly mindedness but refresh and quicken his Spirit by practicing godliness instead?

Should the mighty God and Savior, Jesus Christ, who has borne the cross of the cursed tree, so earnestly invite us to carry an easy yoke for him while we, who profess to be Christians and call him our dear Lord, refuse him and continue to live wild, wanton, and unrestrained lives, without yoke or bond? Should we continue like pagans, breaking his bonds, casting off his yoke, and refusing to take it upon ourselves (Ps. 2:3)? Do we prefer to live according to our own understanding and insight rather than according to the demands of our Savior? Is that in harmony with our supposed Christian faith?

Should Jesus, who created our hearts and who wants to save us and fill us with every heavenly treasure, come to us and knock on our hearts with kind invitations (Rev. 3:20), will we not let him in and trust him to govern our hearts?

Furthermore, if Jesus should seek us and quicken us to true godliness in order to bless us, would we not accept that instead of being righteously cast away to eternal damnation, which he could still justly do even when we decided to seek him, saying, "Lord, Lord" (Matt. 7:21)? Is it not much better for us to accept Jesus' kind call and invitation, take his hand, and follow him where he wants us to go in accordance with his Word by practicing godliness?

Motives for Godliness: The Promises of the Holy Spirit

A New Heart

Because your dull heart is not fit to earnestly practice true godliness, you may say that these things are all very well, but living the Christian life is very difficult for the flesh, so you cannot make a decision yet. If so, let us consider the promises of the Holy Spirit (Eph. 1:13), earnestly reflecting on the three things promised to us when we diligently try to practice godliness. We are promised a new heart to enable us to practice godliness well, merciful consideration of our weakness in the practice of godliness, and the grace toward our sincere practice of godliness. We will discuss all three, beginning with the first promise.

The Holy Spirit promises to give you a new heart and a new spirit when you sincerely decide to practice godliness. This helps you develop a stronger desire and more power to walk in God's ways, to keep his commandments, and to act in accordance with them (2 Chron. 16:9; Ezek. 36:25f.).

When your heart has been renewed thus, you will not find it as difficult to practice godliness. Yet you must be on your guard against the remarkable craftiness of the devil at this point, for he keeps many people from paying attention to godliness. He hides the great loving-kindness of the Lord from them and has them believe that they must perform God's spiritual work with the depraved fleshly heart they have by nature. Therefore, it seems impossible for them ever to delight in serving God. It seems more like death to them when they think about it.

Actually, the situation is completely different because the Holy Spirit gives us more grace (James 4:6). Indeed, the loving-kindness of the Lord is so great that as soon as someone decides, by God's grace and in all sincerity, to engage in God's service, then the Lord himself determines to strengthen this person by his Holy Spirit. "For the eyes of the LORD run to and fro throughout the whole earth, to shew himself strong on the behalf of them whose heart is perfect toward him" (2 Chron. 16:9). He helps us carry the yoke, feeds us, and draws us with the cords of love (Hosea 11:3f.). Indeed, "He giveth power to the faint; and to them that have no might he increaseth strength. . . . But they that wait upon the LORD shall renew their strength; they shall mount up with wings as eagles; they shall run, and not be weary; and they shall walk, and not faint" (Isa. 40:29, 31). Is anything then too hard for us? However difficult it may be to serve God in our depraved flesh, the Lord God promises to stretch out his helping arm to us. He makes his yoke easy and his burden light (Matt. 11:30). Why should I be bothered if someone gives me either a ten-pound or a thousand-pound weight to carry when that person also gives me the power to carry both ten pounds and one thousand pounds?

When the Holy Spirit has renewed our hearts thus, then our formerly reluctant hearts will become flowing fountains of all kinds of new and good thoughts, affections, words, and works, for, as Solomon says, out of the heart are the issues of life (Prov. 4:23). As the fountain of our heart is, so will be the stream of all our actions and duties. Before its renewal, the heart was like an evil, poisonous fountain that spewed forth only what was evil. We continuously committed sin from the evil store of our hearts to our greater damnation. Now that they have been renewed by the grace of the Holy Spirit, our hearts will bring forth all kinds of good and holy activities, bringing us assurance (Matt. 12:34–37). Should we then not be zealous in the service of our God, thereby obtaining more and more a renewed heart, to our comfort? We must remember that this same heart, when left to itself, will give us many troubles and sinful urges (Ps. 81:12; Rom. 1:26) and will bring us to ruin.

Moreover, when our hearts are renewed and established in the fear of the Lord, we will persevere in God's service. Many people who at one time made a great show of godliness may not only lose their first love in the course of time but also completely forsake the Lord their God. That is because they never received a renewed heart. Their words, works, and outward behavior may have improved and reformed, but their hearts remained the same. And just like fruit that is bad inside rots quickly, so it goes with people who have only outwardly reformed but lack a renewed heart.

The psalmist says of those who make a great outward show of repentance but turn away like a deceitful bow when they are really tested (Hosea 7:16) that their heart was not right with God; "neither were they steadfast in his covenant" (Ps. 78:37). But those who have God's law in their hearts (Ps. 40:8) and whose hearts are the dwelling places of the fear of the Lord receive a hope that will never make them ashamed, for such people will never depart from the Lord (Jer. 32:40; Rom. 5:5). Should we then not be gladly zealous for the service of God with a heartfelt devotion? For he wants to give us this new heart by the Holy Spirit and out of his great mercy so that we may dwell with him forever, to our eternal comfort. Seeing that the Lord God offers to take away our hearts of stone and give us new hearts and spirits in order to serve him well, how can we still refuse him? May that be far from us!

God's Merciful Consideration of Our Weakness

Our merciful God also promises us that if we earnestly desire to serve him, he will pity us in our many weaknesses and be compassionate toward us, as a father cares for his children (Ps. 103:17; Mal. 3:17). Indeed, he is even pleased with our defective service because of his Son Jesus Christ (Phil. 1:9–11). Should we not then gladly be led by such a kind Lord and do our utmost to serve him as best we can, as true godliness teaches us to do? For we know that we will please him in whatever we offer, even if it is only a little.

Is it not a wonderful privilege that the Lord, the mighty God, ruler of the whole world, treats us as his children and has mercy on us like a father pities his children? While those who do not set their hearts on seeking and serving him will have to give a very detailed account of all they have thought, spoken, and done (Exod. 32:34; Matt. 12:36), he will look upon us believers with great compassion for his Son Jesus Christ's sake. Truly, no sin will be counted against us if we sincerely desire to practice godliness and are able to say to him, who knows us inside and out, that we do not want to succumb to any sin and, indeed, that we sincerely wish to fight against it. This demonstrates a true fear of God, to which Psalm 103:17, as well as other Scripture passages, refer. In relationship to this, we understand that the Lord does not behold iniquity in Jacob, neither transgressions in Israel (Num. 23:21).

Furthermore, since the Lord our God now looks at us with forgiveness, we no longer have to continually ask ourselves with a fearful and trembling conscience whether our life and conduct are pleasing to the Lord. However, those whose hearts have been convicted of not wholeheartedly serving the Lord or of not living a godly life will have a fearful conscience (1 John 3:18–20). We are assured and know on the basis of God's promises that, although we still have many weaknesses and faults, our service still pleases God. We can have great boldness before the Lord our God, despite our weaknesses, when we feel our conscience witness in our hearts that our godliness is unfeigned and sincere. The Lord will have mercy and compassion on those who seek him with all their hearts. Truly, he works righteousness in those who remember him in his ways (Isa. 64:5).

We are comforted by the Lord in this way and assured that despite our many weaknesses our service will be pleasing and acceptable to him for Christ's sake. We are comforted when we serve him sincerely and from the heart and when we practice godliness. So then should we also not be constantly encouraged to grow and become more active and bold in godliness, even if we still have weaknesses? Should we not be encouraged to wholeheartedly and sincerely practice godliness in the way we have been taught above? When the Lord comforts us, should we not walk in the ways of his commandments (Ps. 119:32)?

Clearly, those who lack the assurance that their deeds will please the Lord are easily discouraged and soon give up. Should we who have this assurance therefore not serve God more every day? Would that not lead to an even greater comfort and a richer experience of God's grace toward us and to a more certain assurance of our salvation? Should we not gladly do our best to practice godliness, seeing that we will find so much forgiveness with the Lord? For such assurance is denied to those who find that serving God is too much trouble and will not do God the honor of glorifying him and making service to him their most important work.

God's Merciful Reward

Our faithful God promises that he will mercifully and greatly reward those who practice true godliness (Ps. 19:11; Matt. 10:42), for Jesus clearly declares that those who forsake something in this life for the sake of godliness will be rewarded a hundredfold in this present life by the comfort of the Holy Spirit and will be given everlasting life in the world to come (Mark 10:29–30).

We experience that reward when we do something good. We immediately feel a certain joy, encouragement, and satisfaction rise in our hearts. It is the Holy Spirit's sweet, pleasant oil of joy, which sweetly and gently quickens and gladdens our heart because of the good we did. Listen to what Solomon says about this: "It is joy to the just to do judgment: but destruction shall be to the workers of iniquity" (Prov. 21:15; see also 1 Chron. 29:9). We understand this to mean that a true Christian experiences more joy in giving than a worldly person gets from indulging in worldly pleasures. A believer has more joy in tears of diligence in prayer than a worldly person has in all the laughing and joking at a wedding party. The child of God finds more joy in denying sinful pleasures than the carnal man finds in indulging in them.

Who doubts that Joseph tasted more joy in refusing the provocative wife of Potiphar than he would have received by succumbing to the pleasures of the flesh? Who then will not gladly practice godliness and be blessed with such a suitable reward?

In addition, the Lord, our good God, continues to enlarge and develop our spiritual gifts over time as we do our best to practice true godliness. He adds to this effort such blessings that our two talents produce two more talents, and our five talents become ten. If we know that by following a certain practice, lifestyle, or rule in our profession or trade that our income will greatly increase day by day, should we, therefore, not follow the practice of godliness whereby our spiritual gifts, which are far better, will increasingly develop day by day?

Finally, the Lord God in his great mercy will for Christ's sake increase our glory in heaven in relation to the measure of our zeal here on earth to practice true godliness (Dan. 12:3; Luke 19:17–19; Gal. 6:16). Should we not gladly surrender ourselves completely to our good God, who wants to show us so much good and give us so many blessings if we will only sincerely obey him? Is the joy of the Spirit such a small matter? Are spiritual gifts esteemed so little? Is the everlasting glory of heaven, even more enlarged by grace, so insignificant that we should not make the greatest effort all the days of our lives to practice godliness, which so faithfully leads us heavenward?

We should dedicate ourselves in every way to serve this great God. We should be zealous to serve him when we see the wisdom and loving-kindness of our heavenly Father, especially when we consider how the Son of God became man to be an example to us of a godly life and how God continues to invite us to walk in the way in which Christ walked. Seeing how the Holy Spirit promises to give us a new heart for the very purpose of pardoning our weaknesses and graciously rewarding our efforts out of his grace, we should be zealous of good works.

BOOK
8

Motives to Practice Godliness Derived from Our Own Condition

Our Natural Condition and the Vanity of Life

Christians, you saw how many motives there are to practice true godliness when we considered the attributes of our God. That should be enough to motivate you without any further consideration. Yet you might be even more motivated to practice godliness if you seriously considered your own condition, noticing the following three things:

- your own state of misery in which you live by nature
- the many blessings of God toward you and your special obligation to him
- all the various promises you made to God and are thereby obligated to practice

Take the condition in which you by nature live. By nature you are vain, mortal, and damnable. Your present life is at best utter vanity; your death is certain and sure, as is also your damnation hereafter if you remain in this natural condition and do not change through the practice of godliness. We will discuss this in detail, beginning with the vanity of our present life.

Your life, which is so precious to you, is actually very insubstantial. Does not every day pass by as a shadow? Everything is vain that pertains to this present life: eating, drinking, getting up, going to bed, walking, and being busy doing this, that, and other things. Sometimes you have joy in life, sometimes sorrow, sometimes pain, sometimes happiness. Life includes all kinds of things that pass away with use and are as smoke out of a chimney (Hosea 13:3) or vapor that appears for a little time and then vanishes (James 4:14). None of the things of this life have any real or enduring value.

King Solomon, who possessed great wealth, would have found something of weighty and lasting value in this life if it were possible to be found there. He took much trouble to look for it but finally admitted all his trouble was fruitless. The nature of man's present life according to his own experience was, "Vanity of vanities; all is vanity" (Eccles. 1:2). Thus, we should gladly sacrifice this otherwise totally vain life to God by practicing true godliness so that he, our all-sufficient God, might fill it with true riches. We might be even more encouraged if we also consider the following three things:

1. Happiness in this life is incomplete. Have you ever experienced a day you thought was so happy that you desired nothing else? Even if you tried as hard as Solomon to be saturated with every pleasure and entertainment (Ecclesiastes 2), could you ever say that everything was exactly what you wanted? Could you say, "This is how I want it and no other way?" Was there nothing else you would wish for? You know that you could not be certain how long that happiness would last and that you could not escape from the reality that all this was only passing pleasure—wouldn't that give a bitter taste to the pleasure all along? It cannot be any different, since every day also brings its own trouble and sorrow. The mouth of truth has told us this is so (Matt. 6:34). The life of poor man is therefore utter vanity; he can do what he likes, living an ungodly or godly life, but he will still have to fight battles on this earth. Clearly, the fol-

lowing saying is applicable to man: While he is in the flesh, he will have his sorrows, and as long as his soul remains in him, he will suffer pain.

2. Life is too meaningless to repeat. Look over your past life with all its experiences. Consider what joys and sorrows, pleasures and difficulties, happiness and suffering you have experienced. Think of your hopes, fears, and losses—especially how many days and nights have passed with all their concerns. Tell me, would you want to relive that same life in the same condition and manner—indeed, in exactly the same way, with the same joys, sorrows, hopes, fears, trials, and tribulations—as you lived before? We have never met anyone who would have been delighted to do this. Man's life is so utterly insignificant and futile that he would not want to repeat it.

Even if a man might wish to have his life back again in hopes of using it better, which, in any case, is a vain thought, he still would not want to experience it again in exactly the same way. Even Jacob said of his past life, "Few and evil have the days of the years of my life been" (Gen. 47:9).

3. Life is meaningless without God. Finally, consider this: Is it conceivable that the meaninglessness of life will improve with the years? It is foolish to expect this. Whatever age or stage of life man has reached, he will find all that has passed only vanity if he has not served God. It is not the number of years but godliness that improves our lives. Observe that a holy fear of God and true godliness are the only real and important things that can offer a degree of substance to our insubstantial lives, giving them permanence, honor, and value. Otherwise, life is lighter than a feather and vanishes like vapor. It is but a shadow (Psalms 39; 90).

Since life is by nature total vanity, you can say what you like, but you will always find it contains much futile and useless activity, much trouble and strife (Ps. 90:10). We should therefore sacrifice our utterly vain lives to God by practicing godliness. This is the only way life can become profitable and turn into a living fountain that flows into eternity. Should we not prefer this rather than continuing to live undirected lives and chasing after nothing but vanity and wind?

Motives for Godliness: The Human Condition

The Certainty of Death

Consider death! Is it not true that death, from which worldly people tend to shy away in terror, is sure and inescapable? Death will surely attack you sometime. Even if it does not strike you for a while, you cannot ward it off when it does. Look how uncertain you are in performing the things of this world because of certain and imminent death, even when you do not know how imminent. If you knew for certain that you had only a month to live and that your life would indeed end within thirty days, would you not look at everything differently? Would you not be very careful and conscientious to start living a better life and begin to practice godliness? If you were not sure whether you have only twenty days or one week left, would you still maintain a worldly, carnal lifestyle? That would be very foolish. You certainly would want to avoid such impiety. You should think about the certainty of death in light of the following:

1. Death diminishes the importance of our efforts. Does not the imminence of death make all your activities look more futile? Perhaps today you want to spend time with someone whom you love with all your heart. Perhaps you have won the favor of your beloved and the goodwill of her friends. You have become engaged and are planning to marry. Yet you can never know if death might separate you from the one you love before you are united in marriage. Such cases occur frequently, even with young couples. We can cite several examples of this.

Or you may have concentrated your efforts with great persistence on gaining a position, and you have been told that your promotion will be announced in a few weeks. Poor man, you have no certainty of life, not even the certainty of living for a few more days! Or you may have gathered such great wealth that you say to your soul, "Take a long rest." You fool, you do not know whether this very night your soul will be taken away in death (Luke 12:20). Many people have experienced sudden death. It could also happen to you soon!

2. Death ends all our hopes and dreams. Is it not true that when death comes to you, you forfeit not only all hope of taking on all

kinds of activities and of accomplishing all the things you were so involved in (Ps. 46:8) but also everything you have already obtained and owned outright? When death comes, it separates you from everything you treasure and value here in the world. You may think that you have everything securely in your grasp, but when you die you will have to let it all go and depart naked, just as you came into this world (1 Tim. 6:7).

You know very well and see daily before your own eyes that your glory and wealth, however great they may be, will not follow you when you die (Ps. 49:12). You know that the best friends may follow a corpse to the grave, yet they only watch when it is buried in the ground, then leave it there and go home. You should become wise and strive after the most important thing, the part that will never be taken away from you, the part that will not leave you in eternity and that will follow you even when you die (Luke 10:42). Truly, you must practice genuine godliness (Rev. 14:13).

3. Death separates us from everything we love. Finally, death is the most dreadful of all things to be feared by the person who has not practiced godliness in his life, for when he thinks about death, he sees that he will soon be separated from every precious and cherished thing on which he set his heart. He will go to a place he does not know, indeed, to a place he fears—to the abyss of hell and to eternal ruin, away from the face of the Lord. Such a poor man cries out in intense dread:

> Three things heavily on my heart do lie.
> The first is that I must surely die!
> The second weighs heavier on my heart,
> I do not know when I must depart.
> The third weighs heaviest of all three—
> I know not my final destiny!

Since this is the situation with death, how could you not take this to heart? Should you not consider this and gladly submit yourself to the Lord of life in order to practice true godliness? Should you not live for him who is able to make your physical death an entrance into eternal life? When you see an ungodly person dying in great fear of death and yet being resolutely carried away by death, would you want to be in his place? I think not! Let the thoughts of imminent death motivate you to live differently than you have lived before if you do not want to die as one dies who indeed dreads death.

Eternal Damnation

You have a precious soul within you that will never die. Indeed, this soul will one day be transported by death's fire to another world, where the Lord our God, the King of eternity, reigns and rules. If you doubt this, then you must squarely face this doubt, since this matter is of great importance. Your doubt is sufficient evidence that you know something like eternity exists; otherwise, the thought of it would never have entered your heart. A mere mortal creature, such as an animal, would never have thought of immortality or eternity. There is no mind so deranged that does not possess some fear and notion of the powers of the world to come.

You see, this is the situation: You are not finished when your life on earth ends. This world, this life, which so swiftly comes to an end, is followed by another existence that never ends. Truly, if you remain as you are by nature and do not change in your mind and spirit by practicing true godliness, you will certainly be damned in the next world by God's eternal judgment, which is according to truth (Rom. 2:2), for all men by nature are under sin and God's condemnation (Rom. 3:19).

You do not need to live a loose, reckless life in order to be condemned in the next world. You do not need to be a drunkard, to gamble, or to live unprofitably. No, even if you refrain from all this, keeping what you have inherited and adding to it, while living respectably, you still remain what you are by nature. If you forget about striving for a renewed mind, if you do not practice true godliness as we urge you to do, you and your soul will be just as lost and condemned in the next world as those who are already in hell. This is the word of truth spoken by the Savior of the world: "Except ye repent, ye shall all likewise perish" (Luke 13:5).

Do you not see, poor worldly person, that this world will be followed by the next world as well as eternal judgment (Heb. 9:27)? Do you not see that by nature you surely will be cursed in that terrible judgment of God? Does that not motivate you to give yourself with all diligence to the service of the Lord our God? We urge you to do so, for you will one day appear before God's judgment seat to give an account of how you sought and served him on earth. Yes, we most emphatically urge you to serve this God who also reigns in the next world, where you will eternally suffer if you do not take urgent action now. If you dread this damnation so little that it will not get you to take appropriate action now, consider the following:

1. You will be sent to the abyss. The place to which condemned souls are banished is the abyss of hell, the dreadful lake that burns with fire and brimstone (Rev. 21:8). This place is filled with horrifying, frightful, damned, cursed, and wretched devils and spirits (Matt. 25:41), who are venomous and embittered and prefer to torment rather than comfort one another. They attack one another like serpents, broods of vipers, scorpions, and fiery flying dragons. Whose heart is not frightened by the thought of having to lie among them, even for only one night?

2. You will suffer incredible pain. The anguish and torment that condemned spirits must suffer in that terrible place is greater and more terrible, more fearful and incurable, than anyone has ever seen or heard or imagined or received into his heart. The condemned soul is tormented there in every way possible. It is deprived of all pleasure and delight. Nothing can comfort or refresh it while it is massively afflicted with every possible kind of torture and torment.

Consider what severe punishment the almighty, all-wise, and wrathful God can impose on his enemies, whom he hates with a complete hatred and judges without mercy (James 2:13). Clearly, these poor, miserable, condemned spirits must suffer and endure all of this. Thus, the Lord testifies that in this place of torment there will be "weeping and gnashing of teeth" (Matt. 25:30).

3. You will suffer forever. It would still be good for these poor people, even though their torment is so terrible, if there were a limitation to their suffering. But the truth is their suffering and torment, however great and unbearable, will last forever and will be endless. When they have been suffering this torment for ten thousand years, they will have to start all over again, for they are as far from the ending as when they started. Oh, forever and forever, never-ending, never-ending—how terrible this thought must be to

tormented spirits! Scripture says these condemned souls will be tormented with fire and brimstone. The smoke of their torment will ascend forever and ever so that they have no rest day or night (Rev. 14:10–11).

If people sincerely considered this now, they might take a more careful look at this. But it is the practice of the devil to hide from people's eyes the dreadful horrors of the damned state in the world to come. Thus, when man departs this world, he is unexpectedly hurled into the next, where he will experience all its horrors all at once. He thus will not fear hell until it is too late to escape from it.

Oh, poor worldly person, whoever you are, read this and become wise while you still have time. Find out about your natural condition. Let this be a prod to spur you on to strive for a better life by practicing true godliness. Your life is utter vanity and completely futile, and imminent death makes all your work more uncertain and vain. There is a world that will follow this life, and it is the one that really matters. You will not qualify for a blessed destiny in the next life—rather, you will forever be unqualified, as we have already shown you—if you make no effort to serve the Lord your God and practice true godliness. We invite and encourage you to do this.

It should now be clear that it would be prudent for you to engage in the practice of true godliness before anything else. You should make an effort in the short time left of your life, which is so uncertain and futile, to use it for the service of the Lord your God to escape eternal death and obtain the eternal life that never ends. Make this the highest priority over everything while you are still lovingly invited to do so by the Lord your God by means of his servants. Listen to his voice while it is still the day of mercy (Ps. 95:7–8), "the acceptable year" (Luke 4:19), and "the day of salvation" (2 Cor. 6:2). Indeed, you should redeem this precious time in order to work out your salvation in fear and trembling (Phil. 2:12).

You have now been told enough that you are by nature utterly vain, mortal, and guilty of sin. You know you must grasp the great weight of eternal glory and honor it in your short span of life. If you fail to do this here on earth, you will be thrown into the greatest misery in the hereafter. It will be an everlasting, endless misery that will last forever and ever. Do you still think that eternal glory is to be despised or esteemed so little? Do you fear eternal damnation so little that you make not the greatest effort to escape it? Will you fail to obtain heaven by practicing godliness, knowing that although these things await you in the future you might yet obtain eternal life through grace?

Motives for Godliness: God's Many Blessings

Now look, Christian, are you still not motivated to practice true godliness by all that has been said about the general character of your God and the miserable state of your natural condition? Have you no desire to be holy? Would you rather lead a careless and loose life than direct it according to the rule of true godliness? Come and reason with me how it should be your duty and obligation to practice true godliness because of God's manifold blessings, for they will show you that you no longer belong to yourself or have the freedom to live as you please. You are obligated to serve your God because of his multitude of mercies and manifold blessings that he has given to you.

Everyone should easily understand how all God's blessings to us—there are so many—encourage and motivate us to do what is good, for God's blessings to us are so many that we hardly know where to begin and where to end. Still, let us consider them in three categories: the blessings the Lord our great God has given to us in the past, the blessings God is giving us in the present, and the blessings God will give us in the future if we will practice true godliness in all sincerity. We will give a brief explanation of each category of blessings, beginning with the blessings the Lord has already given us.

Blessings God Has Given in the Past

There are many blessings the Lord has already given to you. We are not speaking here of his eternal love and merciful election, which he has bestowed on you if you are, as you profess to be, a true believer, but about the blessings that are evident to everyone. These are such tremendous and great blessings from the Lord that it is your duty to serve the Lord all your life by practicing true godliness. These blessings include the following.

1. Your very creation. Tell me, is it not your duty to serve the Lord your God by virtue of the privilege and grace of his having created you? Has he not given you everything you possess? Surely, you must admit that all your limbs, senses, and strength are from him. Your hands and feet, your fingers and thumbs, your eyes and ears, your tongue and mouth tell you, when you begin to think about it, who gave them to you. Indeed, they tell you, each in their own language, that you should serve the one who has given you these limbs, these senses, and the ability to use them.

Do you not have more intelligence than the animals of the field? Have you not more beauty and strength and other more precious things? God gave you these. You are able to speak, eat, drink, and everything else only because of the Lord your God. How then could you speak contrary to God's commandments with proud, foolish words? How could you eat and drink in a way contrary to what he desires? Are you not obliged to speak the word of God, whose bread you eat and from whom you have received the ability to speak (1 Peter 4:11)? Indeed, you are obligated to eat and drink to his honor, for it is from him that you received the very ability to eat and drink (1 Cor. 10:31). The rivers swiftly run into the sea from where its waters come (Eccles. 1:7). Do not these waters teach you to dedicate your abilities to God, since you received all of them from him in the first place?

When Moses and Aaron told Pharaoh to let Israel go to the desert to serve their God there because they were God's people, the wicked Pharaoh replied, "Who is the Lord, that I should obey his voice to let Israel go? I know not the Lord, neither will I let Israel go" (Exod. 5:2). When you hear such profane words, oh, Christian, is not your heart incensed by them? When the Lord tells us to sever our senses, abilities, and members from the slavery of sin and devote them to his service, for they are his, far be it from us to respond as Pharaoh did by saying with word and deed, "Who is the Lord, that I should give my members and abilities to his service? I know not the Lord; neither will I sacrifice my members to serve him" (cf. Exod. 5:2).

Instead, when the Lord calls us to separate our senses, powers, and limbs from the slavery of sin and to dedicate them to his service, we must do so because they are his. It is simply unthinkable that we would reply to God with word or deed, saying to him, "I do not know the Lord. Who is the Lord that I should dedicate myself and my abilities to him?" May this godless profanity of Pharaoh be far from us so that his plagues will also stay far away from us! For whom should we reserve our strength and to whom should we dedicate it? Should we withhold it from the Lord, who gave it to us in the first place?

2. Your regeneration and re-creation. The Lord who created you also re-created you, regenerated you when you had ruined yourself and made you a new creature so that you could serve him in all good works (Luke 1:74–75; Eph. 2:10). If you are a true Christian, this is the case. God has given not only his Word but also his Holy Spirit to you for this purpose (Isa. 59:21). And so because of the blessings of re-creation and redemption, you are unconditionally obligated to serve the Lord your God.

If a powerful king saves you from slavery under Turks who had captured you and frees and perhaps even makes you an official in his court, would you not be motivated to serve this benevolent master throughout your life? God has made you a Christian, one of his children, and has taken you into his house and invited you to sit at his table. Since God has done this, why would you not fear and serve him above all? What is more reasonable than a Christian behaving like a Christian and a child of God acting in accordance with God's will? How can we justify our failure to do so?

3. The means to salvation. Suppose you do not yet feel renewed in the spirit of your heart, and you know that you have not yet been made a new creature. Has not the Lord God, whom we ask you to serve, not entrusted you with the means of salvation? Has he not (oh, great blessing!) sent his Son into the world, born of a woman, to save that which was lost (Matt. 18:11)? Has he not proclaimed the word of the kingdom and of salvation to you? Indeed, he has put up with much from you for a long time, while you lived in your sins. Consider how many times the Lord found you in your sins, which are so damnable and deserving of death. Yet he has not torn you away from your sin, struck you down with death, and thrown you into the abyss of hell as you deserved. Rather, God has pardoned you, continued to wait for you still longer, and has given you time to repent. Even when you did not want to serve him, he still

took care of you. Oh, may those whom the Lord sees drunk with wine now and then, those he meets in a house of disrepute where sins too scandalous to mention are committed, those he catches lying and deceiving, and those who are lazy in his service and who desecrate the Lord's Day seriously consider this. May those who know they are guilty of these transgressions realize how long-suffering the Lord has been toward them. May they take this opportunity to respond to his patience by repenting, for God was long-suffering toward you for this purpose (2 Peter 3:9), lest you gather stores of wrath against God's righteous judgment in the day of his wrath (Rom. 2:4–5).

Blessings God Continues to Give Us

There are many blessings that the Lord continues to give us which should greatly oblige us to serve the Lord and practice godliness. They include the following:

1. Continuing provision for our needs. Oh, Christian, is it not your duty to serve God because of his continuing provision for your needs? When you are hungry or thirsty, who gives you food and drink? Is it not the Lord who fills your heart with food and gladness (Acts 14:17)? From whom do you get clothing to cover your nakedness? Is not clothing one of God's gifts (Hosea 2:9)? In addition, the Lord lets his sun rise over you so you may enjoy the light. He lets his rain fall for you so the earth may produce its bounty by which you live. So you see that in every aspect you live because of God's provision. Should you then refuse to engage in his service?

The Lord also gives you the light of his holy gospel, which guides your feet into the way of peace (Luke 1:79). Perhaps you consider yourself better than others. Are you wealthy? Do you have a high position? Great intelligence? Tell me, how did you get this? Did God give it to you or the devil? Tell me from whom you received these gifts. You must admit that everything you have has come from God (Ps. 75:7–8). Your talents are his talents (Matt. 25:15). Therefore, make sure that you are not like the wicked servant who made his master's talents unprofitable (Matt. 25:25–28). You should put God's talents on earth to good use by serving him so that you may be praised and confirmed by God in his judgment hereafter.

2. Continuing protection. Christian, are you not obligated to serve God because of his gracious work of protection? Think how often he has protected you and kept you safe from thousands of possible accidents, most of which you were not even aware of. Consider the misery and sorrow you have been spared from but in which many people are trapped and totally ensnared with their mind, body, hands, feet, eyes, or ears. These are only some of the many blessings you have received from God. Consider also all the awful, disgraceful, and wearisome sins some people have committed but from which you were spared. These, too, are blessings you received from God, for the seed of every kind of sin is also present in you.

Are not God's blessings delivered new to you every morning when you awake? Truly, he enables you to sleep at night so that you may be refreshed in the morning. He also watches over you when you sleep, protecting you from fire and water, the depravity of evil men, and everything that lives in darkness and wants to harm you. You should thus say with the church of God, "It is of the LORD's mercies that we are not consumed, because his compassions fail not. They are new every morning: great is thy faithfulness" (Lam. 3:22–23).

3. His patient waiting for your repentance. Christian, is it not your duty to serve God because of his great patience toward you, which he renews every morning? You cannot deny that you keep sinning daily against your God, which means that every day you deserve to go to hell. Although you anger the Lord and provoke his wrath, he still waits for you. He still blesses you every day and does not throw you immediately into hell. Surely, it is a special blessing from God, flowing from his indescribable patience, that you are still in the land of the living. It is a blessing that you still walk upon the earth, which is full of the Lord's loving-kindness, and that you still see the sun, while you deserve to lie in the darkness of hell, without hope of ending.

Remember, the devil walks about you like a roaring lion that seeks to devour your soul (1 Peter 5:8). If God did not spare you, the devil would slay you and throw you into eternal hell before the end of the day. Satan's schemes and power are so great. So are your heedlessness and weakness. It is due only to the loving-kindness of the Lord that you have been spared from complete ruin. Should you then not serve your good God with all your strength? Should you not serve him who spares you so mercifully, saves your feet from ruin, and delivers you, as it were, from the jaw of the lion? When Gideon delivered the Israelites from the hands of their enemies, some Israelites said to Gideon, "Rule thou over us, both thou, and thy son, and thy son's son also: for thou hast delivered us from the hand of Midian" (Judg. 8:22). How much more are we compelled to speak to the Lord our God, saying, "Rule thou over us forever and ever, for thou hast been so merciful and delivered us from the hand of the devil"?

God's Future Blessings

If we look at the benefits and blessings God will grant us if we wholeheartedly serve him by practicing true godliness, we will find that they are numerous and precious and will continue to come to us. Apart from the blessings we have already mentioned, the Lord, our good God, will give us the following blessings:

1. Assurance of salvation. God will give us greater assurance that we have been justified, as well as of his grace and favor toward us, for this is what the Lord says to us: "Also the sons of the stranger, that join themselves to the LORD, to serve him, and to love the name of the LORD, to be his servants ... even them will I bring to my holy mountain, and make them joyful in my house of prayer: their burnt offerings and their sacrifices shall be accepted upon mine altar" (Isa. 56:6–7).

The apostle John says something similar: "We know that we have passed from death unto life, because we love the brethren" (1 John 3:14). He adds, "Beloved, if our heart condemn us not, then have we confidence toward God. And whatsoever we ask, we receive of him, because we keep his commandments, and do those things that are pleasing in his sight" (1 John 3:21–22). Is it then not worth the effort to practice godliness in order to have greater assurance of our salvation?

2. Increased spiritual gifts. The Lord God will increasingly sanctify us when we earnestly practice godliness. He will also make us grow and increase in spiritual gifts. This is what the Lord says: "I

am the true vine, and my Father is the husbandman. Every branch in me that beareth not fruit he taketh away: and every branch that beareth fruit, he purgeth it, that it may bring forth more fruit" (John 15:1–2). The apostle Paul also refers to this when he says, "And let ours also learn to maintain good works for necessary uses, that they be not unfruitful" (Titus 3:14). We should therefore gladly practice godliness and, by grace, become increasingly more fruitful in all the spiritual gifts God grants (Col. 1:10; Heb. 6:8–10).

3. *The gift of eternal life.* The Lord God will also glorify those who have lived a godly life here on earth and will grant them eternal life by grace alone. The apostle Paul says that godliness is profitable unto all things, for it promises life that now is, as well as that which is to come (1 Tim. 4:8). Sanctification is a matter of great importance, as we may conclude from the following three things:

We will be brought into the presence of God. In glorious heaven, where God brings those he has taken out of this world to glorify them, we will find the most joyous and loving company we could ever imagine, for in heaven the Lord God Almighty—Father, Son, and Holy Spirit—will make himself known to us in a special way. The Lord Jesus Christ, our Redeemer and Savior, will be there. All the holy, glorious angels will be there, as well as all the holy and blessed patriarchs, prophets, and apostles. Abraham, Isaac, and Jacob, the virgin Mary, Paul, and Peter will be there. All the blessed saints and the martyrs who persevered and all true confessors of Christ's name who have left this world will be there. They will be altogether beautiful and shine like the sun as they are profoundly moved to show one another love and kindness.

We will experience unspeakable joy. Everyone whom the Lord glorifies will enjoy sweet, glorious, and unspeakable joy in that heavenly company that no eye has seen, nor ear has heard, neither has it entered into the heart of man to imagine such blessing (1 Cor. 2:9). Just consider what glorious joy the almighty, wise, and loving God can order for his friends whom he acknowledges and accepts as his children and whom he will exceedingly glorify to the shame of all who greatly oppressed them here on earth. Clearly, the godly will enjoy all these blessings in heaven. God compares this glory with earthly deliverance from slavery and exile, saying, "Therefore the redeemed of the LORD shall return, and come with singing unto Zion; and everlasting joy shall be upon their head: they shall obtain gladness and joy; and sorrow and mourning shall flee away" (Isa. 51:11).

We will live in joy forever. The godly will enjoy this glorious joy in heaven forever and ever, eternally, endlessly! That is what the prophet Isaiah means when he says, "Everlasting joy shall be upon their head." This should encourage the hearts of the godly in an extraordinary way because it assures them that these glorious, unspeakable joys, however great they may be, will never, ever end. That is what the apostle Paul speaks of when he talks of the exceeding and eternal weight of glory that is given by grace to the godly (2 Cor. 4:17).

You see, the Lord will provide all these blessings to those who practice godliness. Since we are obligated and bound with so many cords of love to the service of the Lord our God, should we not gladly engage in it by practicing true godliness? Should we not also say with the psalmist, "For this God is our God for ever and ever" (Ps. 48:14)? Indeed, we should also call out to Christ with a sincere heart, as the Israelites did to David, saying, "Thine are we, David, and on thy side, thou son of Jesse" (1 Chron. 12:18). We have chased after the vanity of life long enough. We should now make a sincere resolution to use the remainder of our time in this life according to the will of God and not to the lust of the flesh (1 Peter 4:3).

Therefore, we say to all Christians, as the apostle Paul once appealed in Christ's name to Roman believers, "I beseech you therefore, brethren, by the mercies of God, that ye present your bodies a living sacrifice, holy, acceptable unto God, which is your reasonable service. And be not conformed to this world: but be ye transformed by the renewing of your mind, that ye may prove what is that good, and acceptable, and perfect, will of God" (Rom. 12:1–2).

Motives for Godliness: Our Promises

Promises We Made through the Sacraments

O Christian, we want so much to rouse you to increase in the practice of true godliness! But do you still find your heart so depraved and so unreasonable toward God that his blessings and invitations to godliness that we have talked about still fail to move you to obligate yourself totally to the service of God? Consider then how many times you have testified against yourself. Like Joshua, you have said that you choose to serve the Lord (Josh. 24:15). How often you promised that from now on you would forsake the devil, the world, and the flesh and, instead, serve God and cling to him throughout your life. Consider how solemnly you made this promise of obedience to him when you partook of the holy sacraments and when you prayed on other occasions and in special circumstances.

Consider also the application of the two holy sacraments, baptism and the Lord's Supper. Were you not baptized in the name of the Father, the Son, and the Holy Spirit for the purpose of committing yourself one day to the Father, the Son, and the Holy Spirit and serving them? You forsook the devil, your own flesh, and all the pomp and ceremony of the world in that baptism (Rom. 6:3–4). You were cleansed in that baptism with water that represents the precious blood of Christ so that you may be on your guard and no longer roll around like a washed sow in the filth of sin (2 Peter 2:22). You were pledged in that baptism to observe everything that Christ the Lord has commanded you (Matt. 28:20). You know you must say yes to this. How can you then withdraw from this pledge?

You may try to excuse yourself, saying, "I was baptized in early infancy; I did not know what I was doing then." What? Do you now wish to repudiate your Christian baptism? Would you regard yourself as an unbaptized piece of waste? In that case, hand in your notice to God's holy church that you have disowned your baptism and Christianity altogether.

However, if the thought of doing so disturbs you and puts fear into your heart and you still want to be regarded as a Christian, then you should truly accept your baptism. Make an effort to observe all that Christ has commanded you so that you will not receive a more severe judgment from God in the day of his visitation than will an unbaptized pagan. Do this so that you will not be severely punished during God's judgment of the world as an evil covenant breaker and deserter.

Consider also, have you ever participated in the Lord's Supper? Many baptized Christians who are now advanced in years once partook of the Supper, but everyone should have been eating at the table if they conducted themselves as they should have and according to what their Christian baptism required of them. Well now, you who have tasted the Lord's Supper, have you not pledged your soul and renewed your obligation to live a good Christian life by earnestly performing God's service in the practice of true godliness? You have eaten the Lord's bread on that condition and on that condition have drunk the Lord's wine. By doing this, you have pledged your soul to the service of the Lord. What is left to you now besides practicing what you promised? If you don't, you will be labeled as a violator and desecrater of the Lord's Supper and will be punished as such.

It is the Christian's duty to engage in the practice of godliness because of the vows he has made by partaking of the sacraments. This bond may be strengthened by these deliberations:

1. The sacraments verify our promise to serve God. The Lord God instituted the holy sacraments to bind us, by a solemn vow, to serve our God with godliness, under the banner of Christ our Lord. It is written that we are buried with Christ by baptism into death so that as Christ was raised from the dead by the glory of the Father, even so we should walk in newness of life (Rom. 6:4). Should we then miss God's purpose by neglecting godliness or, rather, robbing ourselves from his blessing thereby?

2. The sacraments verify our membership in Christ's church. God's holy church admits us to its community when it allows us to partake of the holy sacraments. It administers to us the precious jewels the Lord has entrusted to it with the hope and expectation that we will always earnestly promote the welfare of God's church. We will seek its happiness and work to edify and build up true fellowship in it as much as we can by means of the practice of true godliness, for it is written, "Then they that gladly received his word were baptized: and the same day there were added unto them about three thousand souls. And they continued stedfastly in the apostles' doctrine and fellowship, and in the breaking of bread, and in prayers" (Acts 2:41–42).

Truly, the Holy Spirit intended the holy sacraments to be given to Christians in order to lead them to Christian practices (1 Cor.

1:17; 12:13; Eph. 4:5–6). Would we then dare to shame the hope and expectation of God's holy church for us? Would we not prefer to practice godliness with all our strength so that we may fulfill the expectations God's church has placed upon us?

3. The sacraments strengthen us in godliness. We must admit that because of our evil, depraved flesh, which so quickly wavers in the service of the Lord, it is very necessary to be bound with a sacrament and a sincere vow to the service of God. When we realize that the Lord God, in his great wisdom, has ordained his holy sacraments to bind us to the service of the Lord, should we not take advantage of this? Should this not stir us to be completely devoted to the service of our God? When a soldier is uneasy in the service of his commander and is inclined to be unfaithful to his banner, remembering the oath of allegiance he took before his commander and all its ramifications is a great deterrent for him and should help restrain him from being unfaithful. It is like a spur to urge him on in the service to which he has committed himself.

Jephthah, the judge of Israel, rashly promised to sacrifice to the Lord the first thing he met. When he saw it was his own daughter, he resolved to keep his promise, no matter how heavy this weighed on him, for he said, "Alas, my daughter! thou hast brought me very low, and thou art one of them that trouble me: for I have opened my mouth unto the Lord, and I cannot go back" (Judg. 11:35). Clearly, we Christians should remember the promise of faith we made to God in earnest when we partook of the holy sacraments and be stimulated even more to practice godliness, for it is by godly living that we best show our allegiance to God.

Vows We Made in Prayer

Almost every time you go to God in prayer, do you not commit your soul to forsake unrighteousness and engage in the service of God? Does Scripture not teach us that everyone who names the name of the Lord must depart from iniquity (2 Tim. 2:19)? Therefore, when you pray as you should, you commit your soul to God to serve him. You should also promise God that you will no longer be antagonistic to his commandments and, as it were, "ride upon horses" (Hosea 14:3). That means you no longer want to be led by your desires but will follow God's counsel in your life instead. Every time you pray to God, you should commit your soul to forsake unrighteousness, hear his laws, and act accordingly so that the Lord God may hear you and bless your prayers.

Since you have so often placed yourself in God's service when you have prayed, what is left to do besides practice it? You see, the Christian is committed to the practice of godliness by the private promise he has made in his prayers to God. This commitment can be strengthened by the following considerations:

1. God blesses the prayers of the godly. Scripture clearly shows us that the Lord will not listen to the prayers of those who do not want to practice godliness. David says out of his own experience, "If I regard iniquity in my heart, the LORD will not hear me" (Ps. 66:18). The man who was born blind knew very well on the basis of general religious principles that God does not listen to sinners—those who are workers of iniquity rather than godliness (John 9:31). Should we not then gladly observe God's commandments so that he will bless our prayers? Should we not gladly do the things God wants of us so that the Lord will also do what we desire from him?

It is written that the Lord "will fulfill the desire of them that fear him" (Ps. 145:19). It is sad when our daily prayers are a complete waste of effort because we neglect to practice godliness, for we must practice godliness if we want our prayers to be blessed.

2. God rejects the prayers of the ungodly. Scripture tells us that the prayers of the person who turns his ear from hearing God's law are an abomination to God (Prov. 28:9). It is very sad when a Christian who neglects to practice true godliness makes his own prayers, by which he seeks to gain God's favor, a revulsion and abomination to God. The very thing he thinks might appease God becomes even more repulsive to God. Those who think about this every time they pray should be motivated to become more resolute in making living a truly godly life their first priority.

3. The prayers of the ungodly become a curse. The Christian will be even more motivated when he considers that a curse has been uttered against those who do not engage in the practice of godli-

ness but brazenly continue to do evil, for their prayers will be cursed and regarded as sin (Ps. 109:7). Whoever does not want to incur this severe and most terrible judgment, in which he curses himself by his own prayer—which is the best work he thinks he can do— should realize that he is just a hypocrite and a mocker of God and his holy ordinances if he prays but neglects to practice godliness daily.

Promises We Made to Walk in Godliness

Regarding other individual circumstances in your life, you know there were many times when you promised God that you would start living a godly life. Apart from the things we have already discussed, you have often promised the Lord your God that you would become more holy and live a better Christian life. You promised to give up drunkenness, or being immoral, or being mean. You promised to stop gossiping, or lying, or slandering, or being lazy, or failing to be attentive in the service of God. You promised instead to diligently engage yourself in the service of the Lord. You know you have done this. But you have done so particularly in these situations:

1. When you were rebuked for ungodly conduct. You made promises to change your ways when you were rightly rebuked and warned because of your ungodly life, whether because of your drinking and quarreling, your deception, your pretension, or your feeble attempts in the service of the Lord. You often promised the good Christians who warned you that you would do better and behave as they instructed you. In rebuking you, they were like angels sent by God to protect you from ruin (James 5:20), in much the same way as Lot was taken from Sodom by angels (Genesis 19).

Well then, remember that you have opened your mouth. You cannot go back on your vow to walk in true godliness, as Jephthah realized (Judg. 11:35), for God has no pleasure in fools who promise to pay but do not pay what they promise. It is most important that you keep your promise. You made a good promise, after all, and you should not regret it. It was a promise in which you were already bound with many cords. Unless you want the Lord to find you guilty of not keeping that promise, what else is left but to do what you have promised?

2. When you were in great distress. When you were in some trouble that threatened your life at sea or on land, or when you were very sick and anxious in bed and found yourself sorely pressed because of the hand of the Most High, you promised to serve the Lord diligently once you were delivered. Now the Lord has restored you. He has brought you back to health as you asked. He has listened to your prayer and answered it. What else is left but to listen to God's commandment and say with the psalmist, "I will go into thy house with burnt offerings: I will pay thee my vows, which my lips have uttered, and my mouth hath spoken, when I was in trouble" (Ps. 66:13–14)?

You must pay your vows to God the Most High (Ps. 50:14). You have obligated yourself by the words of your mouth (Prov. 6:2), and you must now pay your vows or risk God's displeasure. You should take care in this, or you may remain in adversity. Indeed, you may be sure that if you promise to serve the Lord when you again become ill and break that promise when you become healthy again you will find out how God will not be mocked (Gal. 6:7). You will discover that worse things will come upon you on the last day than all the sicknesses and troubles you have ever experienced in life (John 5:14).

3. When the Spirit urged you to change. You should also remember that you have not been a stranger to the good spiritual leading, admonition, and prompting of the Holy Spirit for you to amend your ways (Rev. 3:20). You may have received a warning to better yourself when you went for a walk in the field or lay upon your bed. You may have thought about your mortality or about the final judgment or something like that, for that was when you made up your mind to break with your sinful life and serve God.

In any case, you have committed your soul to practice godliness. If you now do not want to grieve the good Spirit of God, from whom those good promptings came, you should no longer default to keep your vows; rather, do everything you can to keep them. You are committed and bound by several promises to the service of the Lord. What else remains but that you observe them? You will do so if you do not want to be judged as an evil servant and condemned out of your own mouth.

You worldly people may have made such promises to the Lord in your baptism, or perhaps in partaking of the Lord's Supper, or in your daily prayers, or when you were in some trouble, or when you powerfully experienced some desire in yourselves to forsake the world and its delights. You also promised God that you would deny your own flesh with its lusts and would earnestly engage in the service of the Lord. But do you really think that your daily conduct, showy clothes, excessive eating, boastful drinking, frivolous chatter, silliness, slander, slothfulness, carelessness in holy exercises, envy, hate, malice, and stubbornness are in accord with your promises?

By promises, I mean those promises you made to God through your baptism, renewed in the Lord's Supper, and further confirmed in your daily prayers and in special needs and circumstances in which you vowed to better yourself and devote yourself totally to the service of God. If you discover that the lifestyle you lead is nothing but a continual breach of all the solemn and special promises you have ever made to God, then be most careful. Indeed, be very careful not to behave foolishly before the Lord God. Because you constantly break the promises to better yourself and serve God, you may be unexpectedly destroyed by God's fierce wrath.

Every person who calls himself a Christian should be attentive to engage in the practice of godliness, for he is always lovingly invited to do this. Please remember also that because of your natural condition, life is futile, your death is sure, and your damnation is certain if you neglect to practice godliness. Be mindful of God's many blessings that he has bestowed upon you, continues to bestow on you now, and will continue to bestow so that you might be motivated to earnestly practice godliness. Do not disregard the promises you made to God when your fellow Christians admonished you, when God allowed you to be afflicted, or when you were secretly admonished by the good Spirit of the Lord to amend your life. All these blessings were given to you so that you would not follow the course of the world or give in to the lusts of the flesh but would serve the Lord your God, who has given you a living soul to serve him. Amen.

BOOK
9

Three More Reasons
for Practicing Godliness

Clearly, everyone who calls himself a Christian should be greatly moved by the reasons we have presented for making the practice of true godliness the most important work in life. Yet we notice that in spite of all we have said, many professing Christians remain just as weak in the practice of godliness as before. Therefore, we will discuss three more things that should be carefully considered regarding this practice. They are:

- the excellence of the godly life
- the dreadfulness of the ungodly life
- the futility of all earthly things that distract and divert many people from true blessedness and godliness to walk in ungodliness

Reasons for Practicing Godliness: The Excellence of the Godly Life

Concerning the first point, many people neglect to practice true godliness because they have never seriously considered how glorious the godly life can be. This is because the devil hides this glory from their eyes, with the result that they have neither the will nor the desire for living a godly life. But it is necessary for us to open our eyes to behold the beauty, excellence, and value of the godly life so that we may see these wonderful qualities of the godly Christian life and be increasingly won to the practice of godliness. In this, we should give special attention to three things. By practicing true godliness, we are being trained to serve the best master, to do the best work, and to bring forth the best fruits. We will discuss each of these, beginning with the first.

Trained to Serve the Best Master

As soon as you sincerely start practicing true godliness, you actually enter into the service of the great Triune God—the Father, the Son, and the Holy Spirit. That is when you serve the best of all employers, masters, and lords. There is no Lord more excellent than these:

1. God, your heavenly Father. Tell me, who could you better serve than this Father, who has given you a living soul and will have compassion on you like a father if you begin to serve him in earnest (Ps. 103:13; Mal. 3:17)?

2. The Son of God, your Savior. What could be better for you than serving the Son of God, who is your Savior, who gave himself for you, and who bore your sins in his body on the cross so that you, having died to sin, might live unto righteousness (1 Peter 2:24)?

3. God the Holy Spirit. Whom would you rather serve than the Holy Spirit, who regenerates you and makes you into a new creature so that you will be able to perform this new service well? Truly, he will renew you in the spirit of your mind and heart. He will also

continue to renew you day by day so that you may know what is the good, acceptable, and perfect will of God (John 16:7–8; Rom. 12:2).

This is certainly an important matter. The wise and intelligent people of this world try to get their children into the service of a mighty king or emperor at a very early age in hopes that this will provide them with a good career and promotion into high positions. How important it is then to be accepted into the service of the King of kings and the Lord of lords, who gives his servants authority over entire cities and districts (Luke 19:17–19). By practicing true godliness, we will be led to this. We will be permitted to enter the court of the great King, not only as servants but as friends of the King (John 15:15).

At one time, King Saul reprimanded his children for being allied with David. He told them somewhat resentfully, "Will the son of Jesse give every one of you fields and vineyards, and make you all captains of thousands and captains of hundreds?" (1 Sam. 22:7). The Lord our God does much more for his faithful servants. He gives them authority over much indeed, and he also offers them a heavenly kingdom. What Christian heart that seriously considers the greatness of the Lord our God would not regard it as advantageous to remain forever in his service? This is the service for which true godliness prepares us.

The Glorious Work to Which We Are Appointed

A second very important reason for practicing godliness is that as soon as you begin doing so, you do the work of the angels in announcing the virtues of the One who has called you out of darkness into his marvelous light (1 Peter 2:9). You are invited to speak to God daily in prayer and daily to hear him speak to you in his Word. You will be permitted, as it were, to attend God's cabinet meetings, to open the journal of the great God, and to read all about God's mighty deeds, wonderful histories, and otherwise hidden secrets of the heavenly kingdom. You will also be appointed to serve other members of Christ's body in order to promote the edification of God's church. The angels will rejoice when you do this work (Heb. 1:14), especially as they watch you advance and progress (Luke 15:7). In short, you will be called to live in moderation, righteousness, and godliness in this present world (Titus 2:12). Who can think of a more glorious work than to live according to the following:

1. Moderation. It is a good thing for man to live in moderation. It is commendable when a man is able to control his lusts and desires so that he is not a slave to his belly and is no longer driven by the power of his fleshly desires (1 Cor. 6:12). Well, those who earnestly practice godliness can achieve this kind of life. They are called to live in moderation, and they are also strengthened to live in moderation. They dress neatly and respectfully, they eat moderately and gratefully, and they enjoy themselves in an edifying manner, doing all things necessary to maintain or sweeten this life. They do this not to satisfy their lusts but to strengthen themselves (Eccles. 10:17). Is this not a beautiful calling? Yet every day we see many people who are damaged and weakened and shamed in many ways by their extravagances and excesses.

2. Righteousness. It is very important that a man live in righteousness with his fellow man. This means he does not owe anyone anything, he does not cheat or injure anyone, and he stands up for widows, orphans, and others who are unfairly treated. It also means that he pays his workers a good wage, deals honestly with those who trade with him, keeps his word, and shares something of what he has with the needy. Job was much respected, esteemed, and loved as a prince by all devout people in the East because of his practice of righteousness (Job 29–31).

3. Godliness. It is a most excellent matter for a man to live in godliness before his God. This means to perform and practice well those things that are entrusted to him and that are pleasing to our great God. It is important that whatever we poor, frail people do—eat, drink, or anything else—we do it all to the glory of God (1 Cor. 10:31). Indeed, it is a most excellent privilege that we are considered worthy to take God's name and covenant in our mouths, for he does not permit the ungodly to do so (Ps. 50:16). We are called to engage in the great things of God's law, in the wonders of his Word, in the excellent things of his kingdom, in his gospel, in calling upon his name, and in the use of holy baptism and the Lord's Supper. In this, we must do everything unto God, who does not

need us but exalts and glorifies us when he condescends to be served by us and entrusts us with taking care of his affairs.

Since we are called and appointed to the wholehearted practice of true godliness, should we then not gladly devote ourselves to this glorious work?

Glorious Fruits Produced by the Works We Are Called to Do

When we begin to practice true godliness, we engage in work that produces the most desirable fruits in great abundance, for godliness is profitable for all things (1 Tim. 4:8). It greatly serves to honor God, to edify God's church, and to promote man's well-being. We will go on to consider each of these things.

A Godly Life Honors God

The Lord our God, whom we serve in spirit, is "a God that hidest thyself" (Isa. 45:15). Worldly people restlessly continue their course in life without paying attention to God as they should. However, godly people seek to manage all their affairs according to his will, thereby showing the entire world that they see him, the unseen, and that they keep the hidden Lord before their eyes. They are willing and prepared to be reviled, insulted, and despised for his sake and for the sake of keeping his commandments. Truly, this greatly exalts and extends the glory of God. Although God hides himself from the eyes of the world, he is still honored and served by the godly, some of whom are very busy people who, besides giving time to attend the needs of their neighbors, have many other things to occupy their time.

We should then gladly and willingly practice godliness, since it honors our great God, who is most deserving. He has promised, has he not, to honor those who honor him (1 Sam. 2:30)?

A Godly Life Edifies the Church

When many people who practice true godliness are together in one location, they serve as God's voices to call people to sincere repentance and into God's church. Such people who practice godliness serve as lighthouses to warn others away from the sandbars of wickedness and to show them the right path to life. Indeed, they serve as many faithful witnesses to speak to all their friends about the things of their God and to help them understand how necessary it is to make God's work their most important occupation. They show by their actions to everyone everywhere that there is a God who wonderfully works in the hearts of men and who continues to reveal himself in the powerful changes he produces in their lives.

Many people are brought to their senses when they notice that those who lived in unrestrained excesses, as they do now, have begun to draw back from such a lifestyle. They have begun to live as people who have seen something better and have begun to change their direction. This often leads people to think more seriously about such matters. Although these worldly ones once spoke scornfully of godly people (1 Peter 4:4), they changed their minds in the day of visitation and now praise the Lord God (1 Peter 2:12).

We may compare them to schoolchildren who, when their teacher steps out of the classroom, become very rowdy, but when a few children stop playing around and settle down to their lessons, the rest are influenced to change their minds. So it is with people who see the godly girded with the zeal of the Lord, take advantage of the situation, and redeem their time. In doing so, they bring sinners to repent of their erring ways. Truly, such godly people consider and believe God's promise to "turn many to righteousness as stars for ever and ever" (Dan. 12:3).

Therefore, we should eagerly practice godliness, for it is through this that the church of God, the most beautiful thing in the world, is most edified and by this that most souls are persuaded to change their ways. Indeed, that is our most valuable pledge.

A Godly Life Heightens One's Well-Being

Godliness greatly heightens a person's well-being in the following three ways:

1. In the present life. The person who practices godliness in his life will improve it in many ways. You see, all other ways in which the children of men occupy their time, no matter how great and excellent they may be, serve only to beautify and improve them in external ways, whereas the practice of godliness improves people themselves. How foolish it is to spend so much time, effort, and money to increase our income, possessions, houses, gardens, earn-

ings, or business while neglecting godliness, by which we ourselves may be improved. Godliness improves us in these ways:

It restores the image of God in us. Godliness increasingly restores the image of God in us. In this way, we are renewed day by day in the spirit of our minds (Rom. 12:1–2; 2 Cor. 3:18; 4:16).

It frees us from enslavement to sin. As we are thus renewed, we are liberated from serving sin with its curses. Therefore, we are freed from a thousand troubles, entanglements, and errors in which worldly people are involved by their own foolishness and thus fail to follow God's wise counsel for their lives (Prov. 5:12–23). If you investigate the cause of all the troubles and complaints people have about their greatest mishaps, you will find that the root of them is sin. The truly godly are saved from such troubles by the power and strength of godliness (Prov. 27:8–27). Thus, they are blessed in all their affairs—in fortune or misfortune or in whatever situation they find themselves—for godliness has the promise of this life and the life to come (1 Tim. 4:8). It has such power that I cannot even begin to describe how it can make all things work together for our good (Rom. 8:28). It does this in such a way that even those situations that increasingly lead the godless to ruin will eventually work out to the spiritual good and profit of believers who endure them.

It gives us peace, comfort, and boldness. If we are renewed in this way and carefully watch our steps, we may expect to keep receiving every good thing from the Lord our God, in whom we put our faith (Rom. 8:32; 2 Tim. 1:12). We will become increasingly more disciplined in godly exercises and become more pleasing to God through our Lord Jesus Christ (Phil. 1:11). Our prayers, church attendance, giving, acts of mercy, performance at work, and whatever else we may do will now please the Lord our God. Once a person has found favor with God, his actions will please God.

2. In death. The person who faithfully practices true godliness in life will also enjoy the fruit of much good in death. We know that in dying there is nothing more comforting than a good conscience. When we practice godliness, our conscience is well kept to the end (Acts 24:14–16). You see, the truly godly person daily strives to increasingly conquer sin in himself. Does this not take away the sting of sin? After all, Scripture teaches us that the sting of death

is sin (1 Cor. 15:56). To the degree that we ward off sin through the practice of godliness, we also break its strength and decrease the bitterness of death.

Therefore, while death creeps up on the ungodly like a deadly adder with its sting intact, it approaches the godly like a bee without its sting. It actually brings the godly nothing more than honey. Thus, the godly often consider death a friendly messenger sent by their heavenly Father to lead them out of this sorrowful world into the heavenly kingdom. By contrast, the ungodly view death as a merciless executioner sent to drag them, despite their desperate struggles, from this world to eternal damnation.

3. After death. After death, the person who truly practices godliness will still enjoy the benefits of many blessings. You see, when everything else fails us and passes away—even our bodies, which are buried in the grave—the only things that will follow us are our godly works (Rev. 14:13). These godly works will go with us to God's tribunal to testify that we have faith and are true members of our Lord Jesus Christ (James 1:18). When God gives the sentence, only those who have shown that they have practiced true godliness in this world will be acquitted from eternal destruction and awarded eternal glory. Meanwhile, those who have been great and mighty and wise in the eyes of the world and who thought they would fare well before God's judgment seat because they conquered thousands on earth, ruled great kingdoms, held high offices, or perhaps were very active and prominent in God's church will hear to their unspeakable anguish and terror, "I never knew you: depart from me, ye that work iniquity" (Matt. 7:23).

And so the practice of true godliness is very profitable, for it improves every aspect of life. He who practices godliness is increasingly renewed in the image of God, released from slavery to sin, and delivered from many troubles that worldly people experience because of their sin. He also receives great boldness before God so that his service becomes increasingly more pleasing to God. He is greatly comforted in death and at God's judgment seat. Truly, since all these blessings accompany true godliness, should we then not apply ourselves to practicing it with all our strength? Should we not from now on gladly make the practice of true godliness our most important work?

Reasons for Practicing Godliness: Abhorrence of the Ungodly Life

Many people fail to practice true godliness because they have never considered how miserable the ungodly life can be. If we want to be stirred up to love godliness, we must seriously consider the following points about the nature of the ungodly life:

- The person who fails to practice godliness will be a lifelong slave to the most cruel masters in life.
- These masters will require the most detestable work possible.
- The works will produce the most wretched fruits imaginable.

Lifelong Slavery to Cruel Masters

If you do not want to serve the Lord God Almighty—the Father, Son, and Holy Spirit—by practicing true godliness, you cannot, may not, and never will be your own boss. You will be forced to serve the devil, the world, and your own flesh. Truly, you cannot find more harsh or cruel masters than these, for the following reasons:

1. Our depraved flesh. Is not the old man, the old Adam, a gruesome, loathsome master? It has thousands upon thousands of various spiteful and contradictory lusts and cravings that demand to be served and satisfied. It also becomes very angry when its lusts are not pacified or served (James 4:1–2). Indeed, it would be most depressing to be a servant or slave of such a fierce, difficult, bad-tempered, tiresome, irritable, antagonistic, and agitated old Turk slave master. It becomes a thousand times more difficult to serve the old Adam when we consider this matter in earnest.

2. The evil world. Is not this wicked world a ruthless, loathsome tyrant and a harsh master (1 John 5:19)? Does it not rule in extreme tyranny over its servants and slaves by encouraging them to follow

old habits, wrong customs, depraved examples, and scandalous practices? Indeed, it forces people to perform these practices, even when they do so reluctantly and against their own will. We see this in the various complaints of worldly people; one person complains about lavish dinner parties and how long he has to sit at a banquet table, while another frets about having to partake of various rounds of "toasts" and being pressured to drink too much, just like other worldly people. Some become so drunk or eat so much, even in their friends' homes, that they complain the next day of hurting in every bone as if they had been beaten with sticks.

Some complain about the great expense of desserts or sweets at parties and others about the indulgence and expense of fancy clothing. They say they wish things were different and would give much to abolish such excesses, but in the meantime they revel in them just like everyone else and offer the same kind of lavish display when it is their turn. That is how the world rules in tyranny over those who have not been delivered from it by the practice of godliness.

Indeed, the world knows how to put on evil festivities, carnivals, and fairs to tempt and tyrannize people. These festivals are so enticing that poor people will take their last valuables to the pawnbroker so that they can entertain their worldly friends at them. If a king or prince were to treat his subjects like that, people would soon be crying out that they were being ruled tyrannically. Soon, no one would be loyal to that ruler or serve him.

3. The devil of hell. This tyrannical master puts into chains and fetters all who have not been delivered from his service by practicing true godliness (2 Tim. 2:25), for as Ephesians 2:2 says, he "worketh in the children of disobedience." As an old saying goes, "Whoever serves the devil, serves an evil master." Who is not frightened by the thought that by not practicing godliness, he welcomes the devil of hell as his master and serves him as his henchman? Clearly, those who do not practice godliness are slaves to Satan even if they are of royal blood (John 8:33–34).

Those who do not wish to practice godliness in earnest are condemned to serve the most loathsome masters. Should we not rather gladly walk in godliness in order to be delivered from the service of these cruel masters?

The Most Detestable Work

If you do not wish to wholeheartedly pursue godliness by performing holy, loving, and godly works, then you will be forced to serve the aforementioned evil masters in the disgraceful filthy work of shameful sin. You will be forced by the evil desires, wrong habits, and spiteful harassment of these loathsome masters to slander, curse, do evil, take vile oaths, commit perjury, scoff, mock, quarrel, fight, overeat, get drunk, gamble, throw dice, lie, deceive, steal, maliciously gossip, and do every other awful thing. Can there be more filthy works besides these?

Even if you are more respectable than that, you will still be forced to conform to the evil customs of the world and behave according to its general philosophy, which is also wrong. Whatever you do, you will show that you are "a worker of iniquity" and will be involved in sin in one way or another. Indeed, filthy sin will be your work as long as you are not delivered from it by practicing true godliness (John 8:34). In short, if you neglect godliness, you will serve the lust of the flesh, the lust of the eyes, and the pride of life (1 John 2:16). The immoderate, unrighteous, and ungodly works of this service are most filthy and terrible in the following ways:

1. Serving the lust of the flesh. It is most wicked for someone who is called a Christian and therefore should have been liberated by the Lord to serve instead the lust of the flesh by living immoderately and without discipline. This person does this by immoral living due to greediness, overindulgence, unchastity, whoring, partying, gluttony, and drunkenness. He does it in pompousness, haughtiness, exhibitionism, narcissism, and all such wickedness. Is this not most filthy work for baptized Christians, who claim they have been washed and cleansed by the blood of God's Son? Those who dismiss godliness are drawn into these works, or at least into some of them, to their own wretchedness. They are like washed sows rolling once more in the mud (2 Peter 2:18–22).

2. Serving the lust of the eyes. It is also most wicked for a Christian to serve the lust of his eyes by unrighteousness, deceit, trickery, false measures, inferior wares, shortage of pay, and dishonest weights. All of these are an abomination to the Lord (Deut. 25:13–16), for all involve practicing usury, manipulation, exploita-

tion, and other oppressions of the innocent and the needy. God will not overlook such unfair practices, "because . . . the Lord is the avenger of all such" (1 Thess. 4:6). Do we not see daily that those who disregard the practice of godliness are busy throughout their entire lives with all or some of these filthy and malicious practices?

3. Serving the pride of life. It is ultimately most wicked for the Christian who neglects to serve the Lord our great God to choose to serve the pride of this evil life in haughtiness and the conceit of his heart in all kinds of ungodly, shameful sins. He thereby forsakes his confession of the holy faith and slanders the name of God by committing all that is abominable and corrupt. Does not experience show us and have we not seen that those who are not prepared to serve the Lord their God by practicing godliness have no objection when it comes down to it to leaving the way of godliness? Like Demas (2 Tim. 4:10), they deny the truth of God and embrace a lie. They move away as far as possible to the side "where the sun shines warmest," where they expect to be most promoted and advanced. Can you imagine any filthier work than that?

Moreover, the poor person who will not be engaged in the practice of godliness will be forced to do filthy work. Is that not most deplorable? The noble Israelites regarded the work they were forced to do by the unmerciful Egyptians in making mortar and brick to help build Pharaoh's treasure cities as hard and worthless (Exod. 1:14). Yet how much harder and more degrading is the worthless work of sin, which only serves to build hell! We will not find many people who are willing to undertake the disposal of human or any other foul matter, even if the people themselves are dirty and smelly. They will not be willing to do this even if they like their employers or the wages that are promised to them.

This abominable sin that serves the pride of life involves totally filthy, dirty, and repulsive work with nothing other than polluted, foul, stinking matter that proceeds from the devil of hell. The masters who force us to do such work are very loathsome, as we have already seen. What's more, the wages of this work are most horrible. We will talk more about them later. We should then gladly make it our first priority to diligently practice true godliness so that we may be released from the filthy, disgusting work of sin!

The Harmful Fruit of Ungodliness

As long as the person who neglects to practice true godliness remains a worker of iniquity, he remains busy with work that produces an abundance of evil fruit. This fruit serves to blaspheme God's name, harm his church, and ruin others, according to the following:

1. It blasphemes God's name. The sinful life of people who are Christians in name only blasphemes the name of the Lord our God most outrageously (Ezek. 36:20; Rom. 2:24). When such people claim the true God as their God, thereby impersonating servants of the almighty God while committing sin without concern for him but only to satisfy their own lusts, their actions show that they have a disgracefully low regard for God. These people consider a handful of short-lived pleasures, profit, or honor more highly than the favor of God. They chase after things that they know displease God. Thus, the Lord can rightly lodge a complaint, saying, "How small a price they have placed upon me" (Zech. 11:13), for they have esteemed a handful of filthy lucre, pleasure, or honor that perishes above my favor!

Imagine the scene of people who profess to be Christians having a drinking party in a dirty tavern. Or think of the frivolous and inappropriate behavior of such people at a carnival or festival or sinful wedding feast. Imagine that some Muslims, pagans, or Turks who were present heard these so-called Christians ranting, raving, boasting, and drinking. If they asked what kind of people they were and learned that they were Christians, would this not cause them to despise the God of all Christians, the one who is the true God? When they see so-called Christians lying, deceiving, and cheating, will this not give them the wrong impression of the Christian God? A Christian's sinful lifestyle is a very strong way of blaspheming the name of the mighty and true God.

2. It harms God's church. What is more, the sinful life of people who profess to be Christians encourages others to sin and does great harm to God's people. People get the idea that they are not the only ones who are doing wrong and that it is not wrong to do what is generally done. They bind themselves together as they "draw iniquity with cords of vanity, and sin as it were with a cart rope"

(Isa. 5:18). They say to one another, "Let us eat and drink; for tomorrow we shall die" (Isa. 22:13; cf. 1 Cor. 15:35–54). Such sinning multiplies into more sin and does unspeakable harm to God's holy church.

3. It ruins others. The sinful lives of those who refuse to practice godliness will be thoroughly corrupted in this present life, in their deaths, and after their deaths. Ungodly living in this present life corrupts man in many ways. Because of his sin:

The image of God in him is increasingly defiled and diminished. The soul is like a lovely, costly portrait on which the Lord God, with his proficient hand, has sketched and painted his own image. Our sins are like splatters of mud that we throw upon this picture. That is why David fervently pleaded with God after he had sinned to be washed clean (Ps. 51:2). A man corrupts himself according to the measure that he transgresses God's commandments with his sin (Prov. 8:36). He thus becomes even viler in his defilement. Because he himself is unclean, all things are unclean to him (Titus 1:15). His prosperity, wealth, recreation, pleasures, possessions, honor, respect—everything he considers important, precious, and valuable—are utterly cursed because of his sin (Deut. 28:15–20). He is like an evil, unclean bird that pollutes and corrupts everything it finds and touches (Hag. 2:14).

He becomes like a raving, crazed person in his sin. A person who is so corrupted is out of control, as far as his soul is concerned. He follows his evil lust and the desires of his flesh, giving way to anger, wrath, fury, hate, envy, jealousy, ruthlessness, and revenge. He commits a thousand evil and scandalous deeds. He thus greatly harms and corrupts himself, reaping a thousand troubles, difficulties, and perplexities in this world. He could have avoided many of those troubles if he had sincerely practiced godliness. Eventually, he becomes unfit for the service of God as he increasingly grows contemptuous and confused by sin. In following vanity, he becomes still more vain until even his prayers turn into an abomination (Deut. 13:14).

He becomes totally unfit to serve God. In striving after vanities, the sinful man becomes even more vain (2 Kings 17:15) so that even his prayers are an abomination to God (Prov. 15:9; 28:9). Think how detestable it must be to God to see this person immersed in lying, gossiping, mocking, deceit, slyness, drinking, and similar grievous sins. This person is completely indifferent to sin; he guzzles it like animals slurp up water (Job 15:16).

If a person has not earnestly practiced true godliness, he will also suffer many afflictions at his death. That is what the apostle Paul meant when he said that the sting of death is sin (1 Cor. 15:56). People who do not practice godliness are really workers of iniquity who intensify the sting of death against themselves because of their sinful lives. Therefore, death will sting them even more viciously when it comes. They might have felt a bit of death's sting during their lives, but with the approach of death they will experience such fear, distress, and despair that they will waste away from the dread of what they expect in the hereafter.

Just the thought of death, if it is strong enough, will make them totally despondent. Even if they are still healthy and sound in mind and body, their courage will desert them, and all their joy will be spoiled (Heb. 2:15). Although they, like the godly, realize that they cannot hold on but must fade away like a candle, they will soon realize that their light will go out eternally (Job 18; 20; 21; 27; etc.; Ps. 92:9). They will also receive the most terrible judgment of God after they awaken from their utopic dream. They will arise in terror when they see the wrathful countenance of the one whom they have scorned all their lives and who now sits on the throne in great glory, ready to judge them (Rev. 6:16–17).

Finally, after his death, the person who has not practiced true godliness will experience indescribable deprivation because of his sins. All his joys and pleasures, his income, possessions, position, office that he achieved in the world, friends, and kin—in short, everything he has set his mind on and enjoyed—will be taken away. All that will be left are his evil sins. All his evil shenanigans and wrong, shameful deeds, committed in abundance during his life, will follow him to God's judgment. Those sins include his swearing, omissions, violations of the Lord's Day, vain pretensions, extravagances, fornications and other immoralities, lying, slandering, selfish and miserly conduct toward the poor and needy, and many other aggravations and scandals caused by his sinful and intemperate life. Those actions, whatever they may be, will all follow him. They will fly with him to God's tribunal, where they will array themselves before the judgment seat of the almighty God. They will stand against the soul of every person who has not been delivered from the slavery of sin by practicing true holiness. They will stand there to accuse him and testify that he has never been a true Christian, no matter how much he may have claimed to be one and no matter how much he took upon himself the title of Christian.

Then the Lord God, who judges in truth every man according to his deeds (Rom. 2:6), will pronounce his sentence of damnation. The ungodly man will realize that in failing to pursue true godliness he has increasingly marred God's image in himself and covered his soul with the devil's abominable likeness. God will dismiss this man from his lovely countenance as one who cannot be counted as one of his own. He will deliver him with the devil and his angels into the hellish fire, where there will be weeping and gnashing of teeth forever and ever (Matt. 7:21–23). The ungodly will cry out to the mountains and rocks, "Fall on us, and hide us from the face of him that sitteth on the throne, and from the wrath of the Lamb" (Rev. 6:16), but it will be too late. There will no longer be time for repentance. God's judgment will already have been given and will be executed. The ungodly will have to drink from the wine of God's wrath, which is poured undiluted into the cup of his indignation. They will be tormented with fire and brimstone in the presence of God's holy angels and of the Lamb, and the smoke of their torment will ascend forever and ever (Rev. 14:10–11).

Thus, the neglect of godliness increasingly harms us as we defile ourselves more and more by our sinful lives. The image of God within us is progressively destroyed as we become entangled in more disgraceful and destructive lusts and sins. Because of this, our seemingly religious profession becomes only a stench before God and our so-called good works a curse and an abomination to the Almighty. We strengthen the sting of death against ourselves and bring our whole life under the bondage and fear of death. We also bring upon ourselves God's severe and unbearable judgment after this life in eternal death and damnation. Since the neglect of godliness results in all this, should we not willingly forsake our sinful lives and determine to practice true godliness, to which we are so compassionately called?

Reasons for Practicing Godliness: The Nature of Material Things

Considering the great gain that true godliness brings and the calamity that is hidden in ungodliness, how reasonable it is for us to diligently practice true godliness. Yet in reality, despite all we say or present to try to persuade people that there is great gain in godliness (1 Tim. 6:5–6), many people still have no desire or yearning to practice it, for their hearts are completely filled with loving earthly things that are precious to them. Because of this infatuation, which is against all right and reason, common sense, and all normal insights or prospects of lasting gain, they turn away from the Lord God and cling to the world. Indeed, if we were to take a worldly person's pulse, we would immediately notice that their ailment was (as we have said many times to encourage godliness) that they were bewitched by material things. They have no interest or passion for anything other than the pleasure of riches or high rank, prominent positions in this world, or other worldly things that their hearts suggest to them.

Therefore, if you, whoever you may be, have learned from the preceding teaching how harmful ungodliness is and how beneficial true godliness is yet find that you are slow in practicing true godliness because of your love for worldly goods, think about how empty all these things will prove to be in the end. They may fascinate you now, yet consider how little these things truly will help you in this life, in death, and in the next world.

The Effect of Worldly Things in This Life

Concerning this present life, consider what your situation is at this very moment. You have become a damaged piece of work because of sin, and not a single one of the world's goods can improve you or restore you. Even if you owned all the world's riches, every high position and office, every pleasure and delight that was distributed in small portions to worldly people—even if you had these all to yourself—even then they could not improve your soul or restore your fallen state before God (Luke 12:19–21). The material things that spiritually blind people are so fascinated with are, in the end, completely futile and vain. Moreover, you should further consider the following three things about the true nature of earthly things in this life:

1. They do not bring happiness. Experience shows that a person's earthly life is neither more enjoyable nor more satisfying if he possesses many worldly things such as high positions and offices, great riches and goods, wisdom and learning, or outward merriment, pleasure, and recreation. If you travel around the world, walk through cities, visit people's homes, listen attentively, and see what goes on among the children of men, you will discover that true happiness does not consist of having high positions, great wealth, or learning. Nor does it consist of the rowdy joy and merriment that are so prominently sought after. None of these can make a person's life on earth truly happy and joyful.

Rather, you will notice that there is something else, even among worldly people, that makes life good and pleasant. As the saying goes, "Contentment is better than riches." You will thus find in every town and village people who may not be believers and who do not have high positions, riches, education, or any kind of outward pleasures but who live a much more joyful, content, and cheerful life than those who do have such things. We can apply here what Christ the Lord said: "A man's life consisteth not in the abundance of the things which he possesseth" (Luke 12:15).

It is then very foolish in every aspect for a person to chase after things that will not bring him true satisfaction and to be thereby dissuaded from the practice of godliness, which alone can bring great gain with contentment (1 Tim. 6:6). Oh, foolish chaser after worldly things, if you would only spend half of your efforts to obtain the true godliness and blessedness that bring contentment rather than chasing after vain earthly goods to obtain riches, high positions, pleasures, or the wisdom of this world, which can give you no true satisfaction. If you would chase after godliness in the way that you now chase after vain things, what real gain would be yours in abundance! What rewards you would receive for your labor!

This is one of the secrets of God's kingdom that is hidden from the eyes of worldly people. We wish with a sincere heart that you would consider these things, reevaluate your life, and pray to God about this much so that you might come to your senses.

2. They do not bring freedom from trouble. What is most certain is that sorrow, pain, discomfort, and severe illnesses (such as colic, gout, kidney stones, and gallstones), as well as afflictions such as jealousy, envy, discord, and great anguish, creep into the castles of noblemen, the palaces of kings, and the homes of the rich, as well as into the small dwellings of humble city dwellers or farmers—indeed, sometimes even more so. Moreover, you who are used to living in abundance, esteemed and served by others, would find it quite unbearable to live the lives of poor people who live in cramped and unhealthy conditions, who do not have much to eat and drink, are poorly dressed, and must serve others.

Yet people who live in relative poverty do not have the problems that you have. Since they don't focus on joy and have become so used to sorrow, they probably have more joy in life than you who are used to affluence. The abundance of pleasant things makes you take things for granted and dulls your enjoyment of them. For poorer people, the very scarceness of these things in their lives makes them enjoy them more when they have only a little of them. They thus endure bad times better and enjoy good times more than people who are used to affluence (Prov. 27:7). So it is not really affluence or high position in life that frees us from the troubles and difficulties of life but something else.

3. They often bring sorrow and grief. We might enlarge on this and point out that sometimes those earthly things that people yearn for and chase after drop them into a pit of sorrows once they obtain them. These things thus reward their owners very badly, for many people have died in misery after chasing after them. Panting after things has brought many a gray head to the grave in sorrow. If these people had not tried to climb so high but had been satisfied to live at a lower level, they might not have experienced such disasters. We see this, for example, in the case of Haman in Esther 7.

Some people have had their throats cut because of money that they accumulated with great trouble, while others have been murdered in other ways for the same reason (Prov. 1:11–13). Even if we are young, we can recall such incidents that happened in our time. In addition, we can think of many a sensual man who was killed by following his fleshly lusts. Think, for example, of Zimri and Cozbi in Numbers 25:8. Indeed, there are many people who, by chasing after fleshly lusts, have also fallen into troublesome, fearful, repulsive, and gruesome diseases.

Even if we have not yet experienced such diseases, it is still true that without godliness all worldly positions, riches, entertainment, and pleasures will eventually become a curse to man, for we should understand that the more a person has sought enjoyment in worldly things in life, the more torment and sorrow he will experience after this life (Luke 16:25; Rev. 18:7). All earthly things, however sweet they may taste now, are only the seeds of eternal sorrow and of the most intense suffering imaginable. Could there be any greater foolishness than ignoring, neglecting, or slacking in our search and pursuit of true godliness and blessedness, which is accompanied by every satisfaction and blessing, for the sake of worldly vanities, which are all futile and even harmful?

You poor man, what can the world offer to tempt you more than the excellent things that the Lord God offers you in saving you through the practice of true godliness? Does the world offer you joy or pleasure? God promises you eternal heavenly joys that will never end if you forsake earthly pleasures that pass with use. We are not talking here of every earthly pleasure but only of those that cannot be enjoyed without sin (Heb. 11:25). Have worldly goods and riches bewitched you? God offers you every abundance of his house (Ps. 36:8), indeed, unspeakable riches that are in Christ (Eph. 3:8). In comparison with that, all other things are as loss and dung (Phil. 3:7–8).

Does the devil entice you to love the world by offering you honor and respect? Do you not see the Lord our God standing here to invite you to practice true godliness? He holds in his hand the wonderfully large, incomprehensible weight of eternal glory (Rom. 8:17; 2 Cor. 4:17)! Stop being foolish! Do not lift earth above heaven, flesh above spirit, and worldly things above the things of God, for true blessedness can be obtained only by practicing godliness.

Earthly Things Cannot Benefit Us in Death

Where death is concerned, we know that worldly things can neither save us from death (Prov. 10:2) nor comfort us in death (Ps. 49:6–8). Yet how many people have not struggled as they were dragged from this world by the incorruptible bailiff called death?

Indeed, they were unable to bribe him, even when they were surrounded by all kinds of valuable worldly possessions. Consider this: How many of the world's distinguished people have you known who, although they were greatly honored and esteemed, earned large incomes, had many friends, and called the most experienced physicians to their bedsides when they were dying, were yet prematurely taken from this world? They were taken when they were young, despite their desire to live longer. They would even have gladly paid a fortune to prolong their lives, if that had been possible.

Why then are earthly things so important to a person if he must soon die and leave all that behind, as Esau said in Genesis 25? Indeed, it often happens that in the hour of death, in the most trying time of great crisis, when a man most needs comfort and relief, he cannot find it despite all the riches he has acquired in this world. Instead of providing help and comfort, the things of earth offer more peril and frustration in the face of death. Are these not great obstacles? They have caused him such great harm as:

1. A troubled conscience. Those who are dying recall all their wealth that was gained without godliness—prominent positions obtained by shrewdness and pleasures acquired in sinful ways—as stings in their feet, thorns in their sides, and much pain in their souls. Indeed, the consciences of some of the most successful people trouble them most as they approach death, for their consciences testify against them. They feel remorse because they have chased with all their might after the vain things of the world while neglecting the service of God and declining to do those things commanded and delivered by God for the keeping of a man's poor soul (Luke 10:41–42).

2. The torment of wrong living. In the hour of death, worldly people are greatly tormented when they remember how they have lived without fearing God. They have lived proudly, extravagantly, frivolously, arrogantly, and worldly throughout their lives. They remember times that they despised someone, even offended and oppressed someone because they were proud of their great wealth and possessions. This becomes a thorn in their conscience or a scorpion at their dying heart, especially when they remember that Peter

declares, "God resisteth the proud, and giveth grace to the humble" (1 Peter 5:5).

3. Sorrow at leaving this world. Suppose the conscience of the worldly person who is dying experiences no anguish of conscience that brings him to repent of his sinful life of chasing after and enjoying worldly things. It is still true that the deeper this poor man is rooted in the world, the more sorrow he will experience when he is taken from it. Indeed, no heart can sufficiently express how dreadful it will be for a worldly person who is so cozily settled in this world to leave it and everything else behind, for the more beautiful, lovely, delightful, precious, and desirable his possessions are in this world, the more his heart will ache when he is separated from them. He will feel the most indescribable pain, sorrow, and sadness when he realizes the cost of having to leave everything behind because of death.

Oh, that the worldly person might take this to heart and earnestly think about how foolish it is to chase after the vain things of this world with so much effort! These things will fail to give him any comfort; indeed, they will give him more sorrow in the hour when he needs to be comforted most. How foolish it is to neglect the practice of godliness and those things in which he would have found great comfort, both in life and death!

Worldly Things Cannot Benefit Us after Death

Finally, the possessions a person acquires in this world cannot help him at all in the world to come, for in the world to come, we will neither eat nor drink, neither marry nor be given in marriage (Matt. 22:30). The things of this world will not count there at all. They will not benefit a worldly man or excuse him when he stands at God's tribunal before his judgment seat, where we must all appear in the end. Suppose a person were to say, "Consider, Lord, I have lived only a few years on earth, and yet I have conquered hundreds of thousands of things. I have held many positions and offices and have obtained many distinguished positions for my children, friends, and relatives. I have acquired many qualifications, including an excellent education."

None of that will mean anything at God's judgment seat. We should not even think of saying we have enjoyed many pleasures, such as jolly drinking bouts, banquets, weddings, games, plays, or competitions. I can guarantee you that the Lord will not view such talents or pleasures with merciful eyes at his judgment (Matt. 25:19–29), for worldly things and accomplishments mean nothing to the Lord our God. Rather, they will be a great hindrance to worldly people at God's judgment and for all eternity for the following reasons:

1. We will reap God's judgment because of worldly things. Worldly things will greatly strengthen the case against worldly people at God's judgment seat because, in obtaining them, they ignored all God's warnings in his Word (John 12:48; Rom. 2:15–16). They will be judged for committing all kinds of grievous sins, such as deceit, lies, undercutting the efforts of others, flattery—in short, neglecting the things of God and his holy service, ordinances, and institutes in zealously chasing after the things of this world. They pursued things that were useless and would be taken away from them—some things during their lives and everything else hastily left behind at death. Indeed, the acquisition of things will make their sentence even more severe.

It is understandable that heathens pursue worldly things during their lives, for they have not heard about a better way from the Word of God. The Lord God, in his incomprehensible providence, lets them walk as their hearts see fit, though that will be burdensome to them on the last day. It is beyond comprehension, however, that baptized people who call themselves Christians and have received better things from the Lord pursue worldly things. Their judgment will be indescribably severe.

2. Worldly things will testify against us. Worldly people who possess and enjoy a great abundance of earthly things in this life will be severely burdened with this wealth at God's judgment seat, for when the Lord God gave them an abundance of earthly things to satisfy the desires of their hearts, he did not leave them without a witness of himself. Indeed, he offered good things to them, "rain from heaven, and fruitful seasons, filling our hearts with food and gladness" (Acts 14:17). Yet all those good things did not persuade

them to serve the Lord God and confess, "Let us now fear the LORD our God, that giveth rain, both the former and the latter, in his season: he reserveth unto us the appointed weeks of the harvest" (Jer. 5:24). Surely, then, the Lord could have reasonably expected such people whom he had so blessed to turn to him in such circumstances (Deut. 28:47). Indeed, their failure to do so will make the case against them even more severe at God's judgment, for the more blessings and the greater abundance of desirable earthly things that people enjoy here on earth, the more severe will be the torment and punishment they experience in the hereafter.

To this case and to others we may apply the following: "Unto whomsoever much is given, of him shall be much required" (Luke 12:48). In the measure that worldly people increase their income and improve their positions and occupations, their responsibility will increase before God in that same measure on the last day. And if they neglect godliness for the sake of their earthly goods, their plagues and punishments will increase in the hereafter in the measure that they increased in earthly goods here on earth. Can greater foolishness than this be demonstrated?

3. Worldly things remind us of our neglect of godliness. Worldly people who have neglected godliness and have constantly chased after earthly things will regret this with the greatest anguish in the day of God's judgment because they will never be able to forget how they so carelessly neglected and ignored the most important thing—the practice of godliness, which should have been their most important work during life. They will regret this even more because they were sincerely taught and admonished in various ways to practice godliness but instead chose to chase after vain, insignificant, temporary, and earthly things. Indeed, they did this despite the warnings given to them that their focus was on vain, paltry, and deceitful things. Surely, that will torment and distress them forever and ever. Their failure to repent will cause them to suffer; it will continually consume and eat away at their heart so that they will loathe, hate, and despise themselves. Indeed, they will feel as if a worm that never dies is gnawing at their hearts (Mark 9:44).

Where is your common sense, worldly ones, when you care so little about eternal things? For you must soon die and appear before

God's tribunal, where not one of your earthly things will be able to defend you. Truly, if you chased after these things while neglecting true godliness, they will only accuse you and help to condemn you. How then can you who will soon die and appear before God's tribunal carelessly continue to slog away in the world, cleaving to the vain, earthly things that cannot help you in any way? Once they are in your possession, they will only encumber you in that day when you most need help. What foolishness this is!

How foolish it is for man, who really knows nothing, to entangle his heart in the fleeting, temporal, and vain things of this life, for they come with many problems. By doing this, he also draws down upon himself the crushing judgment of God in eternal damnation. You see, there soon will be a day when you must appear in the presence of God. When all those things that you are so delighted with today disappear and only God remains (who is all in all for his own), there will be nothing other than everlasting, eternal, and endless sorrow for those who did not want to listen to God and practice true godliness.

O worldly people, please be wise while there is still time! Promptly leave those things that you will not be able to keep forever—things from which you will never get true satisfaction, for this is what it is like: You only do what you like, serving the world and yielding to your flesh by covetousness, never denying your heart anything it wants and pursuing only what you desire. You chase after the things of this world, breaking God's commandments and neglecting godliness. You follow your own will and whims in everything. But you must realize that you will one day be taken before God's judgment seat (Eccles. 11:9), where you will be judged for such worldly ways. Even in this life, in spite of your diligent efforts, you will not be able to escape the general lot of this miserable life—vexations, cares, illness, headaches, and heartaches. These troubles will not fail to touch you. You will not be immune to the general common difficulties of this present life.

What madness it is, then, when, instead of practicing true godliness with the certain hope of eternal rest and joy, you prefer to pursue the worldly life, which leads only to eternal grief and sorrow. What more shall we say about this? Will you choose to be wise? Will you wish the best for yourself? Then start practicing true godliness with all your heart and all your strength for the remainder of your life. This alone can give you true satisfaction in this life, in death, and in the world to come, forever and ever in eternity. Only in this can you have glorious and unspeakable joy with the Lord our God, at whose right hand is fullness of joy. There you may enjoy the loveliness of his countenance forever and ever. Amen!

Dutch Reformed Translation Society

"The Heritage of the Ages for Today"
P.O. Box 7083
Grand Rapids, MI 49510

Board of Directors

Rev. Dr. Joel Beeke
   president and professor of systematic theology and homiletics
   Puritan Reformed Theological Seminary
   Grand Rapids, MI

Rev. Dr. Gerald M. Bilkes
   pastor
   Free Reformed Church
   Grand Rapids, MI

Dr. John Bolt
   professor of systematic theology
   Calvin Theological Seminary
   Grand Rapids, MI

Dr. Arthur F. De Boer
   retired surgeon
   Grand Haven, MI

Dr. James A. De Jong
   president and professor of historical theology, emeritus
   Calvin Theological Seminary
   Grand Rapids, MI

Rev. David Engelsma
   professor of theology
   Protestant Reformed Seminary
   Grandville, MI

Dr. I. John Hesselink
   Albertus C. Van Raalte Professor of Systematic Theology, emeritus
   Western Theological Seminary
   Holland, MI

James R. Kinney
   director of Baker Academic
   Baker Book House Company
   Grand Rapids, MI

Dr. Nelson Kloosterman
   professor of ethics and New Testament studies
   Mid-America Reformed Seminary
   Dyer, IN

Dr. Richard A. Mulle
   P. J. Zondervan Professor of Doctoral Studies
   Calvin Theological Seminary
   Grand Rapids, MI

Adriaan Neele
   professor and academic dean
   Institut Farel
   Dorval, Quebec

Dr. M. Eugene Osterhaven
   Albertus C. Van Raalte Professor of Systematic Theology, emeritus
   Western Theological Seminary
   Holland, MI

Henry I. Witte
   president, Witte Travel
   consul of the government of the Netherlands
   Grand Rapids, MI

The board gratefully acknowledges the financial support of individual patrons, foundations, and academic institutions that met the costs of this translation.

Lifetime membership in the Dutch Reformed Translation Society is available for a one-time, tax-deductible gift of $100. Members support the society's continuing work, receive periodic newsletters, and may purchase society publications at the cost of production. Membership gifts may be sent to P.O. Box 7083, Grand Rapids, MI 49510.

DATE DUE

			Printed in USA

HIGHSMITH #45230